S0-AGO-628

Acapulco
Ixtapa-Zihuatanejo and Taxco

A Great Destination

Kevin Delgado
with photographs by the author

The Countryman Press ✳ Woodstock, Vermont

FIRST EDITION

Interior photographs by the author unless otherwise specified
Maps by Erin Greb Cartography, © The Countryman Press
Book design by Joanna Bodenweber
Composition by PerfecType, Nashville, TN

Acapulco: A Great Destination
978-1-58157-115-8

Published by The Countryman Press, P.O. Box 748, Woodstock, VT 05091

Distributed by W. W. Norton & Company, Inc., 500 Fifth Avenue, New York, NY 10110

Printed in the United States of America

10 9 8 7 6 5 4 3 2 1

For Mary

EXPLORE WITH US!

Acapulco: An Explorer's Guide is broken down into sections representing different areas of the state, then into chapters focusing on an individual city or town. Each chapter opens with a general or historical introduction to the city or town, and then continues with information on destinations, accommodations, and restaurants that, largely, are quintessential Acapulco.

We've tried to list independent venues as much as possible, for two reasons. Most readers, first of all, will know what to expect with the franchises. More important, independent businesses are a perfect example of the spirit of Acapulco. We've also done our best to interweave history and fun facts into every aspect of the book, not just the introductions. This, we feel, is invaluable in getting to know a place.

GUIDANCE

This includes the entities—from chambers of commerce to agencies managing public lands—you can refer to for information on the area.

GETTING THERE

Getting There is a handy overview of what roads or other means of transport will take you to town. If public transportation or shuttles are available, we list them in *Getting Around*.

TO SEE

This lists attractions and points of interest you may want to visit, including museums, memorials, scenic drives, and more.

TO DO

To Do features activities you can experience. Note that admission fees are subject to change.

LODGING

These listings will give you ideas of where to find unique and/or consistently good places to stay. In almost every case, if we haven't stayed there, we've paid a visit and checked it out. Often these lodgings come with some great history attached. Sometimes our listings are slim because a town offers mostly franchises.

WHERE TO EAT

Where to Eat lists venues that serve dependably good food. We've divided them into three categories—*Dining Out* (better restaurants), *Eating Out* (casual ones), and *Nightlife* (bars and clubs). Sometimes restaurants have off nights or suddenly change hands and morph into something totally unacceptable. Please do not blame us—but do inform us.

THE ARTS

These listings are featured not only because art and art walks are becoming popular and valuable sources of revenue for towns but also because these forms of self-expression often reveal the personality of the residents and a place. We tell you where to find galleries and art-centered shops, murals, or museums.

ENTERTAINMENT

This section appears now and again, especially when towns and/or their venues are renowned.

SELECTIVE SHOPPING

This is meant to point you in the right direction for shopping, rather than trying to critique individual stores.

KEY TO SYMBOLS

- 🐾 **Pets.** The dog-paw symbol signals accommodations that allow pets and other venues that are unusually pet-friendly. Any stipulations appear in the review.
- ✐ **Child-friendly.** The crayon symbol appears next to lodgings, restaurants, and activities that are welcoming to youngsters.
- ♿ **Handicapped access.** The wheelchair symbol appears beside lodgings and attractions that offer handicapped access.
- ✹ **Pool(s) on the premises.**
- ((ɣ)) **WiFi access.**
- ▼ **Gay-friendly establishment.**
- ⌁ **Eco-friendly establishment.**

We would appreciate your comments and corrections about places you visit or know well in the state. Please address your correspondence to Explorer's Guide Editor, The Countryman Press, P.O. Box 748, Woodstock, VT 05091, or via email at countrymanpress@wwnorton.com.

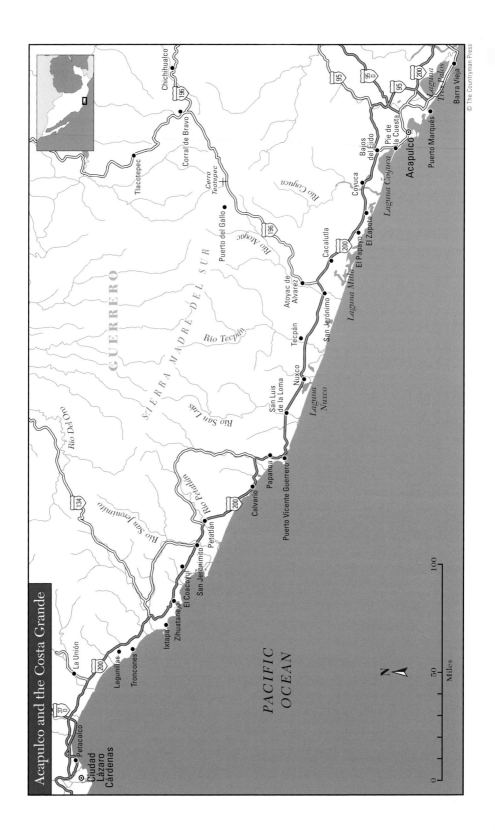

Acapulco and the Costa Grande

© The Countryman Press

CONTENTS

ACKNOWLEDGMENTS

When I was much younger, I took part in that weekend rite of passage that is reserved for San Diego teens, of crossing the border to drink and dance in the clubs along Tijuana's Avenida Revolución. On one such night I was in the company of several co-workers. One was a girl named Mary. I did not know her well, but I had heard she would be there that night and it was the sole reason I had decided to tag along. After several hours of hopping from club to club, we struck up a conversation at the bar. She had just returned from spending a few days in Acapulco with her friends and told me how much fun it had been. The conversation turned to travel. She spoke about her interest in Mexican culture and how she would like to spend some time living in Mexico, traveling to its many fascinating destinations and learning its language. I told her that I had similar ambitions and that I was in the process of planning an extended trip (though in truth the thought had never crossed my mind). You can imagine my surprise when her reaction was, "Take me with you!" Well, that was the beginning of a beautiful friendship, though I never did get around to planning that trip. However, as it turned out, she took me with her about a year later when she decided to chase her dream by studying in Mexico. We both fell in love with Mexico during that trip and it has turned into a journey of cultural discovery that has lasted a couple of decades. Thank you so much, Mary.

I am also in the debt of the cast of characters whose stories and insights have contributed to this book. Thanks especially to Mike Brady for your knowledge and for all of the rides to and from the border. Thanks to John Harten and Mona Klausing for your wisdom and for dragging me along on your adventures.

I am thankful for the kindness, support, and assistance of the hoteliers, restaurant owners, tour operators, and others with whom I visited during my research. Thank you to Betty, Penny, and Todd, as well as Monica and Robert for helping out with the kids; and to Daniel, Riley, Summer, and Isabel for your patience. Thanks to my parents and to my brothers and sisters (Mickey, DJ, Lori, Barbie, Davie, Teddy, Brian, Penny, Darren, Ryan, and Sean) for making me who I am; to my old buddy, Brian Schwartzkopf; and, notably, thank you Simon Lozano and Craig Sodaro for teaching me to write.

INTRODUCTION

To many, the name Acapulco still conjures up images of the city's heyday when it was the resort of choice for A-list Hollywood movie stars and European royalty. Although that vision of the city is no longer the reality, neither is the opposing view, that of a dilapidated destination way past its prime, as may have been the case in the late 1970s and '80s. Today, Acapulco is well on its way to forging a new identity for itself, thanks largely to the addition of sprawling upscale resorts in the Diamante district. The simple fact is that, despite its age, Acapulco still parties hard. Mexicans from the country's interior cities such as Cuernavoca, Puebla, and Mexico City still come here in droves on the weekends to take advantage of the beautiful weather and the lively nightlife.

To the north, Acapulco has a younger cousin that is only now coming into its own as a premier resort destination. The twin cities of Ixtapa-Zihuatanejo offer a completely different beach experience than the one you will find in Acapulco. These cities do not have Acapulco's rich history (heck, Ixtapa didn't even exist 40

ACAPULCO'S RUSTIC BEAUTY HAS LONG ATTRACTED TRAVELERS.

years ago) nor do they yet offer the kind of nightlife that you find in Acapulco. However, the area around Ixtapa-Zihuatanejo features some of the most pristine, picturesque, and accessible beaches that you will find anywhere along the Pacific Coast. In Ixtapa, you will find large resorts built along a well-kept avenue where you can expect to be pampered day and night. The resorts in Zihuatanejo are on a much smaller scale, but exist in an environment that feels much more like a traditional Mexican beach town. Because this area is not nearly known as widely as Acapulco, there are also more opportunities to lose yourself on a secluded beach. Show up between the end of the high tourist season and the beginning of the rainy season and you will find miles of nearby beaches with no one around but the pelicans.

Moving inland from Acapulco, you will come upon one of Mexico's most picturesque colonial cities. Taxco de Alarcón grew in fits and starts as the center of Mexico's silver mining industry. Its relative obscurity over much of its history has allowed it to retain a rustic atmosphere that almost transcends time. Like Acapulco, Taxco has gone through a rediscovery in recent years and is once again a destination for anyone interested in beautiful colonial vistas and silver handicrafts. Taxco has also received plenty of attention for the medieval displays of religious devotion that are demonstrated in the city's processions during Semana Santa (Holy Week).

Wherever you decide to visit along this beautiful corner of Mexico, be sure to take the time to do some exploring. You will find that there is much to see, experience, and write home about.

WHAT'S WHERE IN ACAPULCO

AUTO INSURANCE Under Mexican law, motorists are required to have sufficient currency to cover damages or insurance from a Mexican company in the event of an accident. Non-Mexican insurance does not fulfill this responsibility. If you are involved in an automobile accident, you are basically considered guilty until proven innocent. You will be detained until the local authorities determine who is at fault. If this happens, it is a good idea to contact your nearest consulate immediately. You will be required to demonstrate financial responsibility. Financial responsibility is defined as being in possession of an inexpensive Mexican insurance policy or $5,000 and $10,000 in cash. Therefore, it is not a good idea to drive in Mexico without Mexican liability insurance. If you are renting a car, you will pay for the insurance through the rental company. However, if you are driving your own vehicle into Mexico, you'll need to purchase insurance on your own. It is relatively inexpensive, and it comes with peace of mind. Plenty of companies offer auto insurance at all major U.S.–Mexico border crossings and on the Internet. Here are a few insurance firms located north of the border, just in case: **Adventure Mexican Insurance** (U.S. 1-800-485-4075; www.mexadventure.com; e-mail: info@mexadventure.com), P.O. Box 1469, Soquel, CA 95073; **Instant Mexico Auto Insurance** (U.S. 1-800-345-4701; fax 610-690-6533; www.instant-mex-auto-insur.com), 223 Via de San Ysidro, San Ysidro, CA 92173; **Mexpro Mexican Auto Insurance** (U.S. 1-888-467-4639; fax 928-213-8476; www.mexpro.com), 1300 South Milton Road, Flagstaff, AZ 86001.

BUSES If flying is not the way you like to travel, traveling by bus can be a nice way to get around Mexico and see the countryside in the process. Although Hollywood movies have created an image of Mexican bus travel as being the experience of riding in cramped quarters with several goats and a rooster, many Mexican bus companies provide a more comfortable experience than you're likely to find in the United States and at extremely reasonable rates. **Estrella Blanca** and **Estrella de Oro** are the two major companies there, and provide a pleasant traveling experience with their luxury and first-class service. Estrella Blanca has the bigger footprint in Guerrero, along with its subsidiary bus lines **Autotransportes Cuauhtémoc, Elite, Flecha Roja, Futura, Gacela,** and **Turistar.**

There are many different classes of bus service that run from luxury to something akin to sitting on a vibrating park bench listening to bad mariachis asking for tips. Luxury class may also be known as *de lujo, ejecutiva,* or *diamante.* This is the highest level of service and may include limited seating, refreshments, and headphones. First class, also known as *primera clase,* has air-conditioning and reclining seats and advertises nonstop travel. However, these are apt to stop for roadside passengers if the bus is sufficiently empty. Second class, or *segunda clase,* generally provides clean service but sometimes lack toilets and video monitors. Also, travel by second class can be frustratingly slow because the routes go through small towns and pick up and drop off passengers along the route. These buses generally have no assigned seating and when the bus fills up, passengers may ride standing up. This level or service is sufficient for shorter trips to smaller destinations but you probably want to avoid second class for longer journeys.

Some additional tips: The air-conditioning on these buses can be excessively cool—particularly on overnight trips—so have a sweater handy. However, dress in layers because it's not unheard-of for the air-conditioning to break down. If you plan to travel during the weekend or around a holiday—especially Easter—it's a good idea to buy your ticket a couple of days in advance to ensure you get a seat. It is also advisable to set your travel plans ahead of time if you are going to a smaller town such as Taxco. Do not assume that things will conveniently fall into place when you get to the bus station. For example, there are no direct bus routes between Taxco and Ixtapa-Zihuatanejo. Also, be sure to pack food, water, and refreshments for longer trips.

When you go to buy your ticket, you will often be asked your name. If you have a non-Hispanic name, it is a good idea to have it written down so you can show it to the ticket salesperson. You would be surprised how many names that seem ordinary to your ear sound completely foreign to the Mexican ear. Also, for first-class buses the salesperson may show you a layout of the bus for you to pick out your seat. Ask where the toilet is and choose a seat anywhere but near there. From Acapulco, you can get first-class bus service to various points throughout the country. Ixtapa-Zihuatanejo also has three long-distance bus terminals. Note that there is no bus station within Ixtapa itself. Also, if you are booking bus travel to Ixtapa, be sure to purchase travel to Zihuatanejo and *not* to Ixtapan. If you are unfortunate enough to confuse Ixtapa and Ixtapan, you will find yourself in a village in the mountains southeast of Taxco, many hours away from where you want to be. The taxi drivers here tell stories of tourists getting off the bus here asking to be taken to their resort (of which there are none) and wondering where the beach is.

See *Getting There, Getting Around,* and *To Do* in individual chapters for more information about specific bus lines and their itineraries.

CUSTOMS AND IMMIGRATION

Technically speaking, customs and immigration can be a real pain. You can mitigate some of this inconvenience by either driving in or crossing the border and flying out of Ciudad

Juárez, Tijuana, or some other Mexican airport. Crossing the U.S.-Mexico border on foot or by car is much less of a hassle than making your way through airport security these days. Furthermore, although a passport is required to fly into the United States from Mexico, travelers age 16 and older have the option to present one of the following documents when entering the United States via land or a sea port. Children under age 16 may present an original or copy of their birth certificate, a Consular Report of Birth Abroad, or a naturalization certificate. One of the following documents may be presented to prove both identity and citizenship:

- U.S. passport
- U.S. passport card
- Trusted traveler card (NEXUS, SENTRI, FAST)
- State-issued enhanced driver's license (when available this secure driver's license will denote identity and citizenship)
- Enhanced tribal cards (when available)
- U.S. military identification with military travel orders
- U.S. Merchant Marine document
- Form I-872 American Indian card

For specific details of current passport rules, check out the **Department of Homeland Security** Web site (www.dhs.gov/xtrvlsec/crossing borders/whtibasics.shtm). However, the bottom line is that you should get a passport before you need it—as in *today*. There are ways to expedite a passport if you need one quickly. But getting one via a rush application can be expensive and stressful.

A **tourist card** is an official Mexican document declaring that you have stated that the purpose of your visit to Mexico is tourism and that your visit will last no more than 180 days. This document costs $20 and anyone staying in Mexico for more than 72 hours and traveling beyond the border zone (about 70 miles south) needs to have a tourist card. If you are driving into Mexico, you can get this document at the immigration station just across the border. If you are flying out of a Mexican airport, such as Ciudad Juárez, you will get this document as you pass into the boarding area of the airport. And if you are flying into Mexico from another country (such as Canada or the United States), the cost of this document is included in the price of your airfare and you will receive it, along with instructions on filling it out, while on the plane. Once you disembark, customs and immigration will stamp it, indicating that you are in the country legally.

As a tourist entering Mexico, you are allowed to bring one still camera with up to 12 rolls of film, as well as one video camera with up to 12 blank cassettes. Most historic and archaeological sites allow you to take photographs and video images, though sometimes with a nominal fee. However, special items such as a tripod may be considered professional equipment, in which case you may have to get a special permit to use it at those sites. You can download the permit at the Web site of the national archaeological and historic institution (http://dti.inah.gob.mx/). Smokers entering Mexico may take a carton of cigarettes and up to 50 cigars. Most outside meats, fruits, and vegetables are prohibited, so don't raid the fridge before you head out on your trip. Most important, be aware that guns are illegal in Mexico. There have been cases of Americans unwittingly crossing the border into Mexico while in possession of firearms that are perfectly legal in the United States, only to find themselves locked up for months and even years in a Mexican prison. *Do not take firearms into Mexico with you.*

DINING If you stick to tourist areas, you will have no problem finding restaurants that cater to your every whim. However, if you venture off of the beaten path, you will find that the typical meals and mealtimes that you are used to are not typically observed. In fact, though you may have been taught in your high school Spanish class that *almuerzo* means "lunch" and *cena* means "dinner," these words are often nowhere to be found on a traditional Mexican menu. Breakfast (*desayuno*) is generally light and usually consists of fruit or sweet bread along with coffee, hot chocolate, or *atole,* a thick hot beverage made from rice, oats, or corn. The main meal of the day is called the *comida* and is taken between 2 and 4 PM. This meal often has several courses and many restaurants that advertise a *comida corrida* or *menú del día* will offer this type of dining at a reduced price. Such a meal usually consists of soup or salad, a main dish, and dessert accompanied by *agua fresca* (fruit water). The *cena* (dinner), a light meal often taken between 7 and 9 PM, may simply offer *antojitos* (little cravings), which may be a small plate of enchiladas, tacos, or *sopes* (fried tortillas topped with hot sauce). Smaller snacks are referred to as *botanas,* and can be as simple as salted peanuts or *totopes* (chips) and salsa.

For the most part, you will find that dining out is relatively inexpensive in Mexico. However, prices can vary a great deal, particularly in touristy areas. In the following listings, $ indicates that entrées average less than $7; $$, that they average less than $15; and $$$, that they average more than $15.

DRIVING Depending on your itinerary, it is quite likely that you will discover that a car is unnecessary and even inconvenient in Acapulco and even Ixtapa-Zihuatanejo. However, there is always the chance that you will be in a situation where you need one. The airport is generally the best place to rent a car, though most large resorts offer car rental services in or around the lobby. See *Auto Insurance* in this chapter, and *Getting There* and *Getting Around* in individual chapters for more about car rentals.

In Mexico, speed limits are posted in kilometers. This can be a bit confusing if your speedometer does not include kilometers. However, 60 miles per hour is roughly equal to 100 kilometers per hour, so if you multiply the posted speed limit by 6 and drop the last decimal, that will give you a rough estimate of the allowed speed in miles per hour. For instance, if the posted speed is 65 kph, 65 x 6 = 390, so your speed should not exceed 39 mph.

If you are traveling on public holidays, be aware that Mexican roads can get fairly congested. This is particularly true between Mexico City and Cuernavaca. Also keep in mind that driving in larger Mexican cities can be an intimidating undertaking, with other drivers prying their way into the smallest opening in traffic and putting the onus on you to avoid a collision—as well as treating stop signs and traffic lights as mere suggestions instead of requirements.

Out on the open road, it's much easier to forget that, despite its beautiful views and relative convenience, Mexican roads can be fraught with hazards. One of the most common is the livestock that commonly wander onto the road. This is generally not a problem if you are minding your speed. However, you do not want to come careening through a mountain pass to find a herd of cattle sitting on the road ahead of you. Another, slightly related, problem is the lack of guardrails that exists on the road, even where it winds along steep cliffs. As you drive through areas such as these, it will become abundantly clear that the road was not engineered with the kind of safety standards that are common north of the border. Also keep in mind that many Mexican drivers have never taken formal driving lessons, a fact that leads to some interesting quirks in their driving habits. For example, a Mexican driver may slow and turn on his left turn signal to indicate that either he intends to turn left or that it is safe to pass. You can imagine how this might make aggressive driving a bit more dangerous. Add to this the frequent potholes and steep or nonexistent shoulder, and you quickly come to a bit of advice that should be self-evident: Drive carefully.

There may be times when you will have the urge to throw this bit of advice out the window—say, you have found yourself trailing a slow-moving vehicle for miles before you have the opportunity to pass, and you feel the need to make up some lost time. Resist this temptation. Do not pass along stretches with unbroken center lines (despite what you see locals doing), and make sure you have a good view of the road ahead as you proceed. Also, try not to drive at night. The dangers presented by narrow roads, wandering animals, and unprotected cliffs are exacerbated at night. This especially true of animals, which congregate at the edge of the roadway where the grass grows greenest. One traveler once told me that he has successfully navigated dangerous Mexican roads at night by sidling up behind trucks as a way of protection against loitering livestock. However, that seems like a lot of trust to put in the hands of the trucker in front of you. The best advice is to find a place to get some rest, and get going again in the morning when it's safe.

Mexico has earned a reputation for being a place where tourists are singled out for traffic offenses, though the problem is not nearly as bad as it used to be. However, tourists run the risk of being singled out if they drive recklessly and act rowdy. It is true that in the past, some Mexican law enforcement officers supplemented their low incomes through *mordidas* (bribes), though this has happened less and less as Mexico has enforced anticorruption laws. The chances of this happening to you are slim, particularly if you drive safely and obey the traffic laws. After all, Mexico's economy depends on tourism, and it would not be in the industry interest to shake down every foreigner who passed through. If it does happen to you, you can either pay the officer and move on with your day, or accept the ticket. If you are ticketed, you have the right to ask to pay the ticket by mail. The most common practice, though, is to have you follow the officer to the nearest police station (see "Useful Phone Numbers" *sidebar* in individual chapters), where you will pay the fine. There have been incidents where tourists have refused to go, and the officer has removed the license plates from the vehicle, obliging the driver to go down the station to pay the fine to get the plates back. Bottom line: Drive safely, and don't set yourself apart.

ELECTRICITY Mexico's electrical system is the same as in the United States and Canada: 110 volts AC. The outlets are compatible with any electrical appliance, charger, or extension cords you may bring. However, the outlets in older or smaller hotels may not have outlets suitable for polarized plugs (in which one flat prong is slightly larger than the other). Pick up an adapter at any hardware or discount store before your trip.

GAS Petróleos Mexicanos (PEMEX)—is Mexico's state-owned nationalized petroleum company. Its midgrade unleaded gasoline, Magna Sin (green handle), is rated at 87 octane and should be fine for cars that run on unleaded regular in the United States. PEMEX unleaded Premium (red handle) is rated at 92 octane.

Although PEMEX stations are not as abundant as gas stations north of the border, you will find them in all major stops on your itinerary. They are generally open 24 hours a day, and they do not take credit cards; pesos only here. The upside to this is that PEMEX stations make a great place to break large bills, because the attendants carry a lot of cash. Speaking of the attendants, they will pump your gas and clean your windshield if you need it. It is customary to tip them about 10 pesos, or one U.S. dollar.

HELPFUL PHRASES When it comes to conversation, Mexicans tend to appreciate formalities more than do their neighbors to the north. When approaching someone for information, don't forget to greet the person with the time-appropriate salutation (*buenos días, buenas tardes, buenas noches*), even if it's the only Spanish you can think of at the moment. Avoid using *hola* except among individuals you already know well; although it simply means "hi," it's a casual term and could come across as abrupt. Also, contrary to what you were taught in high school Spanish, if you want to know how much something costs, try not to say "*¿Cuanto cuesta?*" This is a dead giveaway that you're a gringo, meaning that you've probably just added a few pesos to the price of the item. Instead say, "*¿A cuanto?*" This phrase just might pass you off as a *chilango* (Mexico City resident) making the vendor think that you are wise to inflated prices.

Good morning—*Buenos días*
Good afternoon—*Buenas tardes*
Good evening (after 8 PM)—*Buenas noches*
Goodbye—*Adiós*
Please—*Por favor*
Thank you very much—*Muchas gracias*
You're welcome—*De nada*
Do you speak English?—*¿Habla usted inglés?*
I don't understand.—*No entiendo.*
How do you say . . . in Spanish?— *¿Como se llama . . . en español?*
My name is . . .—*Me llamo . . .*
Where is . . . ?—*¿Dónde está . . . ?*
To the right—*A la derecha*
To the left—*A la izquierda*
Straight ahead—*Derecho*
What is the rate?—*¿A cuanto es?*
Bathroom/restroom—*Baño/servicio*
Shower—*Ducha*
Bathtub—*Baño*
Towels—*Toallas*
Soap—*Jabón*
Toilet paper—*Papel higiénico*

Key—*Llave*
Menu—*Menú*
Order—*Orden*
Restaurant bill—*cuenta*
Fork—*Tenedor*
Spoon—*Cuchara*
Knife—*Cuchillo*
Napkin—*Servilleta*
Food—*Comida*
Coffee—*Café*
Tea—*Té*
Beer—*Cerveza*
Wine—*Vino*
Milk—*Leche*
Juice—*Jugo*
Money—*Dinero*
Expensive—*Caro*
Cheap—*Barato*
Post office—*Correo*
Driver's licence—*Licencia de manejar*
Gas station—*Gasolinera*
Border—*Frontera*
Passport—*Pasaporte*

HOTEL RESERVATIONS Sometimes, making hotel reservations in Mexico can be a tricky experience. Larger resorts accept reservations over the Internet with a credit card number. However, many smaller hotels require a process that's a little less organized. Most will accept the initial hotel reservation via their Web site or by e-mail. However, to confirm the reservation, many require that you send a deposit check to a specified address, often inside the United States. In areas where the tourism industry is less developed, such as in Taxco and along the Costa Chica, many hotels require payment by cash only. You may find this to be an inconvenience. Still, the unique ambience offered at these smaller, independent hotels makes the extra effort well worth it.

The cost of lodging is based on an average per-room, double-occupancy rate ($ = less than $100 per night; $$ = between $100 and $175 per night; $$$ = greater than $175 per night.

Note that when calling to make reservations, the direct-dial prefix for Mexico from the United States is 011-52.

INTERNET ACCESS If you plan on bringing your laptop computer, many hotels offer wireless Internet access as part of their amenities. However, there is always an added risk when traveling with a laptop. Alternatively, you can always use the hotel business center or a *cibercafé* (cybercafé) that offers Internet access at a nominal fee. However, this is not a perfect option, either. Hotels tend to charge unreasonable fees for the use of their business centers, and what's worse is the lack of spyware protection on the ancient computers that they offer. Cybercafés tend to be a little better at this, and a lot cheaper; however, you must always be careful with your personal information such as passwords or credit card information when using a strange computer. Log onto your personal accounts sparingly when using public computers. It's always a good idea to click on "Internet Options" and clear the entire cache before logging off.

LANGUAGE It goes without saying that Spanish is the primary language spoken in this region of Mexico (though you do find indigenous people who primarily speak native languages). However, you will likely find that English is spoken by the better-educated upper class, those who have spent time working in the United States, and by locals who deal with tourists on a daily basis. The ability to speak English is a valued skill in Mexico and people often want to practice at every chance they get, but you will often find that those who are not truly fluent will run through the English phrases they know pretty quickly. In more rural areas, your waiter will understand the English names of the menu items, but he probably won't be able to describe the dishes to you in English or tell you exactly how they are prepared. This doesn't mean that you won't be able to get along here without knowing any Spanish. In fact, many expatriates who live in such places as Troncones full-time don't speak Spanish. A good Spanish-English/English-Spanish dictionary is a must-have, especially if you can find one that offers Mexican variants on the Spain-centric Spanish you may have learned in school; you can always point to a word even if you aren't sure how to pronounce it. Being able to speak some Spanish will likely enrich your experience and can really come in handy if you find yourself in a pinch. It is worth your while to make an attempt to learn at least the most basic Spanish words and phrases (see *Helpful Phrases*). Not only will this help you communicate better, it will also go a long way toward ingratiating you with your Mexican hosts. And that's never a bad thing.

MILITARY STOPS If you travel by road in Mexico, you will soon encounter being stopped at a military checkpoint. For the average American who is not used to such things, this can be a jarring experience. After all, you just came down here to have a good time, right? Just keep in mind that everybody goes through this, and it isn't really a big deal. Despite what you may have heard about corrupt

cops demanding payola, Mexico's economy depends on the influx of tourist dollars. It would not be in their interest to have the authorities shaking down every tourist who comes along. As long as you've done nothing wrong, you have nothing to worry about.

Many of these stops are actually largely the result of Mexico attempting to satisfy their allies from north of the border that they are doing everything in their power to stop the flow of drugs northward. Keep in mind that these young soldiers are just doing their job. Many of them come from the poorer parts of Mexico, and they are occasionally even illiterate—meaning that your political opinions about unwarranted searches could hardly have less significance to them. Therefore, it is best just to cooperate so you can be on your way.

Generally, you will be stopped for only a few minutes. The soldiers will likely ask to see your identification and to look in your trunk. (They do have gadgets that can detect the presence of certain kinds of drugs, so you may get a little extra attention if you are carrying prescription medications in your luggage. If they're legal, it's no big deal; to be on the safe side, carry your meds in their original pharmacy-issued containers.) It is always a nice gesture to offer the soldiers a cold soda on a hot day. Assuming that you are not carrying any drugs, guns, or other illegal paraphernalia, you will soon be on your way.

MONEY American dollars are accepted in some places in Acapulco and Ixtapa-Zihuatanejo. However, your money will go much further if you use pesos. To give you an idea of just how much further, the current exchange rate is hovering around 12.7 pesos per dollar. However, usually when you use dollars, prices are usually rounded off to equal 10 pesos to the dollar. This means you will generally be overpaying more than a quarter for every dollar you spend.

Mexican currency notes come in denominations of 20, 50, 100, 200, 500, and 1,000, and are marked with the $ sign (incidentally, the first currency to use the symbol).Breaking larger bills is a persistent problem in Mexico, particularly at smaller independent establishments. I once had to wait half an hour after finishing a meal while the restaurant owner ran around to nearby businesses trying to make change for a 500-peso note. The best strategy to avoid such a situation is to pay with larger bills when spending money at larger businesses and save your smaller bills and *monedas* (coins) for small establishments and street vendors.

The quickest and easiest way to get Mexican currency is to go to a Mexican ATM and withdraw your money in pesos. Like many ATMs north of the border, Mexican ATMs are located in an entrance area between the outer and inner doors to the bank. After normal business hours—as is the case in the United States—insert your card into the slot next to the outer door, and you will be buzzed inside to do your withdrawal. Once you withdraw currency in Mexican denominations, your bank will convert it back to the dollar amount and charge you that way. These machines generally offer cash at the wholesale bank rate instead of the less-favorable tourist rate that you get when you trade cash or traveler's checks, making ATMs both convenient and, on the surface, financially favorable. However-

er, keep in mind when you use your debit card, your bank may charge you a foreign transaction fee of up to 3 percent of the transaction. On top of that, the owner of the ATM will likely charge you a fee of up to 3 percent as well.

Before your trip, it's a good idea to shop around for a credit card that imposes a small foreign transaction fee or none at all. Foreign transaction fees are supposed to be disclosed in the terms and conditions. In any case, it's probably not such a good idea to rely solely on ATMs as your source for money. You should always have a little extra cash on you in case of an emergency. Banks offer respectable exchange rates; *casas de cambio* (exchange houses) a little worse; hotels offer the worst exchange rates. It's always a good idea to exchange at least $50 or $75 into pesos before leaving the United States so that you'll arrive in Mexico with enough pesos for your cab ride or a meal. Credit cards are widely accepted in Acapulco and Ixtapa-Zihuatanejo. However, in smaller towns credit cards acceptance is less common. For example, in Taxco many hotels operate on a cash-only basis. Furthermore, Taxco banks have been known to deny travelers the service of converting their cash dollars into pesos, referring them instead to the more expensive *casas de cambio.* The benefit of using a credit card is that you will receive the more favorable wholesale rate. The drawback is that if you're spending money in a place that accepts credit cards, chances are that it's an establishment that is geared toward serving tourists—and thus you get less bang for your buck than at places that cater to locals.

Immediately following the $–$$$

symbol in this book's listings are the credit cards that are accepted at an establishment (AE = American Express; D = Discover; DC = Diners Club; MC = MasterCard; and V = Visa). If no credit card is listed, no credit cards are accepted there, at the time of writing. However, policies do change, so be sure to double-check with the hotel or other venue whether you may pay using a particular credit card.

POLICE There are so many different types of police in Mexico that you're likely to find that even many Mexicans don't seem to understand them. Mexican law enforcement has a long and spotted history, though the country has tried hard to change things in the last few decades. The four types of police that you are likely to see during your time in Mexico are the *policía de tránsito* (traffic police), *policía metropolitana* (city police), *policía judicial* (federal police, also known as *federalis*), and *policia turistica* (tourist police). Traffic police–usually dressed in dark blue and gray uniforms with flat military-style caps—have a poor reputation for shakedowns. Sadly, city police— dressed in powder blue shirts with navy blue pants and caps—have an even worse reputation for corruption. The *federalis*–dressed in gray and black, often heavily armed, and who travel in official pickup trucks—have improved upon their image greatly in recent years. However, for minor issues in any of Mexico's tourist areas, your best bet is to seek out the tourist police—dressed in white shirts and navy blue shorts. These officers are friendly, attentive, and paid to be your advocate. Keep in mind, however, that they are mainly trained to deal

with petty street crime and that they do not have any real law enforcement authority beyond that. If you are faced with a more serious issue, your best option is probably to go to the embassy.

TAXIS Taxis are a fairly inexpensive option for getting around. As with most places in Mexico, in Acapulco and environs taxis generally charge a flat rate for transportation within certain zones. However, they are not metered, so you will have to settle with the driver on a price. If you are unsure what the rate should be, be sure to ask the clerk at the reception desk of your hotel. Keep in mind that taxi drivers may charge you double the normal price if you call them to pick you up. This covers the trip to come and get you, as well as the trip to drop you off at your destination. Also, fares typically rise between 10 PM and midnight.

Taxis are plentiful throughout the tourist centers and hotel zones, so you shouldn't have any trouble finding one to wave down. Remember to always ask the price of the ride *before* getting in the car—or better yet, know the going rate and state that price to the

driver in the form of a question. Even the most experienced travelers have been known to have been hit by the "gringo tax" every now and then. If the driver quotes you a price that seems too high, don't be afraid to say, *"No, gracias,"* and find another taxi. Also, in Acapulco and Ixtapa you may encounter taxi drivers who approach you with offers to take you to a private beach and free meals and drinks. Don't accept these offers unless you want to spend your day listening to a hard-selling pitch man telling you the benefits of owning a timeshare.

TELEPHONE To call directly to the United States from Mexico, dial 001, then the area code and phone number. Conversely, to call Mexico from the United States, dial 011-52, then the area code and phone number. It isn't a good idea to dial direct long-distance or international calls from your hotel room in Mexico. Hotels often add their own surcharges, even to local calls. This also applies to bringing and using your cell phone while in Mexico. It may seem extremely convenient to pull your phone out of your pocket and dial away, but you will likely wish you hadn't at the end of the month when you get a phone bill packed with hefty international roaming charges. Even receiving calls on your cell phone can result in excessive charges. Public phones in the larger towns are provided by a company called Ladatel; it offers long-distance calls with a *tarjeta de teléfono* (phone card) issued through TelMex, the national phone company of Mexico. You can buy pre-paid Ladatel phone cards in pharmacies, convenience stores, and supermarkets. Another option is to obtain a calling card through your

own phone company before leaving on your trip.

TIPPING As a former waiter, I am all too familiar with the frustration of foreign tourists' skipping out without tipping just because they aren't familiar with the local customs. That's just a bad excuse to be cheap. Furthermore, Mexico does not have the same labor laws that you find in the United States and there may be times when your waiter is earning tips and tips alone. Be polite, and plan on tipping service personnel the customary amount.

Bellboys should be tipped based on the pieces of luggage they carry to your room. Restaurant servers are customarily tipped around 15 percent of the total bill; however, if you're dining with a large group, a service charge may be automatically added to the bill. The tipping of chambermaids is optional though highly appreciated. You should tip the gas station attendant about 50 cents and/or let them keep the change when it equals less than a few pesos. If you take a tour, it's standard to tip the guide about 10 percent the cost of the trip. This is particularly important if you have a guide who goes out of his way to make sure that you are well informed and have a good time. Taxi drivers are generally not tipped in Mexico, except if they give special service or provide you with good advice. Even then, it is at your discretion, as many taxi drivers will bend over backward to give you advice even if you're not looking for it.

TRANSPORTATION How you get to and around this region of Mexico will depend a lot on what kind of trip you would like to have. If you are looking for a relaxing vacation spent by the

pool, transportation won't be much of an issue. In Acapulco, traffic can be a pain and parking in some areas can be a real problem. In Taxco, the streets are serpentine, narrow, and steep and not a lot of fun to drive on. In Ixtapa-Zihuatanejo, the cheap cost of a bus ride or a taxi makes a rental car impractically expensive unless you're going to be on the go. Taxis are plentiful around the airport and the hotels and the larger beach towns offer a variety of public transportation options to get you to and from hotspots and points of interest. See *Buses, Driving,* and *Taxis* in this chapter for general information; also, see *Getting There, Getting Around, and To Do* in individual chapters for more specific information about local transportation and connections beyond.

TRAVELING WITH KIDS This region of Mexico is an ideal setting to take a break from the kids. On the other hand, you will probably find yourself constantly thinking it would have been great to bring the kids. This is especially true if you happen to find yourself at one of the larger beach resorts that offer special services for children. If you do decide to take the kids along, there are extra hoops you will have to jump though. First, new passport requirements for U.S. citizens returning from abroad also apply to children. Getting a passport for a child under the age of 14 requires filling out additional documents as well as having both parents' consent. That said, it is no longer necessary for single parents or unaccompanied minors traveling in Mexico to have notarized documentation authorizing travel, as long as each child has a valid passport and tourist card. Once that is taken care of, just remember to apply plenty of sunscreen.

TRAVELING WITH PETS Bringing pets to Mexico is a common practice for those driving across the border. If you are flying in, airlines have their own rules about this, so you need to check with your specific air carrier for its specific rules and policies. When you get there, Mexico allows dogs and cats into the country as long as the owner has a notarized letter from a veterinarian stating that the animal is in good health and has the proper vaccinations. However, if you're driving, it's unlikely that this will even be an issue.

Keep in mind that there are certain risks to be considered before bringing an animal to Mexico. Very

few hotels allow pets, and those that do generally charge extra. (Be sure to check ahead when making reservations.) Hot weather can also become an issue with some animals that are not used to it. However, the biggest danger with regard to pets is that Mexican towns—from giant Mexico City to tiny towns—have a problem with stray animals. There is always an outside chance that your animal could contract a disease from one of these animals or that some mishap may happen. Unless you are prepared to constantly look after your pets, it might be a better idea just to leave them at home.

WEATHER The coast between Acapulco and Ixtapa-Zihuatanejo is blessed with abundant sunshine and gorgeous weather throughout much of the year. Sunscreen and a hat are a must. The semitropical climate provides 300 days of sunshine annually and temperatures that average between the high 80s and low 90s during the day and low to mid-70s overnight. The humid rainy season can be uncomfortable. It begins in June and continues through September, with July being the hottest time of year. During this time, rainfall is fairly frequent and at times heavy. The heaviest rains come in August and

September, when storms roll in off the Pacific. The rains typically occur during the late afternoon or evenings. The upside to this is that the flora is particularly lush during the rainy season. The downside is that a good umbrella is a must. During the rest of the year, rainfall is relatively rare and brief when it does occur. However, winter evenings have cool breezes that come off the ocean, so pack a sweater or light jacket if you're visiting between December and March.

Taxco's climate is a bit milder. Temperatures average between the high 70s and low 80s throughout most of the year, though highs dip into the low 70s in December and January. Likewise, low temperatures average in the low 50s throughout most of the year, but dip into the high 40s in December and January. As on the coast, the rainy season comes between June and September with the heaviest rains coming toward the end of the season.

WEDDINGS As "destination weddings" have become more of a popular practice in the United States, Acapulco and Ixtapa have become increasingly popular places in which to hold such events. Not only do they provide the perfect setting for a storybook wedding, but they also make for a great honeymoon. And if you're going to ask your guests to do some traveling anyway, why not bring them to a tropical paradise to share your special day.

As with any wedding (outside of Las Vegas), getting married in Mexico requires planning, coordination, and the completion of documents. One solution to make the process easier is to complete the legal paperwork in the United States and simply perform the ceremony in Mexico. However, if you want your ceremony to be more than symbolic, there are several requirements that you need to fulfill at the location in Mexico where you will be married.

Keep in mind that religious weddings are not officially recognized in Mexico and thus do not change your legal marriage status. Therefore, for your wedding to be legally recognized in Mexico and back home, you'll need a civil ceremony performed by a Spanish-speaking judge who resides in the city where you are getting married. You can also arrange to have this ceremony performed at an outside site for an additional fee.

In addition to the judge, you'll need at least two witnesses who are 18 or older, plus you will have to fulfill several other requirements for your marriage to be legally binding; to accomplish them, it is necessary to arrive in Mexico two to three working days before the ceremony to apply for a marriage license and to have your paperwork and documents processed. You'll need certified copies of your birth certificates as well as passports and copies of your tourist cards. If you have been married previously, you'll need papers indicating that you have been legally divorced for at least a year. There is also medical lab work that needs to be performed in Mexico.

With all of these ancillary details, it's probably a really good idea to hire a wedding coordinator to help you out, especially if you don't speak Spanish. Several wedding planners work out of the larger resorts in Acapulco and Ixtapa or are affiliated with some of the boutique hotels in Zihuatanejo. Check the hotel Web sites for more details.

WHAT TO BRING Obviously, if you are traveling to Acapulco, Ixtapa-Zihu-atanejo, or Taxco, you are going to want to bring a camera, a bathing suit, some flip-flops, and a comfortable pair of walking shoes. And just because you're in Mexico, it doesn't mean that you can buy all of your ancillary items at a cheaper price than you would in the United States. For example, if you plan on going snorkeling, it's a good idea to pick up a mask and snorkel before leaving for Mexico because you'll often find a much larger selection—and better prices—at your local sporting goods store or on the Internet than at the beach, where they know they can charge exorbitant prices because you need your equipment.

Some other items that you'll need if you plan on touring around are sunscreen and a roll of toilet paper. The sunscreen is obvious. As far as the toilet paper goes, some off-the-beaten-path restrooms will charge you a few pesos and give you a couple of squares, and at some places there just *isn't* any. Better to come prepared than find yourself in a situation where you have to improvise. Additionally, you'll want to have a tube or bottle of disinfectant hand lotion or disinfectant wipes to freshen up with. This comes in handy in a variety of situations.

One saying seems to have gotten truer in recent years: There are two types of luggage: carry-on and lost. We all know people who have taken trips and ended up spending days waiting for their luggage to arrive at their destination. It's best to pack light and carry all of your belongings aboard with you as you make your way south. But this is not always a possibility. A good trick is to make arrangements with your hotel and ship your belongings ahead. This costs extra, of course, but the peace of mind that it buys is really priceless.

HISTORY AND CULTURE

Each year, thousands of sun worshipers from all over the world flock to the beaches along Mexico's southern coast in and around Acapulco and Ixtapa-Zihuatanejo. Besides being among Mexico's premier resort destinations, these locales offer visitors a rich history of native culture, conquest, high adventure, and wealth gained and lost. This is a place where forms of relaxation were invented, whose beauty has attracted the famous and powerful alike, and where the paths of empires have crossed. This is not to say that the history of the Mexican state of Guerrero has been all glory and consequence. With Mexico's independence, Acapulco's importance as a trading port waned and the region was largely forgotten for a time. Again in the 20th century, Acapulco saw its splendor rise and fall only to begin to rise again. The mountain town of Taxco has a similar story to tell. With the establishment of Ixtapa, Mexican developers were able to preserve the pastoral charm of the seaside fishing village of Zihuatanejo while

ACAPULCO BAY HAS BEEN THE SITE OF EVENTS THAT HAVE CHANGED THE COURSE OF MEXICAN HISTORY.

SPEAKING SPANISH: GIVE IT A TRY

When speaking Spanish, no matter how meager your vocabulary may be, it is always best to attempt to pronounce the words with your best Latino accent rather than with your everyday American twang. You may feel a little silly rolling your *r*'s and truncating your *o*'s when it's obvious you know only a few words, but doing so will make these attempts infinitely more understandable to the ears of your Mexican hosts. Here are some tips on pronunciation:

Vowels

A—Pronounced as a soft *o* as in *got* and *hot.*

E—Pronounced as a soft *e* as in *egg* and *elephant.*

I—Pronounced as a hard *e* as in *keep* and *eel.*

O—Pronounced as a hard *o* as in *toe* and *row* but with a hard stop.

U—Pronounced as a hard *u* as in *true* and *blue* but with a hard stop.

Y—As in English, this letter is usually pronounced like the *y* in *you* and *yellow,* but by itself (as meaning "and"), it makes the hard *e* sound.

Other Letters

H—Silent, as in the American pronunciation of *herb.*

J—Pronounced as an aspirated *h* as in home and *health.*

LL—Pronounced like the *y* in you and *yellow.*

Ñ—Pronounced as an *ny* as in the name Tanya.

R—Pronounced as a hard *r* with your tongue at the top of your mouth. To an American ear, this makes it sound more like a *d.*

RR—Pronounced with a rolling sound with your tongue at the top of your mouth with air forced through it to make it vibrate (a lot of fun).

creating a world-class resort on the edge of a tropical paradise. Yet, despite these attractions, Guerrero remains a poor region of Mexico. Each year, a significant portion of its population travels north in search of a better life while others crowd into the hills around Acapulco hoping to find a future in the tourism industry. But for travelers of all kinds, Acapulco and the surrounding region continues to offer them what it always has: a beautiful paradise.

NATURAL HISTORY

At about the same size of West Virginia, the Mexican state of Guerrero sprawls for about 250 miles more eastward than southward along Mexico's southern Pacific coast. This long stretch of beaches and rolling hills is so extensive that Mexicans have dubbed the longest stretch, which lies between Zihuatanejo and Acapulco, the Costa Grande (Big Coast); accordingly, its adjacent sister has been dubbed the Costa Chica (Little Coast). To the northeast, Guerrero extends inland for approximately 150 miles and rises progressively into the mountains of the Sierra Madre del Sur. This provides for a fairly diverse landscape moving from the sun-drenched sandy beaches and tropical mangrove swamps along the coast to the rugged deciduous forests of the Sierra Madre foothills to the beautiful clout forests of the mountains themselves. This also makes for a rapid climactic change as one travels the state, moving from the temperate weather of the highlands to the tropical setting of the Pacific Coast.

Although Guerrero is best known for the city of Acapulco, Mexico's gateway to the Far East and original resort destination, visitors wanting to get away from the bustle of the tourist centers can find moments of profound serenity and diversion in just about any direction. In the highlands to the north, you will find gorgeous vistas, rustic colonial towns, and well-maintained points of interest such as the immense caves of Grutas de Cacahuamilpa. Along the coasts of La Costa Grande to the west and La Costa Chica to the southeast, you will find vast undeveloped beaches and sleepy seaside villages. But wherever you venture in Guerrero, you will find that there is still a trace of the region's rich history everywhere you look.

THE COAST Their names notwithstanding, the Costa Grande and Costa Chica are both extensive and have much to offer travelers. The Costa Grande extends to the northwest for 150 miles, past Ixtapa and Zihuatanejo to the Río Balsas, which marks the border with the state of Michoacán. The Costa Chica runs a hundred miles to the southeast to the state of Oaxaca. Both coasts are speckled with sandy beaches and blue lagoons lined with mangroves. Occasionally, the foothills of the Sierra Madre run up against the shoreline, providing spectacular views of the beaches below.

The region's many lagoons have formed from the opposing forces of ocean waves lapping against the fresh water flowing down from the sierras. During the rainy season lasting from the summer through the early fall, the rivers flood the lagoons, breaking the shoreline sandbars and allowing the ocean currents in, depositing a bounty of sea life and nutrients and turning the lagoons into a kind of briny soup. As the rainy season gives way, the waves rebuild the sandbars, allowing the lagoons to become fresh water and clear again. These lagoons are populated with hundreds of species of birds, including colorfully billed lily-

GUERRERO HAS A DIVERSE NATURAL ENVIRONMENT.

DISASTER STRIKES: HURRICANE PAULINE

Although hurricanes are most commonly associated with the eastern coast of North America, in 1997, Hurricane Pauline demonstrated that the western side of the Americas is not immune to their dangers. This storm originally formed as a tropical wave in mid-September off the east coast of Africa and only organized into a hurricane after traversing Panama and entering the eastern Pacific Ocean. It initially moved farther out to sea before making a right turn to the northwest. The storm winds strengthened to a peak of 135 miles per hour before weakening as it skirted the Mexican coastline. On October 8, Pauline made landfall at Puerto Ángel, Oaxaca. However, the storm's most devastating effects were felt in Acapulco, where it began pouring in the early morning hours of October 9. The hurricane drenched the city with more than 16 inches of rain in a 24-hour period. Disastrously, Pauline's rains came only a week after Tropical Storm Olaf had saturated the city. The crowded hillsides that surround Acapulco began to give way. Along these cliff sides, where the city's poorest residents live, severe mudslides and flash flooding occurred, washing many shanty dwellings out to sea. Huge rocks, more than 6 feet in diameter, were dragged from high ground, destroying houses below. A tunnel connecting Parque Papagayo with Playa Hornitos was filled with mud and debris and has never been rebuilt. Seventy-five people were killed in the debris flow and more than 200 were declared missing or washed out to sea. Although the resort hotels near the beach were largely unaffected, 10,000 people in and around the

walkers, preening egrets, and herons with fanlike wingspans. This is to say nothing of the more familiar American and Canadian species of ducks that winter in the lagoons of Guerrero, such as the gadwall, shoveler, and pintail. Out along the shoreline, you will likely have no trouble spotting other species of birds, such as brown pelicans and pterodactyl-like frigate birds.

The waters off the coast of Guerrero have always been abundant with sea life and that continues to be the case today. Shoals of fish abound here, making the region a prime location for sport fishing. Billfish such as swordfish, sailfish, and blue and black marlin roam the deep-sea waters several miles offshore, as do dorado, mackerel, and yellowfin tuna. Several species of shark are also found in these waters, including hammerheads, leopard sharks, and threshers, as are huge Pacific manta rays. Closer to shore are found such species as snapper and sea bass. Along the shore, mullet and groupers can be found rummaging in the sand. Fish are not the only wildlife to be found here. Pacific bottlenosed dolphins are occasionally spotted from tour boats, as are humpback and blue whale, which roam the waters from Acapulco to Hawaii.

PAULINE'S HEAVY RAINS AND ACAPULCO'S BOWL-SHAPED TOPOGRAPHY WERE A DEADLY COMBINATION.

city were left homeless and 70 percent of the city was without clean drinking water for days. Because of this, many have viewed this event as a symbol of the inequality that Acapulco and Mexico as a whole continue to deal with to this day.

THE HIGHLANDS Moving inland from the coastal strip, the foothills of the Sierra Madre del Sur rise gradually to an elevation of about 3,000 feet. This area is dominated by the Southern Pacific dry forests that extend from the coast up through the foothills. These forests are so named because they are deciduous and look dry through the long arid winters. Here is where you will find rustic towns rich in tradition, famous for their lumber, mangoes, and handicrafts. These towns include Atoyac and Petatlán on the Costa Grande, and Acatlán and Ayutla on the Costa Chica. The foothills occupy an area roughly as wide as the coastal strip before giving way abruptly to the Sierra Madre del Sur mountain range. This range runs east–west through the state from the Michoacán border through Oaxaca. The peaks of this range reach heights of over 10,000 feet. The tallest of these peaks, Cerro Teotepec, sits in the center of the range and rises to a height of 11,647 feet.

Moving higher into these mountains, at around 5,000 feet, the Southern Pacific dry forests give way to the Sierra Madre del Sur pine-oak forests. These forests contain all manner of tree ferns and colorful maples, as well as pine and

THE PLIGHT OF SEA TURTLES

The Mexican Pacific coast and the adjoining waters have been home to many species of sea turtles for many millions of years. These species include the leatherback, hawksbill, Kemp's ridley, olive ridley, loggerhead, green, black, and flatback sea turtles. Each summer, these turtles hoist themselves out of the surf and awkwardly crawl beyond the high tide mark to dig a nest on the beach. After laying their eggs, they immediately head back to the sea. Although a single turtle can deposit a clutch of up to 200 eggs, scientists estimate that only a fraction of a percent of these survive to adulthood, even under the best conditions. Once the eggs are deposited in the sand, certain conditions of humidity and temperature are needed for them to hatch. After a couple of months of incubation, the baby turtles finally emerge from the eggs and immediately make their way for the water. This short journey from the sandy nest to the water can take up to a half an hour as the tiny turtles are repeatedly thrown back by waves lapping against the shore. During this time, the babies are in constant danger from predators.

The beaches of Guerrero once teemed with sea turtles going through this annual ritual. However, in the 20th century Mexico's sea turtles and their eggs were been hunted to near extinction. They were slaughtered for their oil and meat, and their skin was used to make shoes, handbags, and wallets. Their eggs are high in protein and believed by some to have aphrodisiac properties. Dishes featuring turtle meat and eggs were once featured on the menus throughout Acapulco. Then in the 1990s, the Mexican government implemented some of the world's strictest laws against killing turtles or taking their eggs. Despite these laws, however, the decimation of sea turtles has continued, pushing them ever closer to extinction. Besides the threat of poachers, other human encroachments have added to their plight. For example, the bright lights of beachfront developments sometimes confuse newly hatched babies, drawing them away from the water. In recent years, however, conservationists have been busy promoting ecotourism, education of locals, and public campaigns to reduce the threat to these endangered animals. Conservationists largely continue to fight an uphill battle, but at least these efforts have been successful in stabilizing olive ridley populations. Several turtle sanctuaries along the Guerrero coast offer visitors the chance to volunteer in the protection of turtle nests, to view hatchlings in various stages of development, and, when the time comes, to personally set the baby turtles down onto the sand to begin their trek to the sea. (Although it would be easier to release them directly into the surf, these animals actually need the experience of dragging themselves into the water so that they know where to come back to lay their own eggs.)

GUERRERO'S HIGHLANDS ARE HOME TO MANY RUSTIC TOWNS AND A RICH CULTURAL TRADITION.

oak trees. They seem to exist in a cloud, as a cool overhead fog is a constant presence. Here you will also find many species of orchids, butterflies, and lichen, as well as animals such as the puma mountain lion, coyote, and quail. Upon rare occasions, visitors may catch a glimpse of the striped ocelot cat or the smaller margay. These forests are also home to the elusive jaguar. At altitudes of between 9,000 and 11,000 feet, the vegetation transforms into a high coniferous forest of white and Montezuma pine, spruce, and fir intermingling with high grassy meadows. These beautiful swaths are only accessible by horse or foot and visits should only be attempted when accompanied by an experienced guide.

CULTURAL HISTORY

The history of the Mexican state of Guerrero is the story of outsiders. From the Aztecs who conquered the region to the Spanish who in turn conquered them, to the Manila galleon bringing its treasures from the Far East to the British and Dutch pirates it attracted, to the rich and famous that made Acapulco a world-renowned getaway to the everyday tourists that frequent the region today, out-siders have been shaping the fortune of the region for hundreds of years. Nevertheless, this region has long played an undeniably important role in shap-ing the history of Mexico as a whole. During the colonial period, all of the treas-ure that the Spanish had plundered in Peru and the goods they had traded for in the Philippines passed through Acapulco. In Taxco, the Spanish initiated their silver-mining operations in the New World. Centuries later, Acapulco would pio-neer resort tourism and Ixtapa would further revolutionize it. Through it all, the people of Guerrero have persevered and taken pride in the role they and their ancestors have played in shaping the history of Mexico.

EARLY ACAPULCO The area that is today the Mexican state of Guerrero has been home to human civilization for around five thousand years. Archaeological evidence comprised of pottery made of clay, stone, and ceramic indicates that people first inhabited Acapulco Bay around 3000 BC, growing crops and fishing. In fact, fragments found near the beach at Puerto Marqués in Acapulco are not only the earliest known ceramics from Mexico, but possibly the oldest in Mesoamerica.

Around 1500 BC, a nomadic tribe from the northeast known as the Nahuas, a tribe related to the Nahuatl who would go on to become the Aztecs, entered this region. In fact, the word "Acapulco" most likely comes from the Nahuatl word meaning "place of the reeds." However, some people say it means "in the place where the reeds were destroyed," referring to a tragic legend about a prince named Acatl who fell in love with Princess Quiahuitl. Because the prince was unable to consummate his love, he dissolved in

GUERRERO HAS A RICH TRADITION OF PRE-COLUMBIAN HISTORY.

his own tears and became a mud pond in which reeds began to grow. Princess Quiahuitl by then had changed into an immense drifting cloud that floated overhead one afternoon. Seeing her beloved, she, too, condensed into water and poured down, destroying the reeds and killing herself in the mud pond alongside Prince Acatl.

Archaeologists have discovered cave paintings and petroglyphs by the Nahuas dating from around 1200 BC. The paintings indicate the early presence of fishing settlements, with agriculture and hunting as secondary activities. In the Veladero National Park near Acapulco, there have been discoveries of calendar beads and 18 massive granite slabs engraved with anthropomorphic, zoomorphic, and geometric details. They were created between 200 BC and AD 600.

The pre-Columbian societies of Guerrero were also highly affected by the rise of the great civilizations of Mesoamerica. The first of these cultures, the Olmec, inhabited central and southern Mexico between 1500 and 400 BC. This culture introduced the effective cultivation of crops such as corn (maize), beans, chile peppers, and cotton, and left other significant evidence of their presence, such as pottery, fine art, and graphic symbols used to record their history. The Olmecs dominated Mexico's east coast in the present-day states of Tabasco and Veracruz. However, their influence extended into modern-day Guerrero, evidenced by wall paintings in the caves of Juxtlahuaca, 30 miles southeast of Chilpancingo. These paintings date from around 300 BC to AD 400, well after the Olmec civilization had come to an end. However, these paintings feature abstract motifs and iconography that is distinctive to Olmec culture.

The Mezcala Indians established a hold over the Guerrero region in the seventh century. This culture does not appear to have built any significant structures in the area. However, they did introduce the crafts of stone sculpture and ceramics. Most of what is left of their culture today consists of small stone figurines and jewelry. Three hundred years later, factions associated with the Teotihuacán civilization, which built a city of the same name just north of Mexico City, built pyramids in Texmelincán and Teloloapán in northern Guerrero. In the 12th century, the Aztecs conquered central Mexico and divided the region that constitutes modern-day Guerrero into seven districts. The conquering Aztecs brought about tax collection and exerted cultural and political influence over the local natives. However, the area that is now Acapulco was never ruled directly by the Aztecs but instead remained under the control of local *caciques* (chiefs).

Although it is generally accepted that the first nonnatives to set foot in Acapulco were Spaniards led by Hernán Cortés, some historians claim that a Chinese monk named Fa Hsien predated Cortés by a century. There are other theories that describe encounters with the Chinese as early as AD 412. These theories claim that the Chinese referred to Acapulco as Ye Pa Ti (Place with Beautiful Waters). Although testimonies of this exist in several Chinese records, physical evidence is scarce if not nonexistent.

EARLY ZIHUATANEJO Long before Columbus sailed to America, Zihuatanejo was famous for being a place of pleasure and relaxation. The name comes from the Nahuatl word *cihuatlán* ("place of the women"; see below). The old Spaniards usually wrote it as "Ciguatán" because that is how the word sounded to them. Later, they added the diminutive ending of *ejo,* to modify it to mean a "small place" or "place without major importance." Therefore, in old Spanish books, maps, and documents, Zihuatanejo is referred to alternatively as Cigua, Ciguatán, and Ciguatanejo. The current name has been in use for only around 200 years. The society that originally inhabited this beautiful place was apparently highly matriarchal and weaving was its dominant industry. This is evidenced by the abundance of pre-Columbian bobbins and other related artifacts that are occasionally found in the area. Other common relics from this civilization include figurines, ceramics, stone

PRE-COLUMBIAN INDIGENOUS PEOPLE USED ZIHUATANEJO BAY AS A PLACE OF RELAXATION.

carvings, and hieroglyphs that are still being found dating as far back as 3,000 BC.

In recent years, archaeologists have uncovered many ancient ruins close to Zihuatanejo, including a large subterranean pyramid, as well as many relics and carved stones in nearby Petatlán. Some scholars now speculate that this area was once inhabited by a single indigenous civilization that occupied the territory from the city of La Unión, approximately 50 miles northwest of Zihuatanejo, to Tecpán, approximately halfway between Zihuatanejo and Acapulco along the Costa Grande. The archaeological evidence also suggests that this civilization was self-ruled with a culture independent from other nearby indigenous groups.

Around 1,000 BC, the Olmecs left their unmistakable stamp on local ceramics with abstract shapes and high-tech quality. Later, waves of settlers made incursions into this area, including the seminomadic Chichimecs from the north, the agricultural Cuitlatecs, and perhaps an early invasion of Aztecs before they settled in their eventual homeland in the Valley of Mexico. However, it was the armies of Tarascan emperor Hiripán who, in the late 14th century invaded the Costa Grande and established a coastal province with a capital at Coyuca, between Zihuatanejo and present-day Acapulco. Local legend says Hiripán, who ruled from what is now the neighboring state of Michoacán, built a royal bathing resort on Playa las Gatas in Zihuatanejo Bay. At this site, the Tarascans built a rock reef that created a wading pool for the emperor's wives to enjoy the water in safety. Part of this reef still exists today at Las Gatas. Tarascan rulers subsequently came to this area often with their many wives, servants, and guards to bask in the sun and enjoy the sea, making this the first tourist resort in Mexico.

In the late 15th century, when Aztec emperor Tizoc became a powerful force in Tenochtitlán, Aztec armies invaded La Costa Grande and pushed out the Tarascans. Many have speculated that Zihuatanejo acquired its current name during this period, when the Aztec conquerors discovered where the royal wives had been sent there for safekeeping. By the 16th century, the Aztecs ruled the coast from their provincial town capital at Cihuatlán.

ACAPULCO IS BUILT ON ONE OF THE BEST DEEP-WATER HARBORS ON THE WEST COAST OF NORTH AMERICA.

GATEWAY TO CONQUEST Sixteenth-century Spanish writer-conquistador Bernal Díaz del Castillo made perhaps the first Western reference to Acapulco in his *Historia verdadera de la conquista de Nueva España* True History of the Conquest of New Spain). The Spanish conquistadors arrived at the site of present-day Acapulco just four months after the fall of the Aztec empire to Hernán Cortés. This exploration and expansion occurred so quickly because

Cortés immediately wanted to find a new commercial route to Asia. The expedition, led by Francisco Chico, arrived at the small fishing village on December 13, 1521. Coincidentally, this village sat on the western end of a bay that would turn out to be the finest deep-water harbor south of San Francisco. December 13 was the Spanish feast day of Santa Lucía and Chico promptly named the newly found bay after that saint: Bahía de Santa Lucía.

The Spanish soon realized that this natural harbor was the perfect location to launch excursions in search of a trade route to the fabled Spice Islands and to conquer more territories. Cortés himself established a shipyard at Bahía de Santa Lucía. Spanish conquistadors quickly assumed power over other tribes to the west, and in 1523, Juan Rodríguez Villafuerte led an expedition northwest to Zihuatanejo, where he built another shipyard. After producing a number of caravels and brigantines, Villafuerte sailed to Acapulco, where he formally took possession of Bahía de Santa Lucía in the name of the kings of Spain by driving a staff with the banner of Castile and Aragón into the sand. By royal decree, the city was renamed Ciudad de los Reyes (City of the Kings). Later, in 1550, King Carlos V of Spain promoted it to historical city. Several expeditions set sail from this port during the 16th century. For example, Francisco Pizarro used the ships built here for his incursion into present-day Peru; in 1532, Francisco de Mendoza led an expedition to the south Pacific; in 1539, Francisco de Ulloa led an expedition in search of the mythical cities of Cibola and Quivira; and in 1540, Domingo del Castillo's expedition chartered the first map of Mexico's west coast. In 1561, Acapulco became Spain's exclusive port of entry on the Pacific by royal decree. This meant that all Spanish sea traffic would be routed solely through Acapulco, leaving Zihuatanejo and all other Pacific ports to idle for hundreds of years.

TAXCO HAS RETAINED THE FEEL OF ITS COLONIAL PAST.

Michael Brady

THE BIRTH OF TAXCO Soon after their conquest of the Aztecs, the Spanish conquistadors learned of a village called Tlachco where the inhabitants had regularly paid tributes of silver to the Aztecs. Tlachco, whose name means "place of the ballgame," because the region had been represented in pre-Hispanic hieroglyphs with a symbol representing the Aztec ballgame called *tlatchtli*. The village was tucked in the mountains about a hundred miles to the southwest of the

Aztec capital and had been a subject state for nearly a century. Cortés arrived in 1522 and quickly staked his claim to the area. By the end of the century, silver mined from this region would be spread across all of Europe. Most of the region's history since that time has been a repeated story of boom and bust.

The town of Taxco was founded by Rodrigo de Castañeda in 1529, by mandate from Cortés. The town's first Spanish residents included three miners—Juan de Cabra, Diego de Nava, and Juan Salcedo, and a carpenter, Pedro Muriel, who in 1531 collectively discovered a vein of silver just outside of the new town and established the first Spanish silver mine in North America. Within a few years they had mined tremendous lodes of silver. In 1534, they built the Hacienda El Chorrillo, which featured an aqueduct, smelter, and water wheel. Los Arcos (the Arches), over Highway 95 at the north end of town, is comprises of the remains of that hacienda. Because the success of those first prospectors drew more settlers to Taxco, the silver in the original veins discovered by the Spanish were soon depleted. The town of Taxco, which had been Spain's primary source of precious metals in the New World, began to see a gradual decrease in mining as other richer and more accessible mining areas were discovered and developed in such places as Guanajuato. Eventually, Taxco faded into obscurity for almost 200 years.

THE FORT OF SAN DIEGO WAS BUILT TO PROTECT ACAPULCO FROM INVASION.

THE DANGEROUS ROUTE TO THE FAR EAST In 1565, Friar Andrés de Urdaneta sailed east from the Philippines and dropped anchor in Acapulco Bay, becoming the first European to sail from Asia to North America. At the time, trade was common between Mexico and destinations such as Peru. Furthermore, traveling west across the Pacific was not a problem. Portuguese navigator Ferdinand Magellan had first accomplished it in 1521, the same year as the Aztec conquest. However, prevailing winds and ocean currents made the journey east to Mexico exceedingly difficult. Urdaneta's discovery of this route, which came to be known as the *tornavuelta* (turnaround), would make Acapulco the most important commerce and trading port in the New World. For the next 400 years, European trade with the Philippines and other Asian and South American ports passed through Acapulco. This trade had an enormous affect on the physical and cultural makeup of the region.

According to some historians, the coconut palm, which is so pervasive through-out the region today, came from the Philippines. Furthermore, during the 16th century, Acapulco became a center for the slave trade. The importation of slaves from Africa had long been a common Spanish practice and most slaves in this region were put to work in the silver mines. Some escaped slaves established communities in the mountainous regions of southern and western Guerrero. These communities continued to function until the mid-19th century. Today, descendents of those African slaves have settled along the southern Pacific coast.

Soon after Urdaneta's discovery of the *tornavuelta,* ships from Asia began arriving at the port of Acapulco with silks, porcelain, jade, jasmine, and spices. These goods were then carried overland on a narrow trail to the gulf coast town of Veracruz for shipment to Spain. This was an arduous journey fraught with danger. In fact, just the first leg of the overland route, a 250-mile passage from Acapulco to Mexico City, took 12 days to travel. However, the prospect of lucra-tive overseas trade with Asia made this one of the busiest trade routes of the time.

The most famous ship to dock in Acapulco's harbor at this time was the *Santa Ana,* a special trading ship known to the English as a "Manila galleon." For more than 250 years, this ship made an annual trip from Acapulco to Manila, then under the control of Spain. Upon the vessel's return to Acapulco, the city would throw an enormous merchant fair at which traders would barter for its cargo of silks, porcelain, ivory, and lacquerware.

This annual treasure attracted the attention of pirates from England and the Netherlands. They set out from their hideouts in the Caribbean to try their luck in the Pacific. Soon, the waters along Mexico's west coast were speckled with lurking marauders waiting for their shot at a Spanish galleon. During this time, Acapulco became a haven for pirates such as Sir Francis Drake, who hid his ships in the quiet bay of Puerto Marqués and plundered the vessels that were laden with treasure. Since Zihuatanejo was relatively close to the trade route from Mexico to the Philippines, it also became a favorite spot for these maraud-ers to ride out bad weather or trade for supplies. More commonly, pirates came to Zihuatanejo because its coastline offered conveniently concealed places to wait out the opportunity to attack Spanish ships. Many of Zihuatanejo's beaches got their names during this period. For example, Playa la Ropa (Clothes Beach) was so named after a Spanish craft was wrecked in the waters just offshore and its cargo of Chinese silks came washing up on the beach. Playa Madera (Wood Beach) got its name from the fine timber that was exported from the Zihuatane-jo shipyard.

In 1579, Drake set his sights on the famous *Santa Ana* but failed to take its treasure. Nearly a decade later, however, British pirate Sir Thomas Cavendish was successful in seizing the ship off the coast of Cabo San Lucas. With this feat, Cavendish was able to steal more than a million gold pesos, which resulted in severely depressing the London bullion market.

In 1614, after a Dutch fleet led by Admiral Joris von Spielbergen attempted an invasion of Acapulco Bay, Viceroy Diego Fernández de Córdoba ordered a fort built to protect the city. The site of the fort, known as El Morro, provided an effective lookout as well as a prime spot to set signal fires to warn Acapulco's

TAXCO HAS A BOOM-AND-BUST HISTORY.

12,000 residents of approaching danger. Ironically, the viceroy commissioned a Dutch engineer, Adrian Boot, to design the stronghold. The result was a masterpiece of military engineering, a unique irregular polygon with numerous fortified rooms built around a central courtyard. The building was completed in April 1617 and housed 2,000 soldiers, with enough provisions and ammunition to last a year. It became known as Fort San Diego after the man who commissioned it.

TAXCO REDISCOVERED AND FORGOTTEN AGAIN In 1716, a Spaniard of French descent named Don José de la Borda discovered a rich vein of silver in Taxco, making him exceedingly wealthy nearly overnight. Along the way, he managed to introduce new methods of draining and repairing mines. He is believed to have treated his indigenous workers better than did other colonial miners. He expressed his gratitude for this new fortune by developing Taxco's infrastructure with new schools and roads. Among Borda's other gifts to the city was the ornate Santa Prisca Cathedral that now dominates Taxco's *zócalo* (town square). Today, Don José de la Borda is considered the "father" of Taxco. Once again, his success was heralded and a new flood of miners rushed to try their luck in the hills around Taxco. Before long, more than a dozen other churches had been built in this small town as gifts from other successful miners.

Between the 17th and the 19th centuries, Bolivia, Peru, and Mexico generated approximately 85 percent of the world's silver production. However, in the 19th century during Mexico's war for independence, the Spanish silver barons destroyed their mines rather than lose them to the revolutionaries. With this, the art of silver work that had become an integral part of Taxco died out for another century.

THE WAR FOR INDEPENDENCE Largely because of its economic importance, Acapulco played a key role in Mexico's war for independence. In 1810, shortly after Miguel Hidalgo y Costilla made his *grito* (call) for independence in the town of Dolores, he asked José María Morelos to take the independence movement to the south by capturing Acapulco. Morelos quickly proved to be a talented military strategist, defeating Spanish forces throughout what is today the state of Guerrero. Despite the fact that many of the locals sided with the Spanish royalists, Morelos captured Acapulco in December, only three months after the start of the war. However, he failed to take the Fort of San Diego and Spanish reinforcements forced him to lift his siege of the fortress the following month. Despite this setback, Morelos continued to win military victories throughout the region. By employing a strategy of rapid marches, he was able to capture most of the Spanish possessions on the Pacific coast, of what are today the states of Michoacán and Guerrero.

Morelos soon gained a reputation as one of the bravest and capable military men to emerge from the independence movement. In February 1813, he set out with his army from Oaxaca City to once again capture to city of Acapulco. Morelos and more than 3,000 men quickly captured the city of Chilpancingo and declared it the nation's new capital. However, the battle for Acapulco proved more difficult as royalists put up an intense battle that lasted for six months. In the end Morelos prevailed when, in August, Captain Pedro Antonio Vélez raised a white flag over the Fort of San Diego, signaling the royalists' surrender.

While escorting the new insurgent Congress in November 1815, Morelos was captured at Tezmalaca and was brought to Mexico City, where the royalists tried and executed him for treason. However, his lieutenant, Vicente Guerrero, took over his command and continued the war for independence. Guerrero was the only major insurgent leader to remain at large and survive to see Mexico gain its independence from Spain. After his military days, he was appointed as chief of the southern region of Mexico, where he fought fiercely for the establishment of a federal republic. In 1821, the war with Spain officially ended and Mexico emerged as a new nation. Independence from Spain rendered the trade route through Acapulco obsolete. The last galleon arrived to Acapulco in 1815. This once indispensible trading port soon fell into a period of decline.

19TH-CENTURY INSTABILITY The 19th century was a time of great upheaval in Mexico, and the state of Guerrero was no exception. Vicente Guerrero became president of Mexico in 1829 but was assassinated just nine months later. Four years and more than a half a dozen presidents later, government forces continued to struggle to gain control over its territory as indigenous rebels attacked government installations as well as civilian homes and businesses throughout Guerrero, exacerbating the region's political and military instability. Acapulco regained some of its old prominence for a short time during the early days of the California gold rush as hopeful miners used it as a stopover on their journey north from Panama.

In 1862, French forces invaded Mexico to pressure the Mexican government to settle long-standing debts. During this affair, Acapulco was considered a strategic location. In January 1863, invading French troops bombarded the port before occupying the city for three days. In June, the French seized Acapulco once again and remained for more than a year, placing Habsburg emperor

Maximilian I in control of Mexico in 1864, with the blessing of both Napoleon III and royalist Mexicans. In 1865, the French besieged Acapulco once more but this time Mexican forces were successful in holding them off. Many constitutionalist and liberal leaders sought refuge in Guerrero, where they attempted to reorganize their opposition to the new government. Former president Benito Juárez led this opposition, supported by a Nahua writer and journalist from Guerrero named Ignacio Manuel Altamirano. In 1867, Juárez regained control of the country, had Maximilian executed, and remained Mexico's president until 1872.

In the late 19th century, during the presidency of the dictator Porfirio Díaz, conflicts between the national government and powerful *caudillos* (authoritarian political-military leaders), made it difficult for national authorities to govern Guerrero. As early as 1893, Guerrero rebels led by General Canuto A. Neri carried out insurrections against the federally supported state government. The constant presence of militias and a weak state government in Guerrero created a situation in which there was no central authority. It seemed that no one had the power to effectively control conflicts as they escalated throughout the state.

WILLIAM SPRATLING AND THE REBIRTH OF TAXCO In 1926, William Spratling, a U.S. citizen and associate architecture professor from Tulane University, arrived in Taxco by way of the newly built highway from Mexico City. He had come to study Mexico and its culture and was immediately taken by the town's scenic beauty. By 1929, he had made his way into the influential artistic circles of Mexico and decided to move to the city permanently. Several years later, U.S. ambassador to Mexico, Dwight Morrow, commented to Spratling how

WILLIAM SPRATLING FELL IN LOVE WITH TAXCO'S SCENIC BEAUTY.

strange it was that Taxco had never been considered a location for jewelry design, despite the city's long history of silver mining. Spratling decided to do something about it and thus changed the course of Taxco's artistic and economic history.

Spratling encouraged on the town's artisans to rediscover the craft of silversmithing and tapped into the potential talent of the locals, creating an entirely new way of life. He created his own designs and developed an apprentice system to train young silversmiths from the local population. He also brought in a highly regarded goldsmith from the nearby town of Iguala to teach the art of working precious metal. The great beauty and craftsmanship that came out of these efforts once again garnered worldwide recognition for Taxco as an important town for silver handicrafts. As many of his students began to

IXTAPA WAS BUILT TO HOUSE LARGE-SCALE RESORTS.

open workshops and stores of their own, Spratling continued to give them his encouragement and support. Furthermore, as Acapulco continued to develop as a vacation destination for travelers from Mexico City, these visitors began to consider Taxco an important stopover. This is a tradition that has continued to this day.

In 1967, Spratling died in a car accident just outside Taxco. However, Mexicans continue to regard him as "the father of Mexican silver." A silver bust of him can be found in the town's silver museum, and the workshop he created is now the Spratling Museum behind the Santa Prisca Cathedral. This museum houses his collection of silver designs and pre-Columbian figures that he left to the town of Taxco. However, perhaps a more lasting gift that he renewed the tradition of silversmithing that has made Taxco a town of national importance. Today, the number of silversmiths in and around Taxco number in the hundreds and their work is prized throughout Mexico.

THE PRESERVATION OF ZIHUATANEJO AND CREATION OF IXTAPA

As the 20th century began, Zihuatanejo was a small fishing village that had been largely forgotten by travelers from the outside world. In fact, it was much more famous for its fine woods than its beautiful beaches. Because there was no good road into the town, ships sailed out of the bay to Acapulco loaded with hardwoods, coconut oil, shellfish, and fish bound for ports around the world. For the most part, only the occasional adventurer ever braved the overland route to this ancient resort town, and what they found was a sparse village abutting the seashore. Because there were no hotels, visitors generally stayed in the private homes of local fishermen. Then in the 1950s, the city constructed a small airport for DC-3s to increase commercial trade. This had the unintended effect of bringing more tourists to the region. This prompted the town to begin construction of several small hotels. However, it was not until a highway was constructed from Acapulco in the 1960s that Zihuatanejo's indigo bay began to be discovered by a wide range of paradise-seekers.

Beginning in the 1960s, the number of hotels in Zihuatanejo began to grow exponentially, as did the quality of services. Additionally, the entire region became much more accessible during this time. It was no longer necessary to be a millionaire to vacation in Acapulco, and the foreign and Mexican middle-class was now crowding its hotels. The burgeoning tourist industry brought new residents as well, and by the middle of the decade, the town was home to about 5,000 people. In light of its growing popularity, government developers proposed a plan to turn Zihuatanejo into a resort town similar to Acapulco. However, the townspeople refused to idea of drastically changing the look and feel of their small fishing village. Therefore, the Mexican Federal Bureau for Tourist Development (FONATUR) came up with a plan to create a world-class resort for tourists averse to big cities and mega-destinations. In 1968, FONATUR expropriated a large seaside coconut tree plantation northeast of Zihuatanejo for this purpose. In keeping with the tradition established in Cancún of giving new Mexican tourist destinations indigenous names, this site was christened Ixtapa (the Nahuatl word for "the white place") because of the beautiful white sand beaches found here. Investors poured in, putting up money for drainage, roads, and utilities, not to mention a brand-new airport. The in 1971, the Aristos opened its doors, becoming the first modern high-rise resort in Ixtapa. This hotel stayed open until 2003 when it was demolished to make room for new developments.

ACAPULCO RESORTS HAVE STRIVED TO REGAIN SOME OF THEIR OLD LUSTER.

ANNUAL EVENTS

The following notable holidays and festivals are celebrated throughout the region. Dates may vary. See also *Special Events in individual chapters.*

January: **Jan. 1—Año Nuevo** (New Year's Day), a national holiday. **Jan. 6— Día de los Reyes** (Day of the Kings), when traditionally gifts are exchanged.

February: **Feb. 2—Día de Candelaria** (Candlemas): On this day, plants, seeds, and candles are blessed, followed by processions and bullfights.

March: **Mar. 21—Birthday of Benito Juárez**, a national holiday.

April: **Semana Santa** (Holy Week). This week before Easter is celebrated with many processions, particularly in Taxco, Petatlán, and Iguala.

May: **May 1—Día del Trabajo** (Labor Day), a national holiday. **May 5—Cinco de Mayo**, a national holiday in celebration of the defeat of the French at Puebla in 1862, is a big day in Acapulco.

August: **Aug. 6–7—Fiesta del Padre Jesús**, a celebration of Petatlán's beloved patron and religious symbol.

September: **Sep. 16—Día de la Independencia** (Independence Day), a national holiday.

October: **Oct. 12—Día de la Raza**, a national holiday in celebration Mexico's ethnic diversity.

November: **Nov. 1—Día de Todos Santos** (All Saints' Day), in honor of the souls of departed children, is celebrated with the placing of sugar skeletons and skulls family altars. **Nov. 2—Día de los Muertos** (Day of the Dead), in honor of departed ancestors, is celebrated with festivals and the decoration of gravesites with the deceased person's favorite food and drink. **Nov. 1–15—Feria de la Nao de China** is a celebration of the colonial trade route that linked Acapulco with China via the Philippines. **Nov. 20—Día de la Revolución**, a national holiday in honor of the Mexican revolution of 1910–17.

December: **Dec. 1—Inauguración Presidencial (Presidential Inauguration)**; in Mexico, the national government changes hands every six years (the next occurrence will be in 2012). **Dec. 12—Día de Nuestra Señora de Guadalupe** (Festival of the Virgin of Guadalupe) is celebrated with processions, with a particularly impressive one in Acapulco around the *zócalo*. **Dec. 16–24—Semana de Navidad** (Christmas Week), celebrated with piñatas and posadas, or candlelit processions. There is traditionally an important midnight Mass on Christmas Eve. **Dec. 25—Día de Navidad** (Christmas Day), a national holiday.

ACAPULCO'S CONTINUED DEVELOPMENT In the 1970s, as the Mexican government began to promote the development of more tourist destinations from the Yucatán Peninsula to Baja California, competition caused Acapulco to suffer. Gradually, the city began to fall into a state of disrepair. This only bolstered the notion that Acapulco was a city that had lost its luster. Resort towns such as Cancún, Ixtapa, and Cabo San Lucas, which were built solely to serve as resorts, provided visitors with a utopian feeling of isolation from the problems of the world, whereas Acapulco remained a fully functioning city—with all the complications that go along with that. However, the residents of Acapulco were not ready to cede their reputation as a world-class resort destination, and rejuvenation efforts began in earnest in the 1990s. These efforts were stymied in 1997 when Hurricane Pauline slammed into the city, causing deadly mud slides in the hills surrounding the city. The damage only served to highlight the great economic abyss between the Zona Hotelera (Hotel Zone) and the rest of Acapulco, which is largely poor, crowded, and polluted. In recent years, renovations in the resort area have resumed, along with efforts to improve the standard of living of the local residents. These renovations include the development of Acapulco Diamante, a huge resort district along Puerto Marqués Bay, which was previously a beachfront shantytown. Additional luxury hotels and resort condominiums have gone up near the airport and Old Acapulco. The rural area west of downtown called Pie de la Cuesta, with its beautiful Coyuca Lagoon, has developed smaller inns that cater to travelers looking for a more laid-back ambience, far from the crowds of the Zona Hotelera.

Today, the locals throughout the state of Guerrero offer visitors a wide variety of attractions. Accommodations and services that are second to none can be found not only in the obvious places such as Acapulco and Ixtapa, but in hideaways such as the popular expat-American getaway Troncones just north of Ixtapa, or the astounding caves of Grutas de Cacahuamilpa southeast of Taxco. Throughout this region of Mexico, visitors find it easy to lose themselves in a surprisingly wide variety of diversions. However, it is much more challenging to escape the history and tradition of this wondrous place.

Acapulco 1

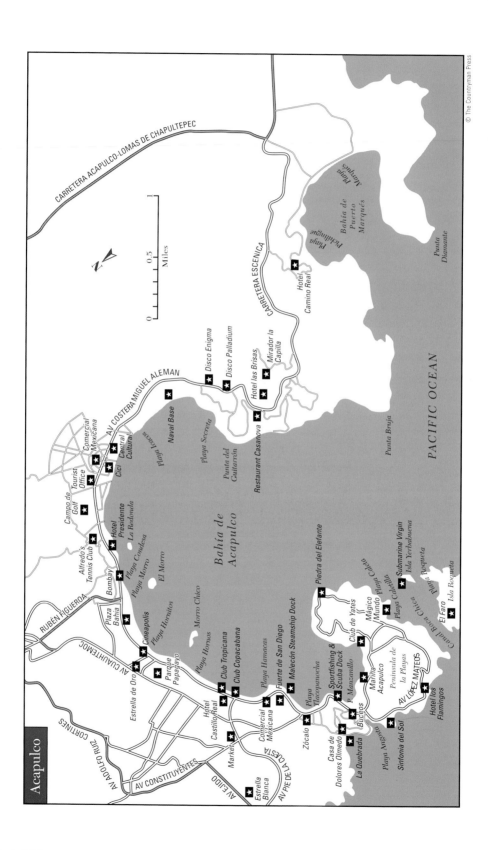

Acapulco

ACAPULCO

Acapulco's rise to become one of the world's the top vacation destinations can be traced back to 1920, when the city received a visit from the Prince of Wales (best known to us now as the late Duke of Windsor). Acapulco's charm captivated him and his royal entourage, and he returned to Europe with stories about the serene beauty of the place. Then in 1928, the narrow path that had once served as the trade route to transport goods from the sea to Mexico City was turned into a real road. Although the trip from Mexico City took more than a week, it allowed easier access for a greater number of tourists. Before long, fashionable Europeans and wealthy Mexicans were spending their winters in what was then a sleepy seaside village.

The first serious effort to generate tourism in Acapulco came from a Texan entrepreneur named Albert B. Pullen, whose real estate investments led to the development of what is today referred to as Old Acapulco. Pullen was able to garner investments from such men such J. Paul Getty, who is said to have purchased 900 acres of oceanfront property at three cents an acre. Today that property is the home the lavish Fairmont Pierre Marqués Hotel on Playa Revolcadero. Pullen's development also attracted writers looking for a pleasant hideaway, such as Malcolm Lowry (author of *Under the Volcano*), B. Traven (author of *The Treasure of the Sierra Madre*), and Tennessee Williams, who set his play *Night of the Iguana* in Acapulco.

Acapulco's development took another major step forward in 1928 with the construction of an airport providing direct international flights from major U.S. cities. In 1933, Carlos Barnard, an accountant for an oil company in Tampico who had traversed his way to Acapulco by mule, opened the first section of Hotel El Mirador with 12 rooms on the cliffs of La Quebrada. In their idle hours, the boys who worked at the hotel began to diving off the 126-foot cliffs behind the hotel into the channel where they dumped the hotel trash. The boys quickly realized the attention they were attracting and began passing the hat for donations. This activity at the cliffs of La Quebrada would go on to become the worldwide symbol of Acapulco.

In 1946, Miguel Alemán Valdés assumed the Mexican presidency and set about promoting economic development in the state of Guerrero. The prize of his vision was to establish Acapulco as a major tourist destination and thus he began devoting resources to accomplish this goal. Today, the main thoroughfare running along Acapulco Bay is named after him. Also around this time, Carlos Barnard opened La Perla restaurant adjoining the Hotel El Mirador and overlooking La Quebrada. Before long, jet-setters, Hollywood celebrities, and other wealthy travelers began to arrive. Jackie and John F. Kennedy honeymooned here, as did Brigitte Bardot. Regulars included the likes of Frank Sinatra, Judy Garland, Johnny Weismuller, John Wayne, and Errol Flynn. It was a place where both Hedy Lamarr and Liz Taylor came to get married and Lana Turner came to live.

In the 1960s, the city saw a new explosion of development. Until that time, the only attraction east of the Fort of San Diego was a bull ring and the city jail. With the construction of Avenida Costera Miguel Alemán, that all changed, as new high-rise resort hotels began popping up along beaches such as Playa Condesa and Playa la Redonda. Furthermore, the city airport was moved from Pie de la Cuesta to a new site just southeast of town and began offering jet air service from the United States. Acapulco reached the pinnacle of its splendor in 1968, when it hosted the yachting events in the Summer Olympics. However, the glimmer of these innovative new resorts did not last long. If anything, the overcrowded swimming pools and kitschy tourist establishments helped diminish the city's reputation as an exclusive destination. Then in the 1970s, Acapulco's reign as the gem of Mexican tourism began to fade as developers looking to create a super–tourist destination from scratch broke ground in the Yucatán Peninsula on a site that would come to be known as Cancún.

Today, shadows of the spender of those bygone days of jet-set and glamour can still be seen around Acapulco, but it has undeniably faded. The city remains a major port of call for cruise ships and it occasionally continues to add larger and ritzier resort hotels. However, its main purpose today seems to be as a quick getaway for *chilangos* from Mexico City. Instead of playing host to crowds of

AVENIDA COSTERA MIGUEL ALEMÁN IS THE MAIN THOROUGHFARE IN ACAPULCO.

international tourists as it once did, the majority of Acapulco's visitors today are Mexicans from other nearby cities.

If your itinerary will keep you close to the coast, Avenida Costera Miguel Alemán is a street you will get to know well. The Costera (Coast), as it is called locally, hugs the oval Bahía de Santa Lucía from the naval base at the southeast end to Old Acapulco, also known as the Caleta at the northwest end.

Old Acapulco was obviously not designed for cars. It is far too dense, with narrow crooked streets, few right angles, and balconies overhanging the street. However, this makes it an interesting area to take a stroll. Among the attractions that are worth taking a walk to see is the Fort San Diego, straight up Avenida Morelos from the Costera and to the right. In about one block, the street veers to the left. Continue straight ahead on the pedestrian walkway. Just before you reach the iron gates of the fort grounds, you'll see the mask museum on your left. The Museo de la Máscara houses well over a thousand masks, principally from the state of Guerrero. Fort San Diego is now a museum that is mostly dedicated to the city's history as a trading port. The *zócalo*, formally known as the Plaza Juan Alvarez, is a block and a half west of the corner of Escudero and Morelos. Here, you can sit in the shade of huge rubber and mango trees, enjoy the sights, listen to the fountains, or get your shoes shined. The art deco Catedral de Nuestra Señora de la Soledad at the far side of the Plaza was built in 1938. The *malecón* (seaside promenade) is across Avenida Costera Miguel Alemán from the *zócalo*. Follow the *malecón* to the northeast into the Zona Hotelera for bars, restaurants, and beaches.

GUIDANCE Secretaria de Turismo (744-440-0170), Calle Hornitos s/n, Acapulco, GRO 39350. This office will help you with maps, service listings, and any other tourism related questions or concerns.

GETTING THERE *By air:* **Juan N. Álvarez International Airport** in Acapulco (airport code ACA) is located about 15 miles southeast of town and is serviced by many domestic and international airlines. Several American airlines operate out of ACA, with most routes going through Mexico City. These include American Airlines out of Dallas, Continental out of Houston, Delta out of Atlanta, and U.S. Airlines out of Phoenix. Mexican airlines connecting to ACA include Aeromexico, Aviacsa, and Mexicana Airlines. This bustling airport generally does a good job of

ACAPULCO'S *ZÓCALO* PROVIDES SHADED RELAXATION.

AIRPORTS IN ACAPULCO AND ZIHUATANEJO PROVIDE CONVENIENT ACCESS TO THE REGION.

quickly processing international visitors through immigration.

There are several booths located in the airport terminal where you can rent cars. If you do not plan on renting a car, obtain taxi service through the agent booth near the terminal exit. This will assure that you pay the standard rate and do not get ripped off. It is generally not a good idea to accept a ride from the taxi drivers offering service on their own. If you do decide to go with these independent drivers, be sure to settle on a price before you get in the car. A ride from ACA to the Zona Hotelera in a compact car runs between $25 and $40, depending on the distance. A ride in a SUV seating up to seven people will cost you between $30 and $45. You can also save yourself a few bucks by riding *colectivo,* meaning that you share a taxi with other passengers. This runs about $8 per person. However, be forewarned that this will be a tight ride for both you and your luggage.

By car: **Cuernavaca-Acapulco Highway 95D,** also known as the Autopista del Sol (Highway of the Sun), is a toll road that runs from Mexico City to the port of Acapulco through Cuernavaca, Taxco, Iguala, and Chilpancingo. The drive from Mexico City to Acapulco takes about four hours and the tolls run about $50 each way. Despite the fact that the tolls along this route are steep, this is the best way to get to Acapulco from the interior. It's a modern highway with four to six lanes and significantly quicker and more convenient than the alternatives. If money is a bigger factor than time, there is a route along a two-lane road called the **Cuernavaca Libre (Highway 95),** which runs parallel to Highway 95D. However, this is a much more treacherous drive that takes about six hours.

By bus: You can get to Acapulco by bus from almost any major city in Mexico. Buses run all day to Acapulco from Mexico City's **Central de Autobuses del Sur** (Mexico City has four bus stations, so make sure you go to the right one). The trip takes about five hours.

GETTING AROUND *By bus:* Acapulco's local buses tend to be a bit shabby but are frequent and plentiful, do and are a very economical means of getting around locally. Several bus lines operate along Avenida Costera Miguel Alemán, and the specific route is painted on the windshield: "Caleta/Hornos/Base." An alternative route, "Caleta/Cine Río/Base," leaves the from the *zócalo* and runs through the business district along Avenida Cuauhtémoc, then returns to the at Costera at La Gran Plaza Mall. This route is convenient if you want to shop at Home Depot or Sears. Keep in mind that the route is always painted on the windshield. (Some buses also have "Costera" painted on the side but be careful: this indicates the bus company, not the route.) There are bus stops at intervals all along Avenidas Costera Miguel Alemán and Cuauhtémoc, but most drivers

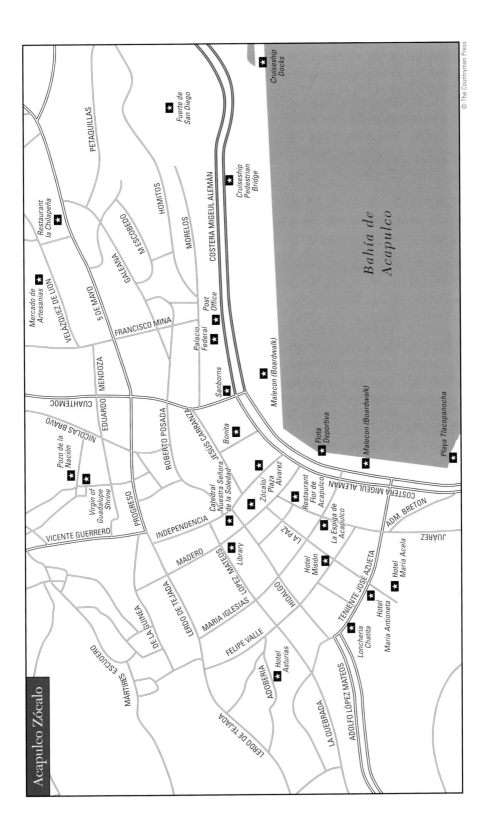

Acapulco Zócalo

Bahía de Acapulco

Cruiseship Docks

Cruiseship Pedestrian Bridge

Fuerte de San Diego

PETAQUILLAS

HOMITOS

MORELOS

COSTERA MIGEUL ALEMÁN

Restaurant la Chilapeña

Mercado de Artesanías

M ESCOBEDO

GALEANA

5 DE MAYO

VELÁZQUEZ DE LION

FRANCISCO MINA

Post Office

Palacio Federal

Sanborns

Malecon (Boardwalk)

MENDOZA

CUAUHTEMOC

EDUARDO

NICOLÁS BRAVO

Pozo de la Nación

Virgin of Guadalupe Shrine

ROBERTO POSADA

JESÚS CARRANZA

Bonita

Catedral Nuestra Señora de la Soledad

Flota Deportiva

Malecon (Boardwalk)

Playa Tlacopanocha

PROGRESO

VICENTE GUERRERO

INDEPENDENCIA

Zócalo/ Plaza Alvarez

Restaurant Flor de Acapulco

COSTERA MIGEUL ALEMÁN

ADM. BRETON

MADERO

LÓPEZ MATEOS

Library

LA PAZ

Hotel Misión

La Espiga de Acapulco

Hotel Maria Acela

JUÁREZ

DE LA GUINEA

LERDO DE TEJADA

MARIA IGLESIAS

HIDALGO

TENIENTE JOSÉ AZUETA

Hotel Maria Antioneta

ESCUDERO

MÁRTIRES

FELIPE VALLE

ADOBERIA

Hotel Asturias

LA QUEBRADA

LERDO DE TEJADA

ADOLFO LÓPEZ MATEOS

Loncheria Chatita

will stop virtually anywhere if you signal that you want to board or get off. City buses run from about 5 AM–about 11 PM. If you want to trek out to the tranquil resort village of Pie de la Cuesta just northwest of Acapulco, you can board a bus in front of Sanborn's Centro and the central post office along the Costera. Look for a green and white bus with "Pie de la Cuesta" or "Playa Luces" painted on the windshield. It's a scenic, half-hour ride along the cliffs overlooking the Pacific at the extremely reasonable price of only five pesos.

Car rental: **Alamo Car Rental** (744-484-3305; www.alamo.com), Avenida Costera Miguel Alemán #2150, Acapulco, GRO 39850. Open daily 8 AM–10 PM. Additional locations: Airport (744-466-9444) and Hotel Mayan Palace (744-469-6075). **Avis Car Rental** (744-466-9190; www.avis.com.mx), Avenida Costera Miguel Alemán #97, Acapulco, GRO 39850.Open Mon.–Fri. 9 AM–8 PM, Sat. and Sun. 9 AM–6 PM. Additional location: Airport (744-466-9190). **Budget Car Rental** (744-481-2433; www.budget.com.mx), Avenida Costera Miguel Alemán #121-L-27, Acapulco, GRO 39850. Open Mon.–Fri. 8 AM–7 PM, Sat. 9 AM–7 PM, and Sun. 9 AM–4 PM. Additional location: Airport (744-481-2433). **Europcar** (555-207-5572; www .europcar.com.mx), Avenida Costera Miguel Alemán #121, Acapulco, GRO 39850. Open daily 8 AM–11 PM. Additional location: Airport (744-446-9314). **Hertz Car Rental** (744-485-8947; U.S. 1-800-709-5000; www .hertz.com.mx), Avenida Costera Miguel Alemán #137A, Acapulco, GRO 39850. Open daily 8 AM–7 PM. Additional location: Airport (744-485-8947).

By taxi: Taxis are abundant and cost 10 to 15 pesos for most destinations within the city. A ride to the Quebrada cliff divers should not cost more than 30 pesos. In Acapulco, the taxis are not metered, so you will have to negotiate a price. Being able to speak some Spanish will help but is not essential. Keep in mind that the taxi drivers who hang out in front of resort hotels can be pushy. If you are not looking for a taxi, don't feel bad about walking right by without an

AVENIDA COSTERA MIGUEL ALEMÁN FILLS UP WITH FOOT TRAFFIC AT NIGHT.

acknowledgement. If you do need a taxi, negotiate your price and stick to what you need. Ignore unsolicited offers of great deals in booze or anything else. Also, if the taxi driver quotes you a price that you feel is too high, just walk away. There will be another taxi waiting down the street, so there is no need to waste your time on someone who is trying to rip you off. The Volkswagen Beetle taxis tend to be cheaper than sedans. Your driver may ask you if you want *aire* (air-conditioning). Air-conditioning will increase the price of your ride. **Cipres Juárez Yedid** (744-485-6728), **Norberto Giovanni Taxi** (744-485-4292), **Sitio de Autos Acapulco** (744-482-0007), **Taxi Web Sapi** (744-466-9437). *Tour service:* **Tour by Van** (744-110-4324; www.tourbyvan.com), Avenida Costera Miguel Alemán #116, Acapulco, GRO 39690. This knowledgeable tour group offers tours and transportation around Acapulco and the surrounding environs. Tours are fully personalized with itinerary tailor-made to suit your personal needs. Select the places you want to visit, the activities you want to enjoy, and the period of time that you are interested in taking advantage of their services. Transport is made in fully air-conditioned vans that can accommodate up to 15 people. Smaller vehicles are also available. All our tours and transportation services include driver, fuel, insurance, and taxes.

MEDICAL ASSISTANCE *Hospitals:* **Hospital Centro Medico** (744-482-4692), José Valdez Arévalo #620, Acapulco, GRO 39670; **Hospital General** (744-445-5877), Avenida Ruiz Cortines #128, Acapulco, GRO 39670; **Hospital del Pacifico** (744-487-7180), Calle La Nao #4 y Fraile, Acapulco, GRO 39670; **Hospital Privado Magallanes** (744-485-6194, Wilfrido Massieu #2, GRO 39670. *Pharmacies:* **Farmacia Hidalgo** (744-482-1772), Calle Hidalgo #24A, Acapulco, GRO 39300. Open daily 7 AM–11 PM. **Farmacia del Puerto** (744-483-1339), Avenida Cuauhtémoc #9-B, Acapulco, GRO 39300. Open daily 7 AM–11 PM. **Farmacias de Similares** (744-483-2166), Avenida Costera Miguel Alemán #3, Acapulco, GRO 39300. Open daily 7 AM–11 PM.

BANKS Banamex (744-486-1678), Avenida Costera Miguel Alemán #2085, Acapulco, GRO 39300. Open Mon.–Fri. 9 AM–4 PM, Sat. 10 PM–2 PM. **Banco Santander** (744-486-4395), Avenida Costera Miguel Alemán #2088, Acapulco, GRO 39300. Open Mon.–Fri. 8 AM–3 PM. **Bancomer** (744-483-7293), Avenida Ejido #5, Acapulco, GRO 39550. Open Mon.–Fri. 8:30 AM–4 PM. **HSBC** (744-485-8621), Avenida Costera Miguel Alemán #2077, Acapulco, GRO 39300. Open Mon.–Sat. 8 AM–7 PM.

USEFUL PHONE NUMBERS

Emergency: 078

Direct-dial prefix, U.S. to Mexico: 011-52

Direct-dial prefix, Mexico to U.S.: 001

Highway Patrol: 744-441-3438

Missing Persons: 744-481-1100

Municipal Police: 744-485-0650

Tourist Police: 744-485-0490

Fire Department: 744-484-4122, 744-460-2112

U.S. Embassy: 744-481-0100

Canadian Consulate: 744-484-1305

Red Cross: 744-445-5912

INTERNET CAFÉS Acanet Internet Café (744-486-8182), Avenida Costera Miguel Alemán #1632, Acapulco, GRO 39300. Open daily 10 AM–9:30 PM. Located in the Gran Plaza, this cybercafé offers several computers for general use. **D Byte Internet Café** (744-483-2755), Avenida Hidalgo #20, Acapulco, GRO 39300. Open daily 11 AM–8 PM. This cybercafé is located a block north of the main church. They offer about five computers for general use, as well as a printer and video conferencing. They charge about 30 pesos for an hour.

LAUNDRY SERVICE Lavanderia Wash & Wear (744-484-9365), Avenida Costera Miguel Alemán #78, Acapulco, GRO 39300. Open Mon.–Fri. 9 AM–8 PM, Sat. 9 AM–2 PM. **Lavanderia y Tintoreria Bahia** (744-483-9200), Calle las Playas #28, Acapulco, GRO 39300. Open Mon.–Sat. 9 AM–8 PM.

✳ To See

For many visitors to Acapulco, all the culture they need comes in a salted glass. However, this city is older than any in the United States and there are cultural attractions here that are well worth taking the time to enjoy. Foremost among these is the old military fort, which is now the city's history museum. Beyond that, there are many interesting and historic locales throughout the city to enjoy if you need a break from the fun in the sun.

Capilla de la Paz (744-434-0170), Calle de la Paz, Acapulco, GRO 39900. Tourists are welcome 10 AM–6 PM. This modern, nondenominational chapel located in the Las Brisas hills, just off the Carretera Escénica. It stands 1,200 feet above Acapulco Bay and features a 130-foot bronze cross that can be seen throughout the city below. The chapel sits among a series of manicured gardens with a series of paths with small terraces and artificial waterfalls. These gardens provide a beautiful and quiet spot for reflection and meditation. The location of this church provides an excellent view of the city.

You can get here by either bus or taxi. By car, take the Carretera Escénica from the city and make a hairpin left at the Los Arcos gate, about a quarter mile past the Las Brisas Resort. Follow the signs uphill for about another half mile.

Casa de la Máscara (744-484-4416), Calle Hornitos y Morelos s/n, Centro, Acapulco, GRO 39300. Open Tue.–Sun. 10 AM–4 PM. This museum is located about a half block west of the Fuerte of San Diego, down Calle Morelos. Although this collection of masks is often overlooked by visitors to the History Museum, it is definitely worth a stop if you are interested in Mexican culture. Inside, you will find six rooms displaying more than 500 colorful masks and other works of folk art.

Masks have played an important role in the ceremonial life of many Mexicans, especially in the state of Guerrero, which produces Mexico's best examples of this type of cultural art form. In fact, the ceremonial mask is considered the artistic symbol of the state. This former private residence was converted into a museum in 1999 by René Juarez, the then governor of Guerrero, as a tribute to the mask makers of the state. All of the masks here have been handcrafted for various fiestas. This includes traditional jaguar and tiger masks as well as less tra-

ACAPULCO FOR GAYS AND LESBIANS

Generally speaking, Mexico is a fairly conservative and widely Catholic country. Particularly among the smaller towns, much of the population is traditional and provincial in their views. That said, there are areas of the country that have long traditions of being very accepting gays and lesbians that go all the way back to pre-Columbian times. For example, in the neighboring state of Michoacán, some small towns have festivals that celebrate their gay and tans-gender residents. Likewise, gay marriage was recently legalized in Mexico City. And in Acapulco, there is a small but thriving gay community. In fact, in recent years the city has begun to develop a reputation for being an attractive destination for gay travelers. Also, the section of Playa Condesa that fronts Beto's Condesa Restaurant from the area known as Las Piedras eastward to the end of the beach is generally considered Acapulco's gay beach. Look for the ▼ symbol for gay-friendly establishments.

THE EAST END OF PLAYA CONDESA IS ACAPULCO'S GAY BEACH.

ditional masks depicting gruesome faces and red devils. Although in modern society, these masks hold little significance beyond the theatrical, there are still rural areas in Mexico where they retain their pre-Columbian meaning. According to indigenous belief, donning certain masks allows the wearer to take on certain supernatural powers. This practice of wearing such masks can commonly be seen depicted in Mesoamerican codices and stone glyphs. Most of the masks here are from the various regions of Guerrero, but there are also examples from the Mexican states of Puebla, Michoacán, and Morelos. Be aware that the art descriptions are all in Spanish. Admission is free, though donations are appreciated. Additionally, photos are permitted without charge, which is unusual in Mexico.

Fuerte San Diego (744-485-3404), Calle Hornitos s/n, Centro, Acapulco, GRO 39300. Open Tue.–Sat. 10:30 AM–4:30 PM. Okay, people don't come to Acapulco for the historic culture—understood. That said, if you are at all interested in Mexican history and culture, no trip to Acapulco is complete without a visit to the Fort of San Diego. Originally constructed between 1615 and 1617, the fort was rebuilt in 1776 following an earthquake. Primarily used to defend the city against piracy, it is the most relevant historic monument in the region and was the most important fortress along the Pacific coast during Spain's long colonial dominance of Latin America. Today, this old fortification houses Acapulco's **History Museum.** To get to this museum from the *zócalo*, turn left and walk to the northeast along Avenida Costera Miguel Alemán for about three blocks until you come to a large pedestrian bridge. Walk under the bridge and take the stairway on the left. At the top, walk east away from the ocean, crossing a bridge over a large trench, which is actually a moat that was dug around the fort in 1634. After continuing uphill for about a block, you will see the entrance to the fort on the right.

It is located in the heart of downtown Acapulco on a hill overlooking the Pacific Ocean and the city's coastal skyline. A stroll through the museum's 15 galleries located in the fort's original store-rooms will give you a good sense of Acapulco's rich history from pre-Columbian times to the important role it played by being a crucial stop on the lucrative trade route between Europe and Asia. In a counterclockwise arrangement, the exhibitions begin with displays dealing with indigenous culture and move through the conquest and colonial history. The majority of exhibits illustrate Spain's trade with China. The most interesting displays spell out the history of the Spanish galleons and the exploits of such pirates as Francis Drake, Thomas Cavendish, and John Hawkins. Another quite interesting exhibit is the fort's original tiled kitchen, which now displays a stove, utensils, and methods of cooking, as well as dried ingredients. The fort's chapel has also been restored to its

THE FORT OF SAN DIEGO HOUSES ACAPULCO'S HISTORY MUSEUM.

HISTORY OF FUERTE SAN DIEGO

Viceroy Diego Fernández de Córdoba commissioned Fort San Diego to protect the bay after a 1614 attack by the Dutch. Ten years later his successor, Don Rodrigo Pachero y Osirio, added features to the fort; then ten years hence, engineer Juan de la Torre added a moat whose trench can still be seen today.

On April 21, 1776, a severe earthquake destroyed the fort. The Spanish Crown put engineer Miguel Constanzó in charge of rebuilding it. Within a decade, he had constructed a new five-pointed fort at a cost of 600,000 pesos. The new fort had sloping walls to deflect cannonballs and two large cisterns to collect rainwater. In case of attack, warning salvos from the fort's cannons would alert the population to take cover in the interior parade grounds. Soldiers would then raise the drawbridge over the moat, using chains.

Although pirates never attacked the fort, soldiers patrolled along the ramparts, watching for distant pirate ships. An occasional roar of cannon brought terror to the population of the small fishing village below. In 1813, the fort fell to insurgent forces during Mexico's War of Independence after a siege lasting several months. King Ferdinand II decommissioned the Fort of San Diego in 1816.

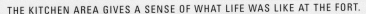

THE KITCHEN AREA GIVES A SENSE OF WHAT LIFE WAS LIKE AT THE FORT.

original state. These exhibits have descriptions in both Spanish and English (even if the English is a bit off at times). There is also a 15-minute large-screen video to help guide you through the museum.

If you walk up to the second floor and step onto one of the lookout points, it becomes clear that the fortress is in the geometric shape of a five-point star, though this is not immediately apparent from ground level. Depending on the season, the Fort San Diego also presents an *espectáculo* (sound-and-light show) entitled "The Silent Vigil," which combines symphonic music and dramatic projections on curtains of water to tell the history of Acapulco. Call ahead to find out specific times; it is usually put on every Thu., Fri., and Sat. evening, in English at 8 PM and in Spanish at 9 PM. Fort admission 30 pesos, free on Sun. A donation of 100 pesos per person is requested for the *espectáculo*.

Jardín Botánico de Acapulco (744-435-0438; www.acapulcobotanico.org), Avenida Heróico Colegio Militar s/n, Acapulco, GRO 39300. Open daily dawn–dusk. Eastward along Avenida Costera Miguel Alemán, you will find a verdant and intimate setting in Acapulco's semiwild botanical garden. Opened in 2002, it occupies a pair of tropical creek valleys next to Loyola University. Trails wind uphill from the parking lot to the visitors' center, which features a small gift shop and café. This lush, hilly property fluctuates between about 650 and 1,300 feet above sea level. Two streams traverse the garden: whereas one is year-round, the other flows only during the summer rainy season. The garden features a variety of native species as well as flora from around the world, such as palms, cycads, aroids, desert plants, ferns, bromeliads, and orchids. The garden's wildlife is mainly composed of several species of birds, such as parakeets, pheasants, ospreys, and highland guans, and reptiles such as iguanas, lizards, and snakes. The few mammals that exist here include raccoon and ringtail possum. To get to the botanical garden, take Carretera Escénica east toward the airport. At the overpass, go under it turning left. Follow the road uphill until you reach Loyola University. $5 admission.

Nuestra Señora de la Soledad (744-482-1848), Independencia y Quebrada #1, Acapulco, GRO 39300. Open daily 7 AM–9 PM. The official name of Acapulco's cathedral is Parroquia del Sagrario Catedral; however, it is most commonly referred to as Nuestra Señora de la Soledad (Our Lady of Solitude). With its Spanish, Moorish, and indigenous influences, this unique church symbolizes the history of the Mexican people and the rich history of Acapulco itself. Despite that long history, it dates back to only 1930. In a country filled with impressive baroque churches, it stands out as one of Mexico's most modern cathedrals. It is situated in the *zócalo,* one of the oldest parts of Acapulco, tucked away from Avenida Costera Miguel Alemán. Although the view of the church is obscured by the shade trees and hemmed-in buildings that crowd the *zócalo,* the cathedral still manages to dominate this central plaza. It features two distinctive sky blue domes atop Byzantine towers on either side of an arched façade. The interior features a golden-tiled floor and walls in the same blue-and-white color scheme as the exterior. The ceiling is painted to resemble an angel-filled sky. There is a collection of religious statues throughout the church, the most prominent being a Christ lying in a crystal coffin.

Palma Sola Archaeological Site (744-482-3828), Veladero National Park, Acapulco, GRO 39000. Open daily, 9 AM–5 PM. This site sits at an elevation of 1,200 feet and is located on the west side of the city on a hillside overlooking the bay. It features gorgeous views of Acapulco and a treasure of ancient glyphs that have been excavated for public viewing. The site is spread out over about 10 acres and features about 18 petroglyphs large and small, the largest being about 20 feet in height. Some of the designs on these glyphs are geometric patterns, others depict animals as well as human forms. They were created by one of the region's earliest inhabitants, known commonly as Los Yopes. Little is known about these people. They date from between 200 BC and AD 600. The glyphs are scattered over the hillside, linked by a well-maintained paths and stone steps. At the top of the mountain is a cave that the Yopes used for ceremonies. At the cave's entrance, you will find one of the most elaborate glyphs. Archaeologists believe that it depicts the creation myth of the inhabitants of the site. All signs are marked in Spanish and English.

Palma Sola is most easily reached by tour or taxi, up Avenida Palma Sola. This road ends just before the hilltop. From here, take a path the last few hundred yards to the site. There is a visitor center with restrooms, but no refreshments are available. Be sure to take a hat, sunblock, and water, and wear comfortable walking shoes. Local guides will most likely be available on-site. You can also arrange a tour through the local tour companies. If you've visited some of Mexico's more famous archaeological sites, you may find this one to be a bit unimpressive. However, nature lovers will delight in the opportunity to wander the nearby forested paths. The trail leading to the site is rather steep, so be prepared for a workout. $5 admission.

ACAPULCO'S MAIN PARISH IS A UNIQUE EXAMPLE OF MODERN ARCHITECTURE.

Parque Papagayo (744-486-0996), Avenida Costera Miguel Alemán, s/n, Acapulco, GRO 39670. Open daily 5 AM–8 PM. Along the Costera, across the street from Playa Hornitos, lies Parque Papagayo. It is bordered on the north by Avenida Cuauhtémoc, on the east by Avenida Manuel Gómez Morín and to the west by Avenida Juan Sebastián Elcano. This property was appropriated for public use in 1979 and named Parque Ignacio Manuel Altamirano for the indigenous Mexican writer. However, over time it came to be most commonly referred to as Parque Papagayo (Parrot Park). If you think Acapulco is nothing but a collection of beaches and bars catering to young partiers, this park offers an oasis away from that, filled with diversions and families enjoying themselves. Its attractions include two basketball courts, a soccer field, a children's playground, and a couple of small lakes with small boats. In the mornings, the park is rife with joggers; and in the evening from about 4 PM to 11 PM, there are food stands and several inexpensive fair rides. The park also has a zoo, but it's small and poorly kept, and, to be honest, more depressing than interesting. Free admission.

The zócalo. Avenida Costera Miguel Alemán s/n, Frente al Muelle Central, Acapulco, GRO 39390. Across the street from the *malecón,* you will find Plaza Juan Álvarez, Acapulco's *zócalo.* Although it doesn't rank among the best *zócalos* in Mexico, Acapulco's old town square is a pleasant place to spend some time. At one time, this plaza was a central feature of the city's life; today it is a sleepy park with shaded benches, fountains, a large stone gazebo, and Nuestra Señora de la Soledad. Lining the plaza are a number of cafés, a few downscale clothing shops, an ice-cream shop, as well as two low-budget hotels. Many residents come here to relax, get their shoes shined, read in the shade, and people-watch. The plaza is most crowded on Saturday nights and on Sundays, when bands play from the gazebo and street performers entertain crowds with their antics. Just behind the cathedral you'll find the Pozo de la Nación Historic District, Acapulco's oldest neighborhood, where the wealthy merchants made their homes.

✳ To Do

Acapulco is a playground with numerous types of diversions available just minutes from wherever you are staying. It's a place where you can do many things in a single day that you don't otherwise have the opportunity to ever do. For exam-

ACAPULCO VIEJO IS AN INTERESTING MIX OF RESORT ACTIVITY AND OLD WORLD CHARM.

ACAPULCO'S BEACHES PROVIDE A HOST OF DIVERSIONS.

ple, in just one afternoon, you can swim with dolphins before taking a quick parasailing trip in which you rise hundreds of feet in the air while being pulled behind a motorboat. Or you can spend an afternoon horseback riding on a deserted beach after a morning of golf or sport fishing. Most of the resort hotels sell tickets or make arrangements for these activities, but you might consider making your own to ensure that you go with a company that you're comfortable with.

BEACHES The beaches in Acapulco are surprisingly varied in terms of the experiences they offer. When you think of Acapulco, invariably the image of Playa Caleta comes to mind, lined with high-rise resort hotels towering over parasailing tourists and bikini-clad young women riding banana boats. While that image is fairly accurate, with a little looking, you can find beaches nearby that offer a much calmer atmosphere and even beaches that are downright secluded. There are beaches here that are great for families, beaches with a traditional Mexican feel, and beaches that provide an upscale experience. Whatever you are looking for, take the time to do a little exploring because each of Acapulco's beaches has a little something different to offer.

Playa la Angosta is a quiet beach on the west side of Acapulco's southwest peninsula. It is a sheltered cove just south of La Quebrada and is often deserted due to the fact that it is relatively off the beaten path of the major hotels and little known. However, it is a lovely stretch of beach in a beautiful part of town. The name of this place means "narrow beach," and for good reason: it is a narrow swath of sand tucked between two sandstone cliffs. A few fishing launches are on one side of the beach and a food *palapa* (palm-sheltered hut) on the

PLAYA CALETA IS OFTEN CROWDED.

other. This is a great place for a picnic but go into the water with caution, as no lifeguards are on duty here. If you hike up the hillside, you have a pretty good view of the cliff divers as they perform. Up the cliff side to the south along Avenida López Mateos, you will find the Sinfonia del Sol sunset amphitheater. This is a popular gathering point to watch the sunset and the twilight diving performance. Playa la Angosta is a mere 20-minute walk from the *zócalo*, or you can take the bus to Playa Caleta and get off near the Hotel Avenida. Walk east one block and you're on the beach.

Playas Caleta and Caletilla are two small beaches located away from most of the hotels along the southern coast of Acapulco's southwestern peninsula. However, these are perhaps the most popular beaches in town. With that in mind, don't be surprised to find the beach absolutely crowded when you arrive. This is particularly true on Sundays and holidays. These beaches have fairly calm waters due to Isla Roqueta, just offshore, acting as a barrier. This makes it an ideal beach for families and less experienced swimmers. However, stay out of the water during the rainy season of June through October because the rain runoff combined with warm conditions causes the bacteria levels to rise. The beach is lined with beach chairs with tables and umbrellas available for rent. You can order food and refreshments while you bask in the sun. There is also a constant parade of souvenir vendors selling everything from shell necklaces to velvet artwork. Be aware that once you show any interest to one of them, you will be surrounded by an entire flock. Get here by bus marked "Caleta" or by taxi.

▼ **Playa Condesa** is sandwiched between Playa Hornos and Playa Icacos. However, because of all the partying that goes on here, this is the most popular beach along the Costera, beginning at the bungee tower and ends at La Gran Plaza. Because of its location, fronting dozens of restaurants, discos, and bars, Playa Condesa is where the party begins and ends in Acapulco. It is lined with several high-rise hotels that fill the beach with partiers during spring break, holidays, and weekends. However, it is not the best place to swim, due to the steep angle of the beach and the strong undertow. There is a flag warning system in place that displays red flags when the waves are too dangerous to swim. Keep in mind that few (if any) lifeguards are on duty here. However, there are plenty of tour guides wandering the beach ready to take you parasailing, banana boating, and waterskiing. Jet skis can be rented for about $20 for a half an hour, though you may be able to negotiate a better deal. Tour guides and tchotchke vendors are ever present but not too pushy. Just say, "*No, gracias,*" and they will be on their way. Be aware that if you show interest, you will be swarmed by others. The sand is white and kept clean by the abutting resorts. At night, the beach is the scene of a vibrant nightlife.

Playa Hornitos is also known as Playa Papagayo because it is across Avenida Costera Miguel Alemán from Parque Papagayo. This beach does not have the party scene that you will find just a few hundred yards up the beach. The crowds here are generally composed of American tourists and Mexican families, and there are restaurants and vendors here that cater to them.

Playa Hornos is located southwest of Playa Hornitos, not far from Old Acapulco. This beach features clean sand and rows of large coconut palms. The water is also somewhat calmer than at the more popular beaches of the Zona Hotelera, though there does tend to be a strong undertow. Be sure to look out for red flags warning you away from the water. Another way this beach differs from others to the east is that it is quieter. The atmosphere here is distinctly laid back and there are several restaurants along the beach, making it a favorite with locals and tourists alike. This beach is also where local fishermen set out in their boats in the morning in search of the day's catch. If you happen to be passing by, you can purchase fish on the spot, before the fish are taken to market.

PLAYA CONDESA IS LINED WITH RESORTS AND SHOPS.

Playa Icacos is located toward the east side of Acapulco's half-moon bay and is the most extensive beach within it. The beach curves to the south past the naval base, where it is somewhat sheltered from the waves coming straight in off the Pacific. However, it has a steep grade at the water's edge, giving it some surf. The water is pleasant enough to make this one of Acapulco's more crowded beaches. The sand is a bit coarse but it's clean. Due to the nearby luxury hotels, Playa Icacos tends to be more upscale than Playa Condesa. It is lined with *palapa* parasols and beach chairs available for rental. A number of small bars and restaurants offer service. There are lifeguards on duty, though on busy days they have a lot to look after. Available activities here include sailing, waterskiing, and motorboating. Stick around for the sensational sunsets that happen here. To get here from the Zona Hotelera, take Avenida Costera Miguel Alemán toward the airport, past the traffic circle, and turn right at Fragata Santa María.

Playa Morro. This beach is close to the Diana traffic circle and the nearby shops and restaurants. Many of these businesses refer to this beach as "Condesa" because it's a more recognizable name, but no matter. This beach provides a buffer between the rambunctiousness of Playa Condesa and the tranquility of Playa Hornitos. However, it does get packed with young partiers during spring break.

Playa Tlacaponcho is located at the southwest end of the *malecón,* near the Maritime terminal and right down the street from the *zócalo.* It's a tiny, shallow strip of sand with small waves that lap against the shore. Because of this, it is popular with local families. It features several nearby beachfront restaurants as well as public bathrooms and changing facilities. It also provides a convenient place to catch a cab.

PLAYA TLACAPONCHO IS POPULAR WITH LOCAL FAMILIES.

Playa Marín is a remote and undeveloped beach on the east side of the island. You can reach it only by a short hike from Playa Roqueta. This seclusion makes this the best beach at Isla Roqueta. However, because of its location, it is also less sheltered than Playa Roqueta. Enter the water with caution because the surf can be a bit rough and there is always the danger of undertow.

Playa Roqueta. This rustic beach, located just east of the landing pier on Isla Roqueta, is a narrow strip of sand with small waves that lap against the shore. It is advertised as having immaculate sand and water simply because it is relatively undeveloped. This is not really the case. Unfortunately, Mexican culture has not had a Lady Bird Johnson figure to implement a taboo on littering. Consequently, many natural areas that draw crowds in this country tend to suffer. (I have personally witnessed a well-to-do woman standing on a beautiful beach finish a soft drink, drop the glass bottle in the sand, and walk away without a shred of self-consciousness.) Playa Roqueta is just one of these places. It has several seafood restaurants abutting it as well as many beach vendors trying to get you to buy their tchotchkes. The crowds that pour off the boats from Caleta fill up this beach to full capacity, so be prepared to get cozy with your neighbor when lounging on this beach.

Southeast of Town

As you travel southeast away from Acapulco Bay to the, the road curves along beautiful vistas of the sea and drops you toward Puerto Marqués. The beaches out here range from rustic Playa Puerto Marqués to the upscale atmosphere of Playa Revolcadero to the undeveloped beauty of Playa Larga. Generally speaking, these are best reached by car, though there are buses that operate out here. Taxi rides past the airport can get expensive.

Barra Viaje is the place to come to if you wish to spend a day away from the hustle and bustle of a busy Acapulco. Located southeast of the airport, this is a long, wide stretch of sand with a powerful surf that creates a feeling of intense peacefulness. Visitors can swim in the nearby freshwater lagoon. The beach has a line of seafood restaurants, so there is no need to worry about packing a lunch. There are also tour guides here that rent horses for as briefly as a half an hour. Or you can take a boat ride through the nearby mangrove swamps. To get here by bus, take the bus to Puerto Marqués and then take the *combi* to Barra Vieja. Or you can take a taxi and make arrangements to be picked up. Be sure to set a firm price before leaving.

FISHERMEN AT THE NORTH END OF PLAYA LARGA.

⇢ **Playa Larga** (Long Beach) is aptly named because it is a long stretch of open beach about 7 miles east of the Puerto Marqués traffic circle along Highway 200. It is relatively undevel-

ISLA ROQUETA

When you arrive at Playa Caleta, you will undoubtedly find that there is no shortage of fast-talking hustlers trying to get you to hop a boat to Isla Roqueta. This can be a bit unnerving, especially if you show any kind of interest, in which case you will likely find that you have a new sidekick that you just can't get rid of. It's best to ignore these guys and go about your business. If you are in fact interested in a trip to Isla Roqueta, just walk to the pier a few hundred yards to the right and buy a ticket at the ticket office. Everyone who visits Acapulco, it seems, makes a trip to this island. This is apparent not only in the number of people that crowd onto these boats, but also in the litter they leave behind on the island.

Roundtrip passage to this small island runs about $3 and is usually in a glass-bottomed boat, which allows you to occasionally catch a glimpse of a fish in the murky water below. The trip to the island is conducted by guides who generally only speak Spanish. They will likely take a few minutes to stop at points of interest around the island before dropping you off and they will likely take time (a long time) to dock up with one of the lunch boats that cruise the waters off Isla Roqueta. On occasion, the guides will also throw back a few beers during this short boat ride before asking for a tip as you disembark. The ride back to Playa Caleta is direct and only takes about 10 minutes.

Isla Roqueta offers many diversions, the best of which are actually away from the water. The interior of the island has a tropical deciduous forest with several hiking trails. If the day is not too hot, it is a good place to go for a hike. These trails provide quiet, hidden spaces that you will not find at the shore. On the east side of the island, about halfway between Playa Roqueta and Playa Marín, there is a small zoo that features several endangered local species, including spider monkey, jaguar, and mountain lion. However, if you're an animal lover, you will likely just find this zoo

oped, though it does have several campsites, a rustic trailer park, as well as a sea turtle hatchery. During the hatching season of late summer, eco-tourists camp out here to guard over the hatchlings as they make their way to the sea. Waves pulse against the shore here as seabirds quietly go about their business. It's a good place to come if you're looking for some seclusion, as there are no beach vendors and usually few others around. However, there is a *ciclopista* (bike path) that runs parallel to the beach all the way to Barra Vieja. This beach is best reached by car, as a taxi ride here would be fairly expensive and there are no depressing. On the shore, you can go for a banana boat ride or perhaps go snorkeling. Guides will put you in a *panga* (small boat) and taxi you out to one of the nearby reefs. (Be aware that, because the *panga* returns to shore immediately, you have to leave all of your belongings on shore with the tour vendor.) Although these tour companies provide the snorkels and life vests, they do not always provide flippers. In these situations, be sure to either bring your own or, if worse comes to worse, snorkel with your shoes on, as the reefs are extremely sharp. The snorkeling here is decent—actually some of the best in the Acapulco area. At certain spots there are plenty of beautiful tropical fish going about their business. However, the plastic bottles and food wrappers that float by may make you wonder if you'll need a tetanus shot when you get back to the beach.

A GROUP OF SNORKELERS OFF OF ISLA ROQUETA.

taxis waiting around for the return trip. The drive from Acapulco is around 30 to 45 minutes and parking is available.

Playa Puerto Marqués. This small beach sits on the lush green cove of Puerto Marqués. The water here is calm and clean making this one of the better spots in Acapulco to take a dip in the ocean. In fact, this beach is a bit of a locals' secret, as there are relatively few tourists here compared to the beaches on the big bay. Despite that, this is a busy beach that gets crowded on the weekend and holidays. The entire beach is lined with simple seafood restaurants in the nearby

PLAYA LARGA IS A LONG STRETCH OF OPEN BEACH.

village of Puerto Marqués. This beach can be reached by taxi or boat tour. To get here by car, take Carretera Escénica eat toward the airport and turn south at the traffic circle at Boulevard Puerto Marqués.

Playa Revolcadero. This long strand of beach is located 10 miles southeast of Acapulco Bay. It faces the open ocean and extends south from the Fairmont Acapulco Princess and the Fairmont Pierre Marqués, two of Acapulco's most luxurious hotels. This beach is blessed with fine, white sand and is framed by deep blue waters and long groves of coconut palms. On weekends and holidays, it becomes a playground for the wealthy and famous alike. This is a good place to take a dip if you are a strong swimmer, but be careful if you are not. Although the waves here are not small, they are rarely dangerous and rough, either. This beach certainly has less of an undertow than the beaches of the Zona Hotelera. However, look for red flags that are posted on days when the surf is too strong to swim safely. Activities that are available here include jet skiing, horseback riding, and (if you're really adventurous) ultralight airplanes.

BUNGEE JUMPING Paradise Bungee (744-484-5988), Avenida Costera Miguel Alemán s/n, Playa Condesa, Acapulco, GRO 39880. Okay, maybe it doesn't have the cachet it had back in the early 1990s, but if you're a thrill seeker looking for a quick rush, maybe a quick jump off of a 160-foot tower is the thing for you. This bungee jump is located right on Playa Condesa, which means that you will have a stunning view of Acapulco just as you take the plunge. You'll have plenty of time to change your mind between the time you get weighed, take safety instructions, and then take the slow elevator ride to the top of the platform. Although the jump goes by in a few seconds, the whole process takes about an hour. Crowds gather to watch the jumpers, who sometimes get dipped in the giant swimming pool at the base of the platform. One jump costs $50 and comes with a T-shirt. Pictures or a video are about $20 extra.

BUS TOURS Acapulco has three long-distance bus stations that serve different bus lines. The primary of these is the **Central Camionera Station** (also known as the Ejido), located north of downtown at Ejido 47. This station is operated by Estrella Blanca and is very clean. This station also offers service to nearby destinations along both the Costa Grande and the Costa Chica, as well as interior destinations such as Taxco and Chilpancingo. For sadists, this station also offers one or two daily connections with Tijuana via the Pacific coast and Ciudad Juárez via the northern interior. The other two stations, **Estrella Blanca**

Station and **Estrella de Oro Station**, are located to the east on Avenida Cuatuhémoc near Parque Papagayo. The Estrella Blanca at Papagayo offers luxury and first-class service to points north. The Estrella de Oro station offers luxury and first-class transport to Mexico City and points along that corridor, such as Chilpancingo, Iguala, and Taxco. This station also offers service to points along the Costa Grande up to and including Zihuatanejo and Lázaro Cárdenas. This station does not offer service to the south.

Costa Line (744-277-4260; www.costaline.com.mx) limits its routes to destinations in Guerrero, Michoacán, Morelos, and Mexico City. They offer two levels of service: Servicio Plus includes lunch, two bathrooms, plasma televisions, and individual air-conditioning; Servicio de Primera includes a bathroom, television, air-conditioning, and reading lights.

Estrella Blanca (744-482-1107; www.estrellablanca.com.mx). This is one of the largest bus companies in Mexico and they offer service from the border down into Veracruz and Oaxaca. They have by far the biggest footprint in the state of Guerrero. This company operates many different bus lines with varying levels of service.

Estrella de Oro (744-485-5282; www.estrelladeoro.com.mx) offers routes to various destinations with a concentration on points throughout south-central Mexico, though their greatest presence is in Guerrero. Their Servicio Diamante buses have a twenty-four-seat capacity that leaves plenty of room to stretch out. This service includes refreshment, separate bathrooms for men and women, air-conditioning, movies, and nonstop transportation.

TAKING THE PLUNGE AT ACAPULCO'S BUNGEE JUMP.

TuriStar (744-486-7968; www.turistar .com.mx). Except for a few regions such as Baja California and the Yucatán Peninsula, this bus company covers almost all of Mexico. Their service includes snacks, cafeteria service, plasma televisions, bathrooms, and headphones.

DIVING AND SNORKELING

Although Acapulco is not a highly sought diving location, the waters surrounding the city provide opportunities for divers of all skill level. The submerged pinnacles and rocks of this area are home to a large variety of species. With the addition of sea mountains and sunken ships, there is plenty to explore. The water temperature here averages 72 degrees Fahrenheit and visibility changes from one day to the next because of prevailing currents. However, the average visibility varies from 18 to 38 feet. Isla Roqueta provides areas for calm, shallow dives as well as underwater caves and rock formations for more experienced divers. Puerto Marqués is another location that is ideal for beginners because of the shallow water, abundant sea life, and good visibility. More experienced divers should explore the shipwreck of the Rio de la Plata, which sunk off the coast of Playa Icacos in 1944. Several local companies are available to rent equipment and arrange dives both during the day and at night.

Acapulco Scuba Center (744-482-9474; www.acapulcoscuba.com), Paseo del Pescador #14, Acapulco, GRO 39300. A large variety of diving tours including beach dives, night dives, and shipwreck dives. Also offers gear rental, snorkeling tours, and PADI-NAUI courses.

Swiss Divers Association (744-482-1357; www.swissdivers.com), Cerro San Martín #325, Acapulco, GRO 39390. Boat dive tours and night dive tours as well as snorkeling tours and kayaking tours. Also offers PADI diving lessons.

Underwater Dive Center (744-483-8127; www.underwateracapulco.com), Gran Via Tropical #2475, Acapulco, GRO 39390. Diving tours for beginners and certified divers at dive sites all around Acapulco Bay and Isla Roqueta. This includes transportation, lunch, and gear. Also offers gear rental, dive courses, and tank fill-up service.

DRIVING Acapulco is a good base from which to explore by car the central Guerrero countryside and towns such as Iguala, Chilpancingo, and Taxco along Highway 95. From Acapulco, you can also drive to the southeast and explore the Costa Chica. Highways 95 and 200 intersect at a traffic circle just north of Acapulco. Start with a full tank of gas and follow Highway 200 east, where you will find yourself in an isolated, sometimes desolate, land in which kilometer markers along the side of the road are often the only indication of where to find its hidden villages and beaches. There are gas stations in Cruz Grande, Marquelia, Ometepec, Pinotepa Nacional, Jamiltepec, and Puerto Escondido.

To the northeast of Acapulco, the Costa Grande provides seemingly endless miles of lonely beaches perfect for camping, surfing, or just getting away from it all. From Acapulco, follow Avenida Ejido to Pie de la Cuesta and pick up Highway 200. This road is marked better than the road along the Costa Chica.

GOLF Out in the Zona Diamante, golfers will find three world-class 18-hole golf courses that provide a challenge for golfers of all levels. These courses were designed by top golf architects and have been home to prestigious tournaments. Additionally, the Turtle Dunes golf course is currently under construction on the former location of the Fairmont Pierre Marqués golf course and is set to be completed soon after the publication of this book. There is also a **9-hole municipal golf course** located along Avenida Costera Miguel Alemán in the heart of the Zona Hotelera near the convention center (744-484-6583), open daily to the public 6:30 AM–10 PM on a first-come, first-serve basis.

Acapulco Princess Golf Course (744-469-1000), Avenida Playa Revolcadero, Granjas del Marqués, Acapulco, GRO 39907. Open daily dawn–dusk. This 18-hole, par-72 golf course was designed by golf architect Ted Robinson and opened in 1971. Playing at just less than 6,400 yards, this course features narrow fairways lined with coconut palms and water hazards on 12 holes. The design of the course is largely flat with medium-size greens and sand bunkers. The course sits in the shadow of the impressive Mayan-style pyramid of the Fairmont Hotel and provides amazing vistas. Guests of the hotel and nonguests are welcome to play. This is a world-famous, exclusive course—*Golf Digest* has included it as one of the 25 greatest golf resorts. Golf carts are mandatory and lessons can be arranged at the pro shop or by calling ahead.

Mayan Palace Acapulco Golf Course (744-469-6042), Avenida Costera de las Palmas Lote C-1-C, Acapulco, GRO 39900. Open daily dawn–dusk. This elongated 18-hole, par-72 golf course was designed by golf architect Pedro Guereca and opened in 1993. With its rolling hills covered with club-grabbing Bermuda grass, it plays at around 6,156 yards and provides vistas of the majestic Sierra Madre Mountains and the Pacific Ocean. The fairways are wide and fairly forgiving. They are lined with hundreds of palm trees and four gleaming lagoons. This course also has six dog legs and half of the greens are flanked by at least two bunkers. Putting greens, a driving range, and lessons are also available. Both guests of the hotel and nonguests are welcome to play here.

Tres Vidas Golf Course (744-444-5126), Carretera Barra Vieja, Km. 7, Zona Diamante, Acapulco, GRO 39900. Open daily 8 AM–dusk. This 18-hole, par-72 course was designed by golf architect Robert von Hagge and opened in 1995. The course hugs the coastline and has been home to the PGA Chrysler Cup Tournament. It plays to around 7,209 yards and features five holes that are nestled right up against the Pacific Ocean. At these holes, lapping waves break just yards from the green. The course is marked by rolling hills with nine tranquil lagoons, sand traps, and palm-tree -lined, Bermuda-carpeted fairways. It also features a driving range and putting greens.

SPORT FISHING Acapulco is a wonderful place to try your hand at deep-sea fishing. Now that charter companies have opened shop in town in recent years, you will not have a hard time finding an experienced guide to give you that opportunity. The best season to take a deep-sea fishing adventure in Acapulco is generally between November and May, though there is never a really bad time to do it.

BOATS RETURN FROM A LONG DAY OF FISHING.

CHARTER SERVICES

Acapulco Sportfishing (744-469-8537; www.acapulcosportfishing.net), Malecón Fiscal s/n, Acapulco, GRO 39390. This saltwater sport fishing charter service operates out of Acapulco's harbor and specializes in big game fish such as sailfish, tuna, dorado, and marlin. Their boats are also available for party cruises. They operate seven days a week and have more than 20 years of experience. They have a fleet of three boats comprised of a 50-foot Pelangochito Hatteras, a 44-foot Altair Striker, and a 46-foot Victoria Sportfisher. All of these vessels can accommodate 8–10 people on a fishing tour and 16 people on a party cruise.

Fantasy Sportfishing (744-419-9773; www.fantasysportfishing.com), Avenida Costera Miguel Alemán s/n, Acapulco, GRO 39390 operates a number of 40-foot twin–diesel engine boats and specializes in big game fish such as sailfish, marlin, and dorado. They also offer sunset cruises of the bay and can arrange other tours of Acapulco such as scenic tours, horseback riding, scuba diving, and snorkeling. Your tour guide, Lorenzo Bello, is fully bilingual and knows the city well.

Fish-R-Us (744-487-8787; www.fish-r-us.com), Avenida Costera Miguel Alemán #100, Acapulco, GRO 39390. This reputable sport fishing and charter company offers a wide array of services in and around Acapulco Bay. They

A SPEEDBOAT TOWS TOURISTS ON A BANANA BOAT RIDE.

A FISHING BOAT SETS OUT IN THE MORNING WITH A GROUP OF TOURISTS.

have a fleet of fully equipped yachts that they rent for day trips on a variety of cruising plans. These plans include deep sea fishing, scuba diving, and party cruises around the bay. If personal water craft is more your thing, this company has a fleet of top of the line wave runners that top out at around 45 miles per hour. Waterskiing service is also available for all skill levels and even for kids. The professional instructors will ensure that you have an enjoyable time. They even have an authentic Venetian gondola for that perfect romantic evening.

↬ **Shotover Jet** (744-484-1154; http://shotoverjet.com.mx/en/acapulco/), Avenida Costera Miguel Alemán #121, Acapulco, GRO 39390. This tour company offers an eco-tour in the form of a high-speed ride down the Papagayo River in a powerful jet boat. It begins high in the Sierras and passes through a majestic canyon and along the Venta Dam and the Omitlán River. The tour departs from the Diana traffic circle every hour from 9:30 am to 4:30 pm and heads to the Papagayo River base. From there, the tour lasts for approximately 50 minutes. Each boat can accommodate 10–12 passengers.

Sailfish are Acapulco's trademark sport fish, and although they are numerous throughout the year, November through March is the period in which they are most readily available. This fish prefers warm water and can reach 10 feet and 200 pounds in these parts. A hooked sailfish can be dangerous to boat due to its sheer size and the frantic leaps it makes in an effort to spit the hook. Pacific blue marlin prefer deep, cool water. Fishing for this species peaks around Acapulco between April and June. This fish feeds on squid and tuna, using its sharp bill to stun its prey. Blue marlin as big as 15 feet and 1,800 pounds have been recorded in the waters off Acapulco. This, too, is not the type of fish you can casually reel in. They usually retreat in high-speed runs and it is often necessary to pursue them with a boat and reel them in gradually. This process can take several hours. Dorado is another large game fish that can be found around Acapulco throughout the year but are most common from September through March, when the water is warm. Dorado as large as 6 feet and 80 pounds are not uncommon. When hooked, this fish can become aggressive. They are known for aerial acrobatics in an effort to spit the hook.

These are just three of the species of fish to be found in the waters off of Acapulco. When making arrangements for your fishing trip, ask plenty of questions and be sure that you are comfortable with the company you have chosen. A day of fishing on an average-size boat can run $500 to $1,000, so you want everything to be just right. Make sure you know exactly what is included and what the refund policy is, just in case you get to the dock and find a floating jalopy waiting for you. Most trips come with lunch, but you should be prepared to bring your own *cerveza*. Also, you will generally have to buy your own baitfish. Your skipper should arrange for that to be available for you.

WATER PARKS CICI Acapulco Mágico (744-484-1970; www.cici.com.mx), Avenida Costera Miguel Alemán s/n, Costa Azul, Acapulco, GRO 39850. Open daily 10 am–6 pm.

This water park, located along Acapulco Bay, is the biggest and best equipped theme park in Acapulco. It offers families and the young-at-heart the opportunity to frolic in large wave pools, toboggan down twisting water slides, and swim with dolphins. One of the most exciting water rides is the Tornado, a tube that shoots you into a circular bowl where you spin round and round until you are shot out the bottom into a deep pool of water. Another attraction is a hot-air balloon that lifts you more than 150 feet in the air, giving you a stunning view of the surrounding vista. There is also a program that lets you swim with dolphins as you learn about these amazing animals. It includes a brief lesson about dolphin behavior before you spend time in the water with the dolphins and an instructor as they play freely around you and do jumps and other tricks. This park has a lot to offer families as well, with a large children's wading pool complete with water slides and cascades. CICI is located beachside, along Avenida Costera Miguel Alemán next to the convention center. $10 adults, under age 12 free.

Mágico Mundo (744-483-1193), Islote Caleta Caletilla s/n, Las Playas, Acapulco, GRO 39300. Open daily 9 AM–6 PM. This water park is a great place to visit if you are traveling with kids. It is located at a scenic spot between Playa Caleta and Playa Caletilla and offers families for the whole family. Although this park features several waterslides and swimming pools, it is actually more of an aquarium than a theme park. Here, you will see an array of exotic fish, crocodiles, and there is a free dolphin show as well. There is also a collection of trained exotic birds, a video arcade, and a terrace with telescopes to help you admire the magnificent view. $4 adults, $3 children.

✳ Lodging

As Mexico's original resort town, Acapulco has a long history of providing accommodations for visitors from all over the world. Today, the city has an incredibly wide range of hotels providing everything from the most basic lodging to deluxe accommodations that would make a king blush. The city stretches more than 4 miles around the large, half-moon bay. Generally speaking, tourist areas are divided into three sections. On the western end of the bay is Acapulco Viejo (Old Acapulco), the original neighborhood that attracted the jet-setters of the city's golden age. Here you will find the city's historic *zócalo*, a wide *malecón* (boardwalk), and the divers of La Quebrada. The second section of the Acapulco tourist scene is the Zona Hotelera (Hotel Zone), also known as Zona Dorada. This area follows the main boulevard, Avenida Costera Miguel Alemán, as it wraps around the center of the bay. Here you will find towering hotels, restaurants, and shopping centers. Although the large hotels here offer plenty of amenities for families, many of the businesses in and around this area cater to hard-core partiers, with plenty of open-air beach bars lining the streets, offering all manner of drink specials to lure you in. The third tourist section begins just beyond the Hyatt Regency Hotel, where the name of the Costera changes to Carretera Escénica (Scenic Highway).

This is the road that takes you to the airport. In this part of the city you will find Acapulco Diamante, Acapulco's most desirable address. The hotels here are extravagant, with gourmet restaurants and flashy nightclubs that offer dazzling views. And, of course, the Diamante hotels are the most expensive as well. Each section has a distinctive experience to offer. All you have to do is choose which best suits you.

Old Acapulco

✦ **Alba Suites** (744-483-0073; www .suitesalba.com.mx), Gran Via Tropical #35, Acapulco, GRO 39390, $$; MC, V. This family-oriented hotel, on a quiet hillside overlooking the bay, is in a residential section of the city. From this vantage point, you will see the entire bay framed by the Acapulco skyline. This is a very convenient location from which to explore the beaches at La Caleta and the Isla Roqueta. This hotel is also fairly close to the cliff divers at La Quebrada, and a short cab ride away from the action at Avenida Costera Miguel Alemán. There are five pools; a Jacuzzi; and Acapulco's largest waterslide, a 360-foot winder that drops straight down a hillside. The 250 rooms are split among seven white, low-rise buildings surrounded by lush, spacious gardens, and are not fancy but are very comfortable, with two double beds and private balconies overlooking the bay, pool, or gardens, plus a kitchenette, refrigerator, and a dinette set, in case you want to dine in. If you don't feel like cooking, check out the hotel's **Acapulceño Restaurant,** open daily 8 AM–11 PM. This casual dining establishment offers Mexican and seafood specialties After your meal, unwind at the hotel's tropical **Oasis Bar.**

⚑ El Mirador Acapulco Hotel (744-483-1155; www.miradoracapulco .com), Plazoteta la Quebrada #74, Acapulco, GRO 39900. $$. AE; MC; V. Set atop the Quebrada Cliffs, El Mirador is the original resort hotel of Acapulco. It has a storied history in which it has hosted some of the biggest celebrities of the twentieth century. Today, it is a well-maintained landmark and a nice option for those looking for a low-key stay in the city. Its 133 standard rooms and nine Jacuzzi suites are surrounded by terraced gardens. The hotel's three swimming pools, open 10 AM–6 PM, include a saltwater pool down among the rocks. Being an older hotel, El Mirador is not the kind of glass-and-chrome high-rise that Acapulco has

come to be known for. It has much more the look and feel of a boutique hotel. The rooms are small and simple yet clean and comfortable. Services include mail service and dry cleaning/laundry. At the hotel's **Don Carlos Restaurant,** enjoy a buffet breakfast daily 7:30–noon, or lunch and dinner 1–10:30. The hotel's other restaurant, **La Perla,** open for dinner 7–11, is an ideal spot for watching the cliff divers who put on shows every hour on the half-hour, beginning at 7:30 PM. The torch-lit grand finale is at 10:30 PM. Despite the fact that this hotel is one of the reasons that Acapulco is what it is, the Mirador is actually not that close to many of the town's attractions. If you are staying here, you will have to take a cab ride to get to the beach or the *malecón*.

⚓ ⚑ ((ᵞ)) Etel Suites (744-482-2240; www.acapulcoetelsuites.com), Avenida Pinzona #92, Acapulco, GRO 39670. $. MC; V. Located in Old Acapulco, this 12-room hotel offers an authentic boutique experience that is hard to come by in Acapulco, where high-rise

ACAPULCO HAS MANY ATTRACTIVE ACCOMMODATION OPTIONS.

THE HOTEL MIRADOR IS ACAPULCO'S ORIGINAL RESORT HOTEL.

resorts reign supreme. Compared to most of what the city has to offer, this is downright rustic. The spacious rooms are sufficiently spacious, furnished with sturdy handmade cedar furniture, which is truly a rarity as the vast majority of hotels here seem to get their furniture at IKEA. Each room has two double beds. Not all have air-conditioning, so you should request one that does, particularly if you are there during the summer. Some rooms are equipped with kitchenettes, and you can also rent rooms with connecting doors. You will need to get a cab to take you to the main shopping center, though if you are staying at this hotel you are probably the type that likes to avoid crowds anyway. However, it is conveniently located, just a five-minute walk from the cliff divers at La Quebrada, but don't expect any extravagant grounds here. There are three modest swimming pools and a garden on the roof of the hotel. You will also find a children's play area located next to one of the pools.

Along the Costera

✦ (ŋ) **Acapulco Tortuga Hotel** (744-484-8889; www.hotelacapulcotortuga.com.mx), Avenida Costera Miguel Alemán #132, Acapulco, GRO 39670. $$. AE; MC; V. Located right in front of Playa Condesa, this interestingly decorated high-rise, with 250 rooms and suites, is designed to give the impression that you are under the sea. Its central interior courtyard, built around a large fountain, is used as a dining area. Look up—you will see that you are surrounded by long-hanging plants draped from the walkways above, giving the impression of a coral reef. The hotel's two small triangular pools positioned around a swim-up bar in the center. They are a bit small for the size of the hotel and tend to get crowded, so be sure to show up early to grab a spot if you plan on lounging there. The rooms are decorated in a simple but tasteful style with marble floors and colorful sheets. Each has two double beds and a private terrace. The hotel is within easy walking distance of the shops and restaurants of Avenida Costera Miguel Alemán. However, if you don't feel like leaving the hotel grounds, there are a couple of restaurants there. **El Nopal,** open daily 7 AM–11 PM, offers traditional Mexican dishes for lunch and dinner. For a more international menu, go to **Los Portales,** open daily noon–10 PM, which serves items buffet style as well as à la carte.

❀ ☌ ☈ (ᵗᵖᵗ) **Avalon Excalibur Acapulco** (744-504-1157; www.hotel avalonexcaliburacapulco.com), Avenida Costera Miguel Alemán #163, Acapulco, GRO 39670. $$. MC; V. One of the oldest high-rise resorts in Acapulco, this hotel has 400 rooms and suites in a 19-story tower overlooking Playa Hornos, within easy walking distance from the shops and bars of Avenida Costera Miguel Alemán. When it's time to relax, there is a large pool and also a children's pool. Avalon Excalibur offers four different room categories: Standard Mountain View is furnished with either a queen- or king-size bed and a private terrace overlooking the mountains bordering the Pacific. Deluxe Ocean View features a room with a queen- or king-size bed and a private terrace overlooking the ocean. The One-Bedroom Ocean-View Suite is a suite with a kitchenette, living room with a pull-out sofa, dinette set with seating for four, bedroom with a king-size bed, plus two private balconies overlooking the Pacific. The Two-Bedroom Suite offers a kitchenette, living room with a pullout sofa, three televisions, two bedrooms with queen-size beds, and three balconies overlooking either the ocean or the mountains. The rooms are spacious but not extravagant, and are decorated in a colorful but modest

Mexican style. As a true all-inclusive resort, the Avalon Excalibur provides you all of your meals and snacks. You may select from two restaurants. The main one, **Bellavista,** serves buffet-style breakfast, lunch, and dinner. Additionally, **El Cocotero Restaurant,** located near the beach, offers seafood specialties and Mexican and American cuisine.

☈ (ᵗᵖᵗ) **Bali Hai Hotel** (744-485-6336; www.balihai.com.mx), Avenida Costera Miguel Alemán #186, Acapulco, GRO 39670. $$. AE; MC; V. This 121-room Polynesian-themed hotel is an interesting blend of the elegant and the rustic. Located at the center of the action, across the street from the beach, it is a good base from which to enjoy all the attractions of Acapulco. The rooms are small but comfortable, each with air-conditioning and two double beds, as well as a sitting area. Two swimming pools are set in a lush garden area with a *palapa* bar off to the side; they can get quite crowded during the high season, so stake out your poolside territory early. The hotel's casual **Oceanic Restaurant,** open daily 7 AM–11 PM, provides a buffet breakfast, and for dinner serves international dishes and fresh seafood.

☈ ▼ **Casa Condesa** (744-484-1616; U.S. & Canada 800-816-4817; www .casacondesa.com), Bellavista #145, Acapulco, GRO 39690. $$. AE; D; DC; MC; V. Located one block from the beach at the center of Acapulco Bay, this is a gay-friendly boutique hotel with nine tastefully decorated suites and a clothing-optional pool in a private garden courtyard. The hotel offers complimentary airport transportation to guests staying at least three days and breakfast is served daily. This is an adults-only establishment.

✍ ✦ **Copacabana Beach Hotel**
(744-484-3260; www.hotelcopacabana
.com), Tabachines #2, Acapulco, GRO
39690. $$. MC; V. This 18-floor hotel
is located at the heart of Acapulco's
nightlife district. It has 392 rooms and
38 junior suites. Standard rooms are
surprisingly roomy with marble floors,
two double beds, and a seating area.
Junior suites are furnished with a
king-size bed and a sofa and love seat,
and also have marble floors, bamboo
furniture, and private balconies offering spectacular views of the Pacific
Ocean. The pool area faces the ocean
and can get crowded, so get here
early and pick your spot. There is a
kid's club here that provides scheduled activities for younger guests;
patrons may also enjoy the Copacabana's gym, game room, and convention center. This hotel has four bars
and two restaurants, including
Acuario, located on the mezzanine
level, which provides a nice view of
the bay. Serving breakfast 7–noon,
lunch 1–5, dinner 7–11, it offers both
Mexican cuisine and international
dishes either buffet style or à la carte.
Near the lobby, you will find **K'ffe
Zucco,** open 24/7 to serve coffee
drinks and light snacks. If you're in
the mood for something a bit
stronger, swing next door to **El Agave
Lobby Bar,** open daily 6 PM–2 AM,
with a happy hour 7–8, for a wide
selection of domestic and imported
drinks.

✦ ⦙ **Crowne Plaza Hotel** (744-440-
5555; www.crowneplaza.com/acapulco),
Avenida Costera Miguel Alemán
#123, Acapulco, GRO 39670. $. AE;
D, DC; MC; V. This grand old hotel,
within easy walking distance of the

shopping and nightlife of Acapulco's
Zona Hotelera, has come to symbolize
the Acapulco skyline. Its unique pyramid shape rises 26 stories above the
beach, and it has more than 500
rooms furnished with either two
queen, two double, or a king-size bed,
with private balconies overlooking the
beach. The grounds feature a serpentine pool area that wraps around a
poolside bar so you can enjoy the
water properly. However, this area
tends to get crowded, so you may
want to wander down to the beach to
stretch out a bit. Crowne Plaza is an
all-inclusive, so your food and drinks
will be included in the price of your
room. ,This hotel has four restaurants
and a poolside bar. **Los Caracoles**
serves a buffet-style breakfast 7–noon
and lunch 1–5 right next to the pool.
For dinner, go to **Los Arcos** next to
the lobby, open daily 6:30 PM–11 PM,
for steak and Mexican specialties; or if
you're in the mood for something
more fancy, you'll find authentic Italian cuisine and piano music at **I
Pagliacci,** open daily 7 PM–11 PM.

✦ ⦙ **Emporio Acapulco** (744-469-
0505; www.hotelesemporio.com),
Avenida Costera Miguel Alemán
#121, Acapulco, GRO 39670. $$. AE;
D; DC; MC; V. Rising right next to
the Diana traffic circle, in the heart of
the Zona Hotelera, the double towers
of Emporio feature attractive contemporary architecture and are decorated
in tasteful minimalist style. All 419
rooms and suites have private balconies overlooking the sea. Spacious
and well-appointed in a continental
style, all are furnished with either a
king-size or two double beds. Amenities include laundry/dry cleaning service, a gym, and an Asian-style spa, as
well as three outdoor pools, one of

which is exclusively for adults and another that is purportedly the largest swimming pool in Acapulco Bay. All three pools are located in a large, lush courtyard in front of the beach. The large pool is in a circular shape with **La Isla Bar & Grill** in the middle. This restaurant offers poolside fare daily 1 PM–11 PM. The hotel has another restaurant as well as two lounges for your enjoyment. The **Condimento Restaurant,** open daily 7 AM–10 PM, features a variety of Mexican and international dishes in a casual atmosphere. Order off the menu or visit the buffet. The hotel offers an all-inclusive option if you are interested in having the price of your food, snacks, and drinks included in the price of your room.

✍ ✈ (((ᵖ))) **Fiesta Americana** (744-484-5282; www.fiestamericana.com), Avenida Costera Miguel Alemán #97, Acapulco, GRO 39670. $$; AE; MC; V. This large hotel has 500 rooms and suites in a 19-story tower right on the beach at Playa Condesa. It is only a short walk from bars, restaurants, and

THE MAIN POOL AT THE HOTEL FIESTA AMERICANA.

the shopping centers near the Diana traffic circle. The rooms are spacious and nicely outfitted either a king-size or two double beds. Each room is equipped with a private terrace overlooking the ocean or the pool area. There are two fairly large swimming pools; however, even that is not enough when the hotel is booked near capacity. Get here early to get a poolside seat and hold on for dear life. Kids will enjoy the air-conditioned clubhouse as well as an outdoor playground area equipped with a merry-go-round. The hotel also has a gym and a spa, and patrons may enjoy its concierge service. There are three restaurants here, serving international fare, Italian cuisine, and seafood. The open-air **Chulavista Restaurant**, open daily 8 AM–3 PM, offers panoramic views of the bay as well as buffet and à la carte dining.

✍ ✈ **Park Royal Acapulco** (744-440-6565; www.parkroyalacapulco.com), Costera Guitarrón #110, Acapulco, GRO 39359. $$. MC; V. This all-inclusive resort has a total of 224 rooms and suites in thirteen villa-style buildings located near Acapulco's main attractions. All rooms have one king-size or two double beds, and balconies opening onto the ocean, river, or gardens. These rooms are decorated in Mediterranean style with pale solid colors and a marble floor. No bright Mexican designs here. The overall architecture of the hotel provides nice views of the bay. The grounds include two large swimming pools, a gym, and a ballroom with a 200-person capacity. Scheduled events include kids' games for children ages 5–10, alternating disco and casino nights during the week, and karaoke nights on the weekend. Services that come at an additional price include airport transfers, spa and beauty treatments, motorized water sports, and business services. There is also laundry/dry cleaning service, and a doctor is on call. Meals and snacks at the hotel's three restaurants are included with the price of the room, as well as unlimited domestic alcoholic and nonalcoholic beverages. **El Pescador,** open daily from 10 AM–10 PM, is an open-air restaurant with ocean-view dining near the main pool. Here, you will find buffet and à la carte service with dishes such as ceviches, salads, and the catch-of-the-day. The **Bahia,** open daily 8 AM–10 PM, is located just above the lobby and also provides ocean views and buffet service featuring Mexican and international cuisine. **La Trattoria Restaurant,** open daily 6 PM–11 PM, has views of Acapulco Bay with indoor and outdoor dining, and specializes in Italian cuisine.

✔ ✈ **Playa Suites Acapulco** (744-485-8050; www.playasuites.com.mx), Avenida Costera Miguel Alemán #123, Acapulco, GRO 39670. $$. AE; MC; V. This hotel has a great location, as it is located in the heart of the action at Avenida Costera Miguel Alemán. It has 500 rooms and suites in two high-rise towers overlooking Playa el Morro. The rooms here are decorated in a pastel Mexican motif and are furnished with either one king-size or two double beds. They also have private terraces overlooking the beach. Tucked between the two towers is an oval pool that wraps around a poolside bar. This pool tends to get crowded, so show up early and pick a spot if you are planning to spend your day sitting there. The hotel has laundry/dry cleaning servic-

es. Despite the fact that it also has a kid's club and babysitting services, it is not the best choice for families. This is the hotel for you if you are coming to Acapulco to party, though it does tend to skew younger and louder during spring break. There are two restaurants: **Las Gaviotas Restaurant,** open for buffet breakfast 7–noon and dinner (international cuisine) 6–10:30; and **El Morro Restaurant,** which offers a buffet lunch noon–5.

✔ ✈ **El Presidente Acapulco** (744-484-1700; www.elpresidenteacapulco.com.mx), Avenida Costera Miguel Alemán #8, Acapulco, GRO 39670. $$. AE; MC; V. Located right in front of Playa Condesa near the main shopping and nightlife center of Acapulco, this high-rise hotel offers 146 rooms and suites on 11 floors. The rooms are spacious and colorful and come with either a king-size or two double beds. Each room features a private terrace, not all of which overlook the beach. If the view is important to you, be sure to request a room facing the beach. Otherwise, you may find yourself with a view onto the crowded avenue. The pool could stand to be a big larger for the size of the hotel, and is located in a courtyard right in front of the beach. Here you will find a gorgeous view of Acapulco Bay; it's a great place to watch the sun set. However, this area tends to get crowded during the day, so show up early to get a spot. Services include babysitting and laundry/dry cleaning. The hotel also features several restaurants, including **Bugambilias Restaurant,** open daily 8 AM–10:30 PM for buffet breakfast, as well as à la carte lunch and dinner . For a more formal meal, check out **El Gaucho,** open for dinner daily

5–midnight which offers Argentinean specialties.

✦ **Ritz Acapulco** (744-469-3500; www.ritzacapulco.com.mx), Avenida Costera Miguel Alemán #159, Acapulco, GRO 39670 $$. MC; V. This twin-towered, 240-room, all-inclusive resort is at the heart of Acapulco Bay. At the base of the towers is an elongated blue-tiled pool set right up against the beach. This being the hotel's only pool, it can get quite crowded during the high season. Rooms are simply decorated with balconies overlooking the bay. However, keep in mind that some suites have only a partial bay view. There are several options for accommodations, but all rooms are furnished with either two double or one king-size bed. Connected rooms are available, as well as junior suites with two bedrooms. There is gym, plus an on-site theater where you will find nightly magic shows, comedy sketches, and even karaoke. The majority of beverages, meals, and snacks are included in the price of your room. For a nice dinner, visit La Cava Restaurant, open Thu.–Sat. 6:30–10; during the high season, Mon.–Sat. It has a dress code and does not serve children under the age of 12. One meal at La Cava is included in the price of the room for guests staying at least four nights. For more casual dining, the hotel offers buffet-style eating at **Villa Linda Restaurant,** open daily for breakfast 7–11, lunch 1–4, and dinner 7–10 PM. The poolside bar is open 10 AM–midnight and serves snacks noon–6 PM.

✦ ((ᵠ)) **Villas la Lupita Hotel** (744-486-3917; www.villaslalupita.com), Antón de Alaminos #232, Acapulco, GRO 39670. $. MC; V. This well-maintained boutique hotel is a good choice for the budget traveler. It offers 35 warmly decorated rooms in a four-level building just one block away from the action at Avenida Costera Miguel Alemán. The rooms here are small—really small—but still manage to be comfortable if you don't require much room. The building is constructed in an L shape with a central courtyard in the crook. Here you will find a modest-size pool with ample beach chairs for hanging out. There is also a poolside *palapa* for shade. This is a great place for hanging out in the evening while recapping the adventures of the day. If you happen to have brought your laptop with you, there is also free wireless Internet on the patio. There is no restaurant or bar onsite but that's not at all an issue, as there are plenty of those to choose from within easy walking distance from the hotel. There is also free parking. Make your reservations online for the best rates.

Acapulco Diamante

⚓ ✦ ((ᵠ)) **Camino Real Acapulco Diamante** (744-435-1010; www .caminoreal.com/acapulco/), Carretera Escénica Km.14 Baja Catita #18, Acapulco, GRO 39880. $$–$$$, AE; DC; MC; V. This 157-room hotel is located slightly off the beaten path between a steep mountainside and the scenic Puerto Marqués Bay, 15 minutes south of downtown Acapulco. Inspired by contemporary Mediterranean-style architecture, the building was designed to blend with its surroundings, the grounds set against waterfalls that spill into a large pool that appears almost to be an extension of the bay itself. Down a little farther is Lover's Stone, a large, flat rock sticking out of the bay, connected to the grounds with a small wooden bridge. This is the perfect setting for a romantic dinner alone or for wedding pictures. There are several room options, furnished with either a king-size or up to three double beds. They are decorated in a simple but elegant Mediterranean style with solid, natural colors and sparse ornamentation. All rooms have balconies overlooking the bay. During summer, Christmas Week, and Easter Week, the hotel provides children ages 5–10 with guided activities in the Mischief Club. This is a free service and lunch is included. The hotel also offers babysitting service. If you're in need of relaxation, the on-site spa and gym are open daily 8 AM–9 PM. Afterward, pull up a seat at the pool bar without getting out of the water or unwind in the lobby bar, which has spectacular views of the bay. There are a couple of dining options on the premises, including **La Huerta Café,** open daily 7 AM–11 PM, a casual restaurant offering a beautiful view of the bay and an international menu with both buffet and à la carte selections, and for a more sophisticated experience, **La Vela,** open daily for lunch 1–6 and dinner 6–11, an open-air restaurant specializing in seafood and fine cuts of meat. The hotel also offers 24-hour room service.

🐾 ♒ ♿ ✈ **Fairmont Acapulco Princess** (744-435-1500; www.fairmont.com/acapulco), Playa Revolcadero s/n, Colonia Granjas del Marqués, Acapulco, GRO 39907. $$$. AE; MC; V. Built in the shape of twin towering Aztec pyramids, this grand resort is situated among a mangrove of coconut palms, and boasts more than 1,000 rooms and suites. It is located in the Diamante district,

where you will find all of the most stunning resorts of the city. Each room has either a king-size or two double beds. The rooms come in a wide variety of classes, ranging from the 565-square-foot junior suite to the 1,045-square-foot one-bedroom suite, all the way up to the 2,550- square-foot two-bedroom penthouse suite. Each room has a private terrace or balcony overlooking the ocean, gardens, or the hotel's own championship 18-hole golf course. Obviously, there are more amenities than can be listed here, but among them are a health spa, a fitness center, kid's club, and babysitting center. All of the facilities at this hotel are designed to have wheelchair access. Also, this is a dog-friendly hotel, so it is a great choice if you can't imagine vacationing without Fido. The hotel has many restaurants to suite your dining wants and needs. Among them is the poolside **Chula Vista,** open daily 6 AM–11 PM, which offers casual buffet dining with views of a saltwater lagoon. For a more formal night out, the hotel's **Veranda Restaurant,** open daily for dinner 7–11, which serves Italian cuisine in a candlelit setting within view of the Pacific Ocean. This restaurant is resort casual, so no shorts or jeans, please.

♒ ✈ **The Fairmont Pierre Marqués** (744-435-2600; U.S./Canada 1-800-441-1414; www.fairmont.com/pierre marques), Playa Revolcadero s/n, Acapulco, GRO 39890. $$$. AE; D; MC; V. This historic resort was once the private hideaway of J. Paul Getty. Today, it offers guests a relaxing atmosphere with its a cluster of white bungalows and villas set among 480 acres of palm trees, intimate tropical gardens, and three pools just off of

Revolcadero Beach. On the other side of the hotel, you will find the Princess Golf Course, making this hotel an ideal choice for golf enthusiasts. The 229 guest accommodations range from single rooms to spacious bungalows, and there are several dining options on the hotel premises. The swankiest of these is **Tabachin,** open daily 7 PM–midnight. Stylish and specializing in contemporary Mexican cuisine, it is widely regarded as one of the best restaurants in Acapulco. Don't show up in your bathing suit and expect to get a seat. Long pants are required for men and women should dress in smart, casual attire. Reservations are recommended for Tabachin and can be booked online or by calling the front desk. If you are looking for something more casual, try **Pierre's Delicatessen,** a 24-hour café. The Fairmont Pierre Marqués is also an ideal place for special events. It offers a first-class setting for small gatherings as well as a convention center that can accommodate up to 500 people. For even larger gatherings, the hotel can accommodate outdoor banquets of up to 1,000 people. Other amenities include laundry service.

✦ ✦ (ɴ) **Las Brisas Acapulco** (744-469-6900; U.S. 1-800-228-3000; www.brisas.com.mx/), Carretera Escénica 5255, Acapulco, GRO 39867. $$$. AE; MC; V. Famous for its pink-and-white motif, this opulent hotel is situated on the cliffs overlooking Acapulco Bay. It has 263 bungalow-style rooms, each with a beautiful view of the ocean. With too many amenities to list here, Las Brisas offers a luxurious experience with private swimming pools and a fleet of jeeps to transport you around the facilities. This hotel is a great choice

for many types of travelers, including businesspeople, couples on a romantic getaway, as well as families. It has a business center, kids' pool and child-care services, tennis court, health spa, fitness center, beauty salon, and personalized service that is unusual for a hotel this size. **La Concha Club,** open daily 10 AM–6 PM; its open-air restaurant, noon–5 PM, is a private beach club on the bay with two salt-water tide pools and a large freshwater pool with a swim-up bar. This club is a great option for anyone planning a special event such as a wedding or reunion. **Bellavista** is open for breakfast 8–AM and dinner 7–11. Its restaurant and bar have panoramic views of the bay and nearby Sierra Madre Mountains. The breakfast menu features both Mexican and American dishes; dinner switches to fine international cuisine. Keep in mind that there is a dress code; men are required to wear long pants, collared shirts, and closed-toe shoes (no sneakers allowed!).

✦ ✦ **Grand Mayan Acapulco** (744-469-6000; www. mayanresorts.com/the-grand-mayan/), Avenida de las Palmas #1121, Acapulco, GRO 39900, $$$. AE; MC; V. A stunning luxury resort hotel located in the Diamante district, the Grand Mayan is one of Acapulco's grandest, with 450 spacious rooms and suites that come with private terraces. This resort features one of the longest interconnected swimming pools in all of Latin America. But forget the pool—the Grand Mayan Acapulco also has its own water park with waterfalls, slides, toboggans, and hanging bridges. Its kid's club offers a variety of sports, handicrafts, and cultural activities for children ages 4–11. Other amenities include an arcade; a tennis court; an 18-hole, 72-par tropical golf course; and an on-site health spa to rejuvenate you. The variety of restaurants and lounges make sure you are never want for anything during your time here. The **Bakal Restaurant and Café,** open daily 7 AM–3 PM and 6–10, provides an enjoyable breakfast-through-lunch casual buffet that borders on luxury in its assortment of fresh fruits and juices; then in the evening, the tone switches to a more refined dining experience. Another option is **Café del Lago**, open for dinner 6–11, which serves a variety of gourmet meals. Beach formal dress is required here, so don't show up in a T-shirt and shorts.

✔ **Mayan Palace Acapulco** (744-466-2400; www.mayanresorts.com/mayan-palace), Avenida de las Palmas #1121, Acapulco, GRO 39900. $$$. D; MC; V. This sprawling property located at the Playa Diamante district of the city has 360 rooms and suites. These accommodations are roomy and decorated in a modern style, and equipped with private terraces that overlook the ocean. Standard rooms are furnished with two double beds; suites with a king-size and two double beds; and master suites with a king-size, two double, and two sofa beds. The large pool area opens onto the beach, with plenty of seating. The grounds are luxurious and include an 18-hole, par-72 golf course among exotic tropical gardens. There is also an on-site water park. There is a babysitting service as well as a kid's club. This resort also offers six restaurants, including the **Bakal Restaurant and Café,** open daily 7 AM–1 PM, which serves a sumptuous buffet breakfast and lunch. For a more for-

mal dining experience, go to the **Mondo Restaurant,** open daily for dinner 5–10, whose menu lists a variety of international cuisine such as sushi and French crepes. For steak and seafood coupled with live piano music, dine at **Café del Lago,** open for dinner 5–10.

✔ **Mayan Sea Garden Acapulco** (744-469-6001; U.S. 1-800-996-2926; http://grupomayan.com/sea-garden/acapulco/), Avenida Costera de Las Palmas #1121, Acapulco, GRO 39900. $$$. AE; MC; V. Not to be mistaken for the more luxurious Mayan Palace, this resort is still a great option for both couples and families. You will find that the clientele here runs the gamut from young singles to couples of all ages as well as families. With 111 guest rooms, the hotel offers three levels of accommodation: The master room contains two queen-size beds, as is the suite, though suites are larger, with a couch and a kitchenette. The largest option is the master suite, furnished with two king-size and three sofa beds, in addition to a kitchenette. The décor in all is a bit cookie-cutter, with pastel prints and mass-manufactured furniture, but the rooms are comfortable nonetheless. However, with the blue-tiled pool and enchanting hotel grounds beckoning, you may not spend much time in your room. Located on one of the city's most picturesque beaches, Sea Garden Acapulco offers all manner of diversion, including an aqua park with waterslides, 12 clay tennis courts, a gym, private lagoons, and a health spa. There is also an 18-hole, par-72 championship golf course overlooking the ocean. After a full day of activities, you can quench your thirst and fill your appetite at a variety of bars, snack bars, cafés, and restaurants throughout the hotel grounds.

✿ ✔ (⌜⌝) **Villamar Princesa Suites** (744-485-2179; www.hotelvillamar princesa.com), Circuito Olinala Lote 1, Acapulco, GRO 39907. $. MC; V. This boutique hotel is an interestingly designed white building just five minutes away from the Acapulco airport. It is located in the Diamante district, near the Princesa Golf Course and Las Palmas shopping mall and away from the crowds of the *malecón*. However, this also means that it is away from most of the city's attractions, so you will need to either have a car or take a cab ride if you plan on seeing the sights. It also has a garden courtyard with a small circular pool and a connecting children's pool. Room décor is simply, with light tones to enhance the setting. This hotel has four standard rooms with one king-size bed and a sofa bed; the maximum occupancy for these rooms is two adults and two kids. There are also four three-bedroom suites in which one bedroom has two double beds, the other two equipped with one king-size bed apiece.; maximum occupancy for these rooms is eight people. Finally, the hotel has two penthouse suites with two bedrooms each, one with two double beds and the other with a king-size bed. These suites have a sofa bed for an extra person; maximum occupancy for a penthouse room is six people. The rooms are also equipped with complimentary wireless Internet access, a kitchenette, a living room, and a private balcony overlooking the pool area.

✴ Where to Eat

When it comes to eating, Acapulco has it all. It has many fashionable restaurants as well as many good, reasonably priced eateries. Generally speaking, everyday dining options are found all along Avenida Costera Miguel Alemán in the Zona Hotelero. If you happen to discover that you're hungry while walking along this strip, you will not have any trouble finding a place to eat. In fact, it is quite likely that the doormen working some of these restaurants will come looking for you, encouraging you to come in and enjoy their specials. This can get annoying, so don't feel bad about ignoring them. Farther to the south, away from the Zona Hotelero, you will find most of the fashionable restaurants in the Las Brisas hills south of town just off the Carretera Escénica. Here, the atmosphere is distinctly more upscale and you will find some real gems off the beaten path.

DINING OUT

Old Acapulco
El Amigo Miguel (744-483-6981), Avenida Juárez #31, Acapulco, GRO 39880. $$. AE; MC; V. Open daily for breakfast, lunch, and dinner 9:30 AM–8:30 PM. This family-owned restaurant has been a fixture in this city since the early days of Acapulco's golden age. Today, it remains one of the most popular restaurants among the local population. The menu features all sorts of Mexican seafood specialties made with the freshest ingredients and served in a home-cooked atmosphere. This includes many types of soups, grilled shrimp, lobster, and grilled fish smothered in chipotle sauce. If you're not a seafood

lover, this may not be the place for you, though there are a few items on the menu that don't involve seafood.

Mariscos Pipo (744-482-2237), Almirante Breton #3, Acapulco, GRO 39880. $$. AE; MC; V. Open daily for lunch and dinner 1 PM–9:30 PM. This family-operated seafood restaurant is a seafood lover's delight with just about any type of seafood to be found on the menu. This seafood is as fresh as it comes, caught from the sea and prepared daily. The décor here is rustic seafaring cheesiness, with rope nets, plastic fish, and glass buoys hanging from the ceiling. To be fair, they have attempted to provide a sense of history with photographs of Old Acapulco hanging on the walls. The menu is beyond reproach, with a wide selection of seafood dishes, including cocktails, soups, ceviche, quesadillas with all sorts of seafood (including baby shark), and fish prepared anyway you would like. Try the Veracruz-style red snapper, prepared with onion, tomato, peppers, and olives. Or keep it gringo-style with garlic and butter sauce.

Along the Costera
El Cabrito (744-484-7711), Avenida Costera Miguel Alemán #1480, Acapulco, GRO 39880. $$. MC; V. Open daily for lunch and dinner 2 PM–midnight. This restaurant, located south of the convention center, offers a slice of the Mexican heartland right in the heart of this tropical paradise. It has a hacienda ambience, and waitresses in traditional white dresses. This is not the best place if you're a vegetarian. The restaurant's name, meaning "young goat," is a tip to its specialty, which is Mexican *barbacoa*-style charcoal-grilled and delicious. However, the menu also features southern specialties such as Oaxaca-

style chicken mole as well as northern specialties such as shredded beef *machaca* burritos. And don't forget the seafood dishes, made with the freshest catch from the waters off Acapulco's coast. All of this goes perfectly well with a cold Mexican beer and a twist of lime. Try and get a table on the terrace and dine with a view, surrounded by tropical plants.

Hard Rock Café (744-484–2189), Avenida Costera Miguel Alemán #37, Acapulco, GRO 39880. $$. AE; MC; V. Open for lunch and dinner noon–2 AM. This well-known bar and grill may not provide a uniquely Mexican experience, but sometimes there's just something nice to be somewhere that feels familiar. It has the customary Hard Rock décor, with autographed gold records and guitars hanging on the walls as well as a small clothing and souvenir store. Most Thu., Fri., and Sat. nights, the restaurant features live music beginning at around 10 PM. This music is loud, so you may not get much conversation in if you happen to be dining at this time. The menu is typically north of the border, with hamburgers, steaks, and hot fudge sundaes.

Ika Tako (744-484-9521), Avenida Costera Miguel Alemán #99, Acapulco, GRO 39880. $$. AE; MC; V. Open daily for dinner 5 PM–3 AM. This casual dining restaurant is a popular and fun place to grab a bite after a day on the sand. It specializes in Mexican seafood such as tacos made with fresh fish, shrimp, and other seafood. If you've never had a fish taco, this is a good place to start, since they prepare them here in just about any way that suits you and a large selection of salsas are available to spice them up. For the more experienced fish taco-eater, try the octopus and calamari. If seafood isn't your thing, they also offer chicken, meat, and vegetarian choices. A selection of wines and beers is also available. The dining area features several tables overlooking the bay below, though it tends to get hectic in here during busy periods. Place your order and relax because the service can be a bit slow.

El Olvido (744-481-0203; www .elolvido.com.mx), Plaza Marbella, Avenida Costera Miguel Alemán, Acapulco, GRO 39880. $$$. AE; MC; V. Open daily for dinner 6–midnight. Despite the fact that it's located in a shopping mall, the terrace dining area at El Olvido provides beautiful bay views and an elegant ambiance. The Mediterranean décor provides a surprisingly romantic setting in the midst of the Zona Hotelera. It is a wonderful choice, particularly if you don't feel like taking the taxi ride out to Las Brisas. It tucked away on the bayside of Plaza Marbella shopping center located at the Diana traffic circle. The sophisticated dishes offered here are beautifully present-ed with plenty of personal care. Much of the cuisine here is distinctly Mexican, such as the lamb chops with chipotle sauce and sea bass topped with a green sauce of avocado and cilantro. However, the menu also has a French fusion twist, such as the red snapper dressed in a butter and citrus sauce. This restaurant also features a number of specialty drinks to get you in the right mood. Reservations are recommended and try to get here before 10, when the loud music from nearby dance clubs brings down the atmosphere.

Acapulco Diamante

Baikal (744-446-6845; www.baikal .com.mx), Carretera Escénica #16, Acapulco, GRO 39880. $$$. AE; MC; V. Open for dinner Sun.–Thu. 7–1, Fri.–Sat. 7–2. Located at the begin-ning of the bay-view strip at Las Brisas, this restaurant is a great place to come when you're in the mood to splurge. As it is located across the street from the Palladium disco, it's a convenient stop before the party begins. The experience begins right when you enter the front door and descend a spiral staircase into the daz-zling bar and large dining room with an elevated ceiling. The imaginative menu features fusion French and Asian cuisine combined with some Mexican flare. This restaurant also has an extensive selection of wines. How-ever, it is the view that completes the dining experience. The atmosphere is elegant with muted natural colors and tasteful furniture. The restaurant is built into the side of a cliff, which provides panoramic views of Acapulco Bay. Reservations are required.

Casanova (744-446-6237), Carretera Escénica #5256, Acapulco, GRO 39880. $$$. AE; MC; V. Open for din-ner Mon.–Sat. 7 PM–11:30 PM. A fancy dinner in Acapulco is incom-plete without a fabulous view of glit-tering Acapulco Bay, and this restaurant provides it. Located across the street from the Las Brisas resort, just off the Scenic Highway, it is built into a cliff overlooking the ocean and features a beautifully devised dining area accented in marble and stone. The dining experience is comple-mented by live music every night. This restaurant attracts a fashionable crowd, and is not the place to come if you're right off the beach. Casual slacks and loose-fitting collared shirts are fine but leave the flip-flops in your room. The menu offers a large selection of pastas, salads, and seafood, as well as a selection of poultry and meat dishes. There is also an extensive wine list. Reservations are required.

Coyuca 22 (744-483-5030), Avenida Coyuca #22, Acapulco, GRO 39390. $$$. AE; MC; V. Open daily Nov.–Apr. only, for dinner 7 PM–11:30 PM. Tell your cab driver the name of this elegant steak and seafood restaurant and he'll know just where to go. This is not only because the name of the restaurant is the address, but also because this has been one of Acapulco's most popular restaurants for more than 25 years. The inviting open-air dining area is set among a spacious hilltop garden with Doric pillars and a pool of water at its center. There is also a large illuminated obelisk that completes the grand atmosphere. This terrace provides beautiful views of the city and the bay and a great place to enjoy the Acapulco sunset. After dark, candlelight creates a romantic ambience just right for a couple's night out. Prime rib and lobster tails are the specialty here and there is a nice wine list to provide the perfect complement to your meal. It is located in the center of the peninsula on Acapulco's southwest side. Reservations are required.

Madeiras (744-446-5636, Carretera Escénica 33-B, Acapulco, GRO 39880. $$$. AE; MC; V. Open daily for dinner 7 PM–11:30 PM. This beautiful restaurant provides a sophisticated atmosphere accentuated with minimalist natural textures such as chiseled stone walls and calm mood lighting. The owners, Chef Richard Sandoval and Plácido Domingo, the world-renowned operatic tenor, present an innovative menu, which combines European traditions with Asian ingredients and Latin American recipes to create unique dishes such as achiote-hoisin short ribs and chipotle-marinated fillet. The menu changes daily and there is an impressive wine list to perfectly compliment your meal. Set in the exclusive hillside district of El Guitarrón, this restaurant features an open-air terrace that overlooks Acapulco Bay. Dress to impress, with long slacks and nice shoes for men and your best cocktail outfit for women. No one in shorts, tennis shoes, or bathing suites is admitted. Reservations are recommended.

Zibu (744-433-3058), Carretera Escénica s/n, Acapulco, GRO 39880. $$$. AE; MC; V. Open for dinner Sun.–Thu. 7 PM–midnight and Fri.–Sat. 7–1. Located off of the Scenic Highway in the Las Brisas Hills, this restaurant provides a stunning view of Acapulco Bay and a fantastic ambience perfect for a romantic night out. Like the menu, the décor is a blend of Mexican and Thai influences, which results in a unique and memorable dining experience. It features an open-air dining area furnished with rattan chairs and tables warmly lit with tiki torches, candles, and South Pacific–style lamps. The Thai background music completes the effect. Just beyond a small pool is a delightful *palapa* lounge, which serves a variety of interesting drinks. There is a large but pricy wine collection here, including several French wines. The bold flavors of the fusion Mexican and Thai cuisine are surprisingly balanced and delicious.

Old Acapulco

La Cabaña de Caleta (744-482-5007, Playa Caleta Lado Ote, Acapulco, GRO 39880. $. AE; MC; V. Open daily for breakfast, lunch, and dinner 9 AM–9 PM. This beachside Mexican restaurant provides a bohemian atmosphere and a convenient place to grab some good food and drinks when visiting Playa Caleta. There is an open-air terrace with a *palapa* roof for shade as well as covered cabañas right on the beach. Wherever you choose to dine, you will have a nice view of the bay as well as Isla la Roqueta. The menu features plenty of seafood specialties such as shark quesadillas and ceviche. For larger appetites, you can choose entrées such as seafood casserole, dorado fillet grilled with garlic, paella, shark tamales, and shrimp kabob. If you're not a seafood lover, you can choose from a number of more familiar Mexican dishes, such as chicken tacos and enchiladas. If you're in the adventurous mood, you can rent wave runners and arrange banana rides at this restaurant. It also has lockers and showers available to beachgoers.

Along the Costera

100% Natural (744-485-3982), Avenida Costera Miguel Alemán #200, Acapulco, GRO 39880. $. AE; MC; V. Open 24/7, serving breakfast, lunch, and dinner. This is a terrific restaurant that specializes in health food and fresh fruit. It's a good choice if you've overdone it on heavy buffet food and mixed drinks and want something basic and light. It's a particularly good choice to start off the day, with omelets and whole-grain pancakes topped with fruit. For lunch, they have a selection of sand-wiches served on whole-grain bread. This is also a good place to have a big fruit salad topped with honey and granola, or try a *liquado,* a blended Mexican specialty made with fruit and milk or yogurt. The menu has many vegetarian choices as well as more familiar Mexican selections, such as enchiladas and tacos. The atmosphere here is casual and the entire restaurant is decorated with tropical plants. A seat by the window provides a good place to people-watch. And because it's always open, it's always a good place to grab a quick bite to eat.

Santa Clara (744-484-0201), Avenida Costera Miguel Alemán #136, Acapulco, GRO 39880. $. MC; V. Open daily for snacks 9 AM–11 PM. This ice-cream shop is located in the heart of Acapulco's Zona Hotelero near Playa Condesa. They serve a large selection of ice creams and frozen yogurts, as well as smoothies, coffee, and espresso drinks. If you happen to have a laptop with you, drop in to connect to

100% NATURAL IS A FAVORITE IN ACAPULCO FOR ITS JUICES AND *LIQUADOS*.

TACOS AL PASTOR AT TACOS & BEER.

the Internet, which runs for about $1 for 20 minutes.

Tacos & Beer (744-484-2549), Avenida Costera Miguel Alemán s/n, Playa Condesa, Acapulco, GRO 39880. $. MC; V. Open daily for dinner 7–5. The name of this restaurant pretty much says it all. It is located right off of Playa Condesa and serves up a selection of tacos and (what else?) beer. Stop in here for a quick bite to eat either before or after a long night of dancing. It has the décor of a high school cafeteria and the interior lighting is bright enough to bug you out if you happen to stop in a little tipsy at 3 in the morning. Despite all of that, the food is good and rather cheap. The location of this establishment makes it a pretty busy place so be prepared to wait after placing your order.

El Zorrito (744-485-3735), Avenida Costera Miguel Alemán #212, Acapulco, GRO 39880. $. AE; MC; V. Open 24/7 for breakfast, lunch, and dinner. Located next door to a convenience store, you may walk by this simple

restaurant without even noticing it. However, the low-key atmosphere of this small Mexican restaurant is something to be appreciated in this town of high-pressure tourist traps. Besides that, the food is good. Decorated with plastic chairs and tables, and with ceiling fans spinning overhead, this down-to-earth restaurant puts all of the emphasis on providing you with good food cheaply. The portions are generous and the food is on the spicy side, so consider yourself warned. The menu features the old standards such as enchiladas and tacos, as well as traditional Mexican specialties such as *pozole* (pork and hominy soup). A good measure of this restaurant is the fact that you will often find more locals here than tourists. Conveniently located near the clubs in the Zone Hotelera, it's a great choice to wind down the evening after a long night of dancing.

Acapulco Diamante

Carlos 'N Charlie's (744-462-2104), Boulevard de las Naciones #1813, Acapulco, GRO 39880. $$. AE; MC; V. Open for lunch and dinner 1 PM–1 AM. Okay, it's a bit of a tourist trap but sometimes that's just what you're in the mood for. Located in La Isla Shopping Center in the Punta Diamante side of town, this restaurant provides a young crowd, a fun atmosphere, and a laid-back casual setting. And, oh yeah, they have food, too. The menu mostly features Mexican bar food, with such items as fajitas, quesadillas, and fish tacos. However, they also offer several steak dishes as well as a small selection of hamburgers. Decorated much like a TGI Friday's, there are musical instruments, automobile parts, and kitchen utensils hanging from the ceiling and waiters that double as entertainment guides. Be prepared to party when you're here, as guests are encouraged to cut loose among the comical skit performances, singing, and dancing on the chairs done by the staff.

Paciugo (744-466-3058), Boulevard de las Naciones #37, Acapulco, GRO 39880. $. MC; V. Open for snacks Sun.–Thu. 10 AM–9 PM and Fri.–Sat. 10 AM–10 PM. This gelato shop is like Italy's answer to Baskin-Robbins, with 30 or 40 flavors beckoning you in off the street. The wonderful flavors to be found here are just the remedy for a sweltering Acapulco afternoon. They range from Almond Chocolate Chip to Yogurt Raspberry Swirl and everything in between. And if you can't find a flavor to suit you (an unlikely proposition), come back tomorrow because there are actually more than 200 flavors that are constantly rotated.

Senior Frog's (744-446-5734), Carretera Escénica #28, Acapulco, GRO 39880. $$. AE; MC; V. Open daily for lunch and dinner 10 AM–1 AM. This bar and grill is perhaps the most famous tourist trap in Acapulco. It serves a long menu of bar-style food and plenty of drinks, and to top it off, has a beautiful view of the bay. And whether it's the food or the drinks, the portions are generous. The most common order seems to be the yard of beer that comes in a long plastic beaker. And don't be surprised if you suddenly find yourself in the grip of a waiter pouring a tequila shooter down your throat while blowing on a whistle to the cheers of onlookers. Come ready to party because this restaurant has a distinctly loose atmosphere with its own dance club and plenty of rowdy patrons out for a good time. It

is located in the Las Brisas area off the Scenic Highway. The restaurant closes at 1 AM but the club stays open much later.

NIGHTLIFE

Along the Costera

El Alebrije (744-484-5902), Avenida Costera Miguel Alemán #3308, Acapulco, GRO 39880. Open daily 11 PM–5 AM. This cavernous disco claims to be the biggest club in Acapulco, and with a capacity of over 2,500 people, it certainly looks to be. It is conveniently located in the Zona Hotelera and faces Acapulco Bay, with several bars and dance floors on different levels. It draws one of the youngest crowds, with most patrons between the age of 18 and 25. The music here is in English and Spanish, though you might not see a lot of foreigners in this bar unless you're here during spring break. But then again, every bar is packed with gringos around that time of year. Getting a table can be a hassle, especially on Fri. and Sat. nights. And good luck getting a drink when the disco is crowded. Despite the fact that the bartenders prefer to be tipped before they serve you, actually getting the drink can take up to 30 minutes, so you might want to order more than one. There is a cover of $36 for guys and $26 for girls, which includes drinks.

Baby'O (744-484-7474), Avenida Costera Miguel Alemán #22, Acapulco, GRO 39880. Open daily 10 PM–5 AM. This club is one of Acapulco's perennial favorites. It attracts a fairly mixed crowd of various ages, 25 and up. The facilities are high quality and fairly limited, with a capacity of around 250 people. The music played here is also wide ranging, from '80s New Wave favorites to contemporary Mexican dance artists. If you are fortunate enough to get a table, the service here is excellent. However, it is expensive, with a cover charge of between $30 and $60 for men and between $10 and $15 for women. On top of that, drinks run between $6 and $15. This alone makes the crowd a bit more exclusive than most bars along the main strip in the Zona Hotelera.

Baby Lobster Bar (744-484-1096), Avenida Costera Miguel Alemán and Playa Condesa, Acapulco, GRO 39880. Open daily 11 PM–5 AM. This open-air bar is located near Playa Condesa and the bungee jump at Avenida Costera Miguel Alemán, and it has direct beach access. Because of its location, it gets going earlier than most, making it a good place to start the evening. The location also makes

it more casual than most; sandals and shorts aren't a problem. The crowd is generally in their 20s and 30s. The music here is a mix of dance tunes from the '80s as well as contemporary artists. There is no cover and drinks go for between $6 and $12, though there is usually a 2-for-1 happy hour all night.

Barbarroja (744-481-1226), Avenida Costera Miguel Alemán #107, Acapulco, GRO 39880. Open daily 8 PM–2 AM. This is another open-air bar located along Playa Condesa near the bungee jump. You'll know you're there when you stumble upon the giant pirate ship that is crewed by waiters and bartenders in pirate attire. Barbarroja definitely ranks among the most touristy of Acapulco's tourist traps. However, it has a fun atmosphere and is an easy place to hang out if you don't feel like testing out your Spanish, as there are usually plenty of

NIGHTLIFE IN ACAPULCO STARTS LATE AND GOES ALL NIGHT.

gringos here. The music tends to be a mix of Mexican and western pop mixed in with well-known dance tunes. The crowd here tends to be a mix of all ages and it tends to get going very early compared to most clubs. Barbarroja also has a fairly large menu consisting mainly of steak and seafood dishes. There is no cover, so don't be afraid to poke your head in to see if you want to stay awhile.

▼ **Cabaré-Tito Beach** (744-484-7146), Privada de Piedra Picuda #17, Acapulco, GRO 39690. Open daily 10 PM–5 AM. This club was once a straight strip club and the runway from those days is still intact. Today it is a small and spirited gay disco.

▼ **Demas** (744-484-1800), Avenida los Deportes #10, Acapulco, GRO 39690. Open daily 11 PM–5 AM. This large gay dance club has an industrial décor and a lively atmosphere. You will find strippers dancing on the bar and there is a darkroom as well.

Disco Beach (744-484-8230), Avenida Costera Miguel Alemán and Playa Condesa, Acapulco, GRO 39880. Open Tue.–Sat. 10:30 PM–4 AM. This open-air disco is located right on the beach at Playa Condesa. The club plays a variety of dance music, with several raised dancing platforms as well as dancing on the beach. If dancing isn't your thing, there is also a pool table. Drink service is available inside or on the beach. This provides for a casual atmosphere; shorts and flip-flops are no problem here. Every Friday night, there are foam parties down on the beach; and they have bikini contests Wednesday, so dress appropriately. The crowd is on the younger side with most patrons between 18 and 25. The $30 cover charge covers drinks.

Ibiza Lounge (744-484-8230) Avenida Costera Miguel Alemán and Playa Condesa, Acapulco, GRO 39880. Open daily 11 PM–4 AM. This lounge, located next door to Disco Beach, is a good place to catch your breath after a night of dancing. The crowd tends to be in their 20s and 30s, and this bar tends to attract a lot of couples because of the secluded spaces it provides. The patrons here dress casual but not sloppy—no shorts or flip-flops here. This also seems to be a popular hangout for locals. The lights are kept low and you can either lounge on the comfortable couches in the air-conditioned salon or in outdoor tents located on the beach. The biggest drawback is that the throbbing techno music tends to be too loud to permit any kind of comfortable conversation.

Mangos (744-484-4762), Avenida Costera Miguel Alemán and Playa Condesa, Acapulco, GRO 39880. Open daily 12 PM–4 AM. This popular beach-facing bar and grill is located on Playa Condesa, in the heart of the Acapulco nightlife. It is an air-conditioned establishment, which is a good thing on particularly hot summer nights. The crowd tends to be in the 25–40 age range. There are more than a dozen big-screen televisions for sports and music videos and a free pool table located downstairs. Mangos offers good bar food and a large selection of domestic and imported beers. There is a variety of music all night long, from rock to pop, with some Latin songs mixed in. The bar is usually packed on weekend and makes a good place to have a few drinks before hitting the dance floor. There is no cover but try to arrive before 10 PM to avoid waiting for a table. There is no cover charge.

Mojito (744-484-8274), Avenida Costera Miguel Alemán and Playa Condesa, Acapulco, GRO 39880. Open Tue.–Sun. 9 PM–5 AM. This lively club brings a taste of old Cuba to the Acapulco strip. The music is salsa with other Latin influences mixed in and there is usually live music. If you want to dance but don't feel like bumping to techno music or syrupy pop songs, Mojito provides a nice alternative to many of the other clubs along Playa Condesa. It draws a slightly older crowd and there is a $10 cover charge. If you need a little instruction, salsa classes are offered here Mon. and Wed. 7 PM–9 PM.

Nina's (744-484-2400), Avenida Costera Miguel Alemán #2909, Acapulco, GRO 39880. Open daily 10 PM–4 AM. If you are looking for a change of pace from the tourist bars, this fashionable club may be the thing for you. It features live music every night, including cumbia, salsa, merengue, and mambo. A variety of shows begin around 1 AM, including comedians and celebrity impersonators. However, unless you speak Spanish and are up on Mexican pop culture, these entertainments will probably be lost on you. When the show ends, the band takes over and people swarm the dance floor. There is a $22 cover charge, which covers all of your drinks. This club attracts a diverse range of ages, though almost entirely Mexican. Arrive early on weekends because the place gets packed.

Paradise (744-484-5988), Avenida Costera Miguel Alemán s/n, Playa Condesa, Acapulco, GRO 39880. Open daily 6 PM–5 AM. This restaurant-bar is located right next to the bungee tower on the avenue. It has a large open-air terrace overlooking Playa Condesa. This establishment begins each night as a restaurant, with diners relaxing on the terrace enjoying the breeze. If you're beginning your night here, the kitchen serves up a large variety of seafood dishes. When the night gets going, Paradise transforms into a dance club as the terrace fills up with dancers bumping to a wide variety of dance tunes. It attracts a clientele with a wide range of ages, though it tends to skew younger as the night wears on. By midnight, it is usually crowded with mostly 18- to 25-year-olds. Be sure to ask about any promotions they may have, such as 2-for-1 drink specials.

Salon Q (744-481-0114), Avenida Costera Miguel Alemán, #23, Acapulco, GRO 39880. Open daily 11 PM–5 AM. This salsa club features live bands, talented singers, and plenty of salsa dancing. Besides salsa, the music features other Latin styles, such as *cumbias,* tropical songs, and *quebraditas.* Around midnight, there is a break in the dancing for a celebrity impersonators show. The atmosphere here is lively and the crowd is mostly in their 30s or older. There is a cover charge of around $15, which includes Mexican spirits and beers.

▼ **Savage** (744-484-1800), Avenida de los Deportes #10, Acapulco, GRO 39690. Open daily 11 PM–5 AM. This club features lavish drag with elaborate costumes and showmanship that borders on the surreal. There is a drag show at 12:30 AM to English-language beats and a Latin show at 2:30 AM.

▼ **Shurakk** (744-484-8852; http://www.shurakk.com), Avenida de los Deportes #110, Acapulco, GRO 39690. Open daily 11 PM–5 AM. This trendy gay nightspot features an elegant outdoor lounge. They offer 2-for-1 drinks all night on Thu., 2-for-1 beers on Fri. and Sat. 12 AM–2 AM. The cover of about $5 includes one drink.

Acapulco Diamante

Classico del Mar (744-446-6475), Carretera Escénica #2, Acapulco, GRO 39880. Open daily 3 PM–3 AM. From the outside, this bar looks like a giant shanty with derelict additions thrown on with no thought. Inside, however, it's a sophisticated dance club with a stylish bar and lounge complete with ornate chandeliers and velvety lounge furnishings. It is spread over three levels. The first is a standard club with lots of mirrors and lights. There is a small bar on the second level. On the third level is a tiki rooftop deck with a panoramic view of the glimmering lights of Acapulco Bay and bamboo huts on the dance floor. The music here is Latin American pop and international dance hits. This club is a favorite among Mexico's locals and wealthy *chilangos* (Mexico City residents). There is a cover of $28 for men, which doesn't include the cost of drinks. Women are admitted free.

Mandara (744-446-5711), Carretera Escénica Las Brisas, Acapulco, GRO 39880. Open daily 10 PM–4 AM. Located on Las Brisas hillside and high above Acapulco Bay, this large club features a 100-foot glass wall overlooking the bay. However, you might miss if you happen to be here on a crowded night because this club gets busy. It attracts a fairly diverse crowd. On weekends, the club puts on an impressive light show at around 3 AM. The music here ranges from Spanish remixes to electronic music to contemporary American artists.

You have the option of paying a hefty cover charge and having your drinks covered, or having a tab at the bar. Although the main club closes at 4 AM, the El Privado upstairs lounge stays open until well after sunrise, just in case you're in the mood to keep going. Mandara strives to have a classy ambience, so dress to impress when coming to this club. Shorts, jeans, and flip-flops are not okay here.

Palladium (744-446-5490), Carretera Escénica Las Brisas, Playa Guitarrón, Acapulco, GRO 39880. Open daily 11 PM–5 AM. This well-known club is perched on the Las Brisas hillside and has an impressive evening view of the Acapulco Bay. Later in the evening, a shower of sparks cascades down the exterior of the panoramic window looking out over the bay. Then, at around 4 AM, you can catch a fire dancer dressed as an Aztec warrior and painted entirely silver. The music here is mostly techno and the club features a large dance floor and several spots for lounging. The crowd here is mostly in their 20s and 30s and there is a cover charge of $38 for men and $28 for women, which covers drinks.

Pepe's Piano Bar (744-446-5736), Carretera Escénica and Comercial la Vista, Local #5, Acapulco, GRO 39880. Open Wed.–Sun. 10 PM–4 AM. This piano bar offers a more sophisticated atmosphere than most of Acapulco's "party" bars. The music here varies from traditional Spanish boleros to Mexican folk music. The ambience is loose and informal and there is a lot of interaction between the performers and the crowd, which gets into the act by performing karaoke. This crowd is usually of a diverse range of ages. There is no cover.

Zucca (744-446-5690), Carretera Escénica #28, Acapulco, GRO 39868. Open Wed.–Sat. during high season and Thu.–Sat. during low season, weekdays 11 PM–2:30 AM and weekends 11 PM–4 AM. Located in the Las Brisas hills, this popular bar features music from the '70s through the '90s. The crowd here skews slightly older than most bars in Acapulco, primarily because they do not admit anyone younger than 25, though this rule is loosely enforced when it comes to the ladies. It attracts mainly couples and the club provides plenty of intimate spaces, with fabulous views of the surrounding hillsides and Acapulco Bay. Show up dressed to impress. The dress code prohibits shorts, jeans, T-shirts, and sandals. Men should wear pants and collared shirts and, for women, this is an opportunity to wear that cocktail dress that's been sitting in your closet. There is a cover charge of $20 for men and $10 for women. Reservations are recommended.

✷ The Arts

GALLERIES Edith Matison's Art Gallery (744-484-3084),Avenida Costera Miguel Alemán #2010, Acapulco, GRO 39690. MC; V. Open Mon.–Sat. 10 AM–2 PM and 5 PM–9 PM. This upscale gallery specializes in exhibiting and selling works by renowned Mexican and international artists, including an array of paintings and sculptures by prominent regional artists. An extensive selection of high-quality Mexican handicrafts is on display as well.

Galería de Artesanías (744-484-7152), Avenida Costera Miguel Alemán #4455, Acapulco, GRO 39690. Open by appointment. This is a permanent gallery, located in Acapulco's convention center, specializes in fine examples of traditional Mexican crafts handmade by local artisans.

Galería Espacio Pal Kepenyes (744-446-5287), Costera Guitarrón 140, Acapulco, GRO 39690. MC; V. Open by appointment. This gallery features the work of Pal Kepenyes, a Hungarian artist whose sculptures have gained praise for their grace and movement. Examples of his public artwork can be seen in the bronze sculptures around town. Although he has resided in Acapulco for more than 25 years, his works have also been displayed in Paris, London, Tokyo, and Berlin.

Galería Rudic (744-484-4844; http://rudic.com/rudic/), Carretera Escénica S/N, Lote 2-C, Acapulco, GRO 39880. MC; V. Open Mon.–Sat. 10 AM–1 PM and 5 PM–9 PM. This fashionable gallery offers works by a large selection of contemporary Mexican artists, including Armando Amaya, Leonardo Nierman, and Gaston Cabrera. Galería Rudic features oil paintings, acrylics, water-colors, and pencil works, and there are sculptures of marble and onyx as well as lithographs as well. Prices include packing, shipping, and insurance costs.

MURAL Casa de Dolores Olmedo, Camino de la Inalámbrica #6, Acapulco, GRO 39907. Known as the grand dame of Acapulco, Dolores Olmedo was one of Mexico's great patrons of the arts. She was indeed the benefactor of celebrated muralist Diego Rivera. In fact, he spent the last 18 years of his life in this house with Olmedo and painted the inside walls with murals to show his appreciation to his host. In time, she became one of the world's foremost collectors of his work. Although she died in July 2002, her home, known as the House of the Winds, continues to be an important landmark. Along the outside wall, you will find a spectacular mosaic mural more than 100 feet in length, dominated by a depiction of the Aztec feathered serpent god Quetzalcoatl. It also features the pre-Hispanic dog Xoloitzcuintle. The aged Rivera labored on the work for a year and a half, and it is the last he did before his death in 1957. Today, this mural is considered one of the city's most important cultural works. The house is located on a quiet street not far from La Quebrada in the upscale neighborhood of Península de las Playas. You can get here by taxi. However, if you prefer to walk from La Quebrada, cross Avenida López Mateos and walk south about a quarter of a mile up the steep and winding street of Camino de la Pinoza. Take the first right at Camino de la Inalámbrica. After about another quarter mile, you will see the house on the right. Free admission.

✳ Entertainment

BULLFIGHTING Because of the long Spanish occupation of Mexico, the culture here is deeply influenced by the culture of Spain. Consequently, bullfighting has been one of the most popular pastimes in the country for the last 400 years. Bullfighting in Mexico is very similar to Spanish-style bullfighting. The event begins with the *picadors* circling the bull on horseback, jabbing its shoulder muscles with lances. Next, running fighters called *banderilleros* enter the ring, thrusting barbed darts called *banderillas* into the bull's neck and shoulder region. Finally, the *matador* enters

the ring. Matadors perform precise moves to impress the crowd and attract the bull in a manner that is considered graceful. The event ends with the matador's killing the bull with a sword. These events also include other events such as rodeos, pig chases, and dances. However, they have also become a source of controversy in recent years. Animal rights groups have railed against the sport, arguing that it is dangerous for the matador and the horses that the picadors ride, and, of course, that it is inhumane to the bulls. These groups have had their influence and, in fact, for a time it was illegal for anyone under the age of 18 to attend a bullfight. However, that law has since been rescinded. In any case, bullfighting remains a prominent sport in Mexico from November to March. In Acapulco, where bullfighting is more of a tourist attraction than a cultural event of great interest to the locals, the bullfights take place only in January and February, which corresponds with high tourist season. **Plaza de Toros** (744-485-4207), Calle Cotija #56, Acapulco, GRO 39999, is located in near Playa Caletilla in Old Acapulco. It is an impressive venue lined with tropical palm trees. When the matadors enter the arena, brass bands located high in the stands play their music to set the mood. However, because the crowd is primarily composed of tourists whose only experience with bullfighting has been in *Loony Tunes* cartoons, when the killing begins, any excitement that has been built up tends to change to shock and horror. However, by the third or fourth bull, many of the uninitiated have adjusted and one can even hear the occasional ¡Olé! coming from the crowd. Prices vary upon seating, though once inside you can pretty much sit wherever there is a free seat—and there are plenty. Admission $15–35.

La Quebrada Plazoleta de la Quebrada 74, Acapulco, GRO 39390. Open daily with diving at 1 PM, 7:30 PM, 8:30 PM, 9:30 PM, and 10:30 PM. This is Acapulco's most iconic attraction and no trip to the city is complete without attending one of these shows. Each afternoon and evening, young men hang perilously from the jagged cliffs of La Quebrada. When the moment is right, they plummet 150 feet into a narrow inlet between the rocks below, timing their dives to coincide with incoming waves that protect them from landing in the shallows. This tradition began in 1934, when young boys began diving from the cliffs for a few pesos from tourists. As these boys became more skilled divers, they learned how to use the motion of the waves as leverage. Despite the danger of these jumps, there has never been a fatality. La Quebrada divers have become world-famous performers and an important part of Acapulco culture. The show lasts for about a half hour, with some divers making solo jumps and others doing it in tandem. During the evening shows, some divers make their jumps holding lit torches in their hands. The general-admission viewing area can get crowded, so be sure to get here early to get a good spot. Another option is to head over to the adjacent Hotel Mirador, which charges a cover of about $10 to watch the show from their terrace. There are also local tour companies that will take you to the show by boat and anchor in spots that allow you to see the show from the bay. Get here most

easily by bus or taxi. Travel west along Avenida Costera Miguel Alemán, 3 blocks past the *zócalo*, then take Avenida López Mateos uphill to La Quebrada diver's point. General admission 35 pesos; includes a bottle of water or soda.

✳ Selected Shopping

Guerrero's party-central town is also well equipped with shops offering everything from the latest fashions to Mexican handcrafted folk art and find jewelry. There are several shopping centers located around the Diana shopping center and spread out along Avenida Costera Miguel Alemán, so you won't have a hard time finding places to shop. What's listed here is a sampling of what is available.

THE DIVERS OF LA QUEBRADA HAVE BECOME A SYMBOL OF ACAPULCO.

Alebrijes & Caracoles (744-485-1490), Avenida Costera Miguel Alemán #125, Acapulco, GRO 39850. Open daily 9 AM–8 PM.

This shop is located in the Plaza Bahía and is one of the best locations in Acapulco for high-quality gifts, toys, and decorations. *Alebrijes* are intricately painted wooden figures from the indigenous culture located around Oaxaca. They are usually in the shape of interestingly contorted animal spirit figures. A *caracol* is a spiral shell of a snail or other sea creature. This store, which is really divided into two shops, specializes in both types of Mexican folk art but also has other interesting types of *artesenía,* including papier-mâché fruits, wind chimes, ornaments, toys, as well as unusual decorative items for home and garden.

El Abuelo (744-484-2423), Calle Mina #389, Acapulco, GRO 39300. Open daily 9 AM–6:30 PM. This novelty and party supply store has all the products you might need to throw an authentic Mexican fiesta. If you suddenly find yourself in need of a costume, this is the place to come. There

INDIGENOUS FIGURES CARVED FROM OBSIDIAN.

Michael Brady

are all the standard supplies such as napkins, glasses, balloons, noisemakers, and piñatas—oh the piñatas! However, this store also offers some quality Mexican gifts and handicrafts.

Artesanías Finas de Acapulco (744-484-8039), La Costera and Avenida Horatio Nelson, Acapulco, GRO 39850. Open Mon.–Sat. 9 AM–6 PM and Sun. 9 AM–2 PM. A large department store well known enough to have its own local nickname, *Afa-Aca,* as it is commonly referred to, carries a wide selection of all sorts of folk art and handicrafts from all over Mexico. This store is an important stop with cruise ship passengers particularly because it allows you to make one stop and find any kind of *artesenía* that you are looking for, as well as rustic furniture, ceramic pottery, jewelry, masks, onyx figurines, and hand-embroidered clothing. The merchandise is high quality and the prices are reasonable though perhaps slightly higher than some of the smaller shops. However, this shop does offer a mailing service so you don't have to lug your purchase around in your luggage.

El Mercado de Artesanías el Parazal, Calle Cinco de Mayo, Acapulco, GRO 39350. Open daily 9 AM–9 PM. This is the oldest arts and crafts market in Acapulco. This traditional Mexican market is an out-door collection of vendor stalls selling a dizzying array of clothing and handicrafts. This is a great place to find hammocks, ceremonial masks, hand-embroidered dresses, and jewelry. Shopping here will give you the opportunity to try out your bartering chops by bargaining with the vendors. The market is about two blocks east and three blocks north of the *zócalo.* To get here, from the *zócalo,* walk east two blocks and turn north at Juan R. Escadero and continue to Vásquez de León. Turn right and continue for a block. The market will be on your left.

CLOTHING Alkimia (744-484-4830, Avenida Costera Miguel Alemán #3111, Acapulco, GRO 39850. Open daily 10 AM–7 PM. Come here for Bermuda shorts, T-shirts, bathing suits, and beachwear of all kinds. The store specializes in clothes made from fabrics that are light, comfortable, and easy to maintain.

Armando's (744-484-5111), Avenida Costera Miguel Alemán #1252–7, Acapulco, GRO 39670. Open daily 9 AM–9 PM. This store offers its own line of brightly colored women's clothing with a distinct Mexican accent. They are trendy and appropriate for Acapulco's warm climate. This store also sells accessories designed by Luisa Conti.

Blue Jeans (744-484-9501), Avenida Costera Miguel Alemán #154, Acapulco, GRO 39670. Open daily 10 AM–7 PM. This store sells trendy designer jeans for women and work jeans for men. They also have shorts, T-shirts, and blouses, as well as accessories such as backpacks and caps. The store is well stocked and prices are reasonable.

Cusma (744-481-1112), Avenida Costera Miguel Alemán s/n, Acapulco, GRO 39670. Open daily 10 AM–7 PM. This large store specializes in bathing suits for the entire family. It has a large collection of all styles from one-piece to Brazilian, in all sizes. They also have all types of beach accessories such as sunglasses, hats, and flip-flops. This is high-quality merchandise and relatively expensive.

Esteban's (744-446-5719), Balcones #110–2, Acapulco, GRO 39300. Open daily 10 AM–7 PM. This store special-

THERE IS NO SHORTAGE OF CLOTHING SHOPS ALONG ACAPULCO'S SHOPPING DISTRICT.

izes in opulent women's eveningwear and fashionable resort clothing. The designs are original and many pieces have intricate embroidery. Cocktail dresses range between $300 and $4,000, daytime wear is less expensive. There is also a men's department on the second floor.

SHOPPING CENTERS Galerías Diana (744-481-4021), Avenida Costera Miguel Alemán #1926, Acapulco, GRO 39670. This modern shopping center is located at the Diana traffic circle in the heart of the Zona Hotelera. It features many familiar stores including Starbucks, Nine West, and Vans. There are also a lot of small boutiques shops as well as many eating establishments, including an Applebee's. This mall also features a multiplex that plays the latest films out of Hollywood. These movies are presented in English with Spanish subtitles.

La Gran Plaza (744-486-6479), Avenida Costera Miguel Alemán #1632, Acapulco, GRO 39670. This large shopping mall, located on the ocean side of Avenida Costera Miguel Alemán facing Playa Icacos toward the south end of Acapulco Bay, encompasses more than 135 stores in a luxurious two-level environment, ranging from those specializing in international designers to several small handicraft shops selling traditional souvenirs. There is also a large food court and many restaurants offering everything from traditional Mexican cuisine to eclectic international food. This mall also has a movie theater that plays the newest Hollywood blockbusters. This being a tourist area, these movies are screened in English with Spanish subtitles. Most shops accept major credit cards as well as U.S. dollars. However, try not to pay with American cash because you'll get a lousy exchange rate. Often, during holidays, the mall

THERE IS PLENTY OF SHOPPING AROUND THE DIANA TRAFFIC CIRCLE.

schedules free entertainment such as concerts by popular entertainers.

Marbella Mall (744-481-1788), Avenida Costera Miguel Alemán, Diana Traffic Circle, Acapulco, GRO 39670. This small shopping mall is a collection of small retail stores and top-brand boutiques including Tommy Hilfiger and several sporting good stores. There are no fast-food restaurants here but there are a small number of eateries, including the upscale Olvido Restaurant. The Canadian embassy is also located here. There are narrow hallways off the interior central courtyard and the good air-conditioning makes it a good place to window-shop on a particularly hot afternoon.

Mercado Municipal, Calle Diego Hurtado de Mendoza and Avenida Constituyentes, Acapulco, GRO 39350. This is the largest market in town but not really meant for tourists. It is the primary market for local residents to haggle over all kinds of everyday goods such as woven baskets and mangoes. That said, you can get some good deals on leather goods, hammocks, and other crafts. If you do end up here and find something you just have to have, haggle like crazy. The simple fact that you're an out-of-towner means that the price you're quoted is likely significantly inflated and, with a little insistence, you can cut the price by as much as 50 percent.

Plaza Bahía (744-485-6939), Avenida Costera Miguel Alemán #125, Acapulco, GRO 39350. This mall features 65 retail stores that offer everything from perfume, shoes, lingerie, jewelry, and electronics. There are also a number of fast-food restaurants here. In the interior central courtyard, you will find an impressive bronze fountain with bronze horses made by the renowned sculptor Victor Salmones. This mall also has a bowling alley, movie theaters, and go-karts. The air-conditioning makes it a good place to window shop on hot days.

LA COSTA CHICA

Stretching for more than a hundred miles south of Acapulco, the Costa Chica is a tropical land far afield from mainstream Mexican culture. It is populated with thousands of indigenous people who, if they speak Spanish at all, speak it as a second language. Many of these people live in small villages in the foothills of the Sierra Madre del Sur and live their lives in ways that have changed little for hundreds of years. In addition to the indigenous residents, the Costa Chica is also only one of two regions in Mexico that is home to a large Afro-Mexican population (the other being the coastal area from Veracruz to Quintana Roo). Also known as *costeños,* this population mainly subsist through farming and fishing. Although the people of the Costa Chica have in the past had a reputation of being suspicious of outsiders, in recent years they have become more accustomed to tourists passing through, due largely to the development of beaches further south in Oaxaca. Still, accommodations along the Costa Chica are few and far between and generally offer few amenities. If you come to the Costa Chica, it is best to be prepared for a rustic beach experience.

COCONUT PALMS ABOUND ALONG THE COSTA CHICA.

✳ Lodging

✦ **La Caracola** (741-101-3047; www .playaventura.com), Costera Antelmo Ventura #68, Juan Alvarez, GRO 39900. $. This hotel is located in a small town called Juan Alvarez at kilometer 124 on the highway to Pinotepa Nacional and Puerto Escondido. However, it is probably better known as Playa Ventura because a family by the name of Ventura owns most of the beachfront here. This hotel is actually a compound of several simple beach bungalows with bamboo walls and wooden floors. Several are located right on the beach with a full view of the ocean. You will not find any five-star amenities here. The beds are plywood with foam mattresses, though they are clean. Some of the bungalows are equipped with kitchenettes, which is key because places to eat around here are few and far between.

However, this place makes a great hideaway if you are looking for a secluded surf spot. The compound also has a small swimming pool and you can rent a horse and ride up the beach if you're looking for even more seclusion.

✦ **Hotel Bello Nido** (741-412-0141), Avenida Cuauhtémoc #50, Ometepec, GRO 39900. $. Located in Ometepec, the center of the coastal indigenous heartland, this hotel offers 30 simple yet clean rooms in a three-story building about three blocks north of the *zócalo*. The rooms have ceiling fans, cable television, and either one or two double beds. For a more quiet experience, request a room on the upper floors away from the street. These rooms are arranged around a pleasant central courtyard that is dominated by a modest swimming pool.

LA COSTA GRANDE

Running 150 miles northwest from Acapulco to Zihuatanejo, this long, immaculate coastline is a land of coconut groves, cornfields, and small fishing villages. If you have Acapulco and Zihuatanejo on your itinerary, you may be tempted to travel up Highway 200 as fast as you can, skipping La Costa Grande altogether. Although this may dictated by time constraints, the Costa Grande offers miles of secluded beaches, high-quality surfing, and gorgeous vistas. It is well worth it to take some time to enjoy some of the better spots along the way.

Most services along the Costa Grande are concentrated in the far south at the Pie de la Cuesta. Located 10 miles northwest of Acapulco, Pie de la Cuesta is a long, narrow strip of land that separates the roaring Pacific Ocean from the calm fresh waters of the Coyuca Lagoon. Here, you will find a small seaside hamlet easily accessible from Acapulco and perhaps most famous for its beautiful sunsets. This rustic resort village offers a host of diversions in a tranquil setting. These diversions include such activities as kayaking, fishing, horseback riding, and just snoozing in a hammock. You can get here by bus from Acapulco by hopping on any of the buses marked "Pie de la Cuesta" along Avenida Costera Miguel Alemán. To get here by car, take the avenue west from Parque Papagayo and turn right at Calle Diego Hurtado de Mendoza. Follow this street as it quickly becomes Pie de la Cuesta and, further on, Ciruelos. This street curves dramatically as it winds its way west and then north out of town. As this road turns away from the shoreline several miles out of town, turn left onto Fuerza Aérea Mexicana. This road will take you into Pie de la Cuesta.

The 20-mile-long stretch of beach in Pie de la Cuesta is popular among surfers. However, only surf here if you

PIE DE LA CUESTA CAN PROVIDE A NICE BREAK FROM THE CROWDS OF ACAPULCO.

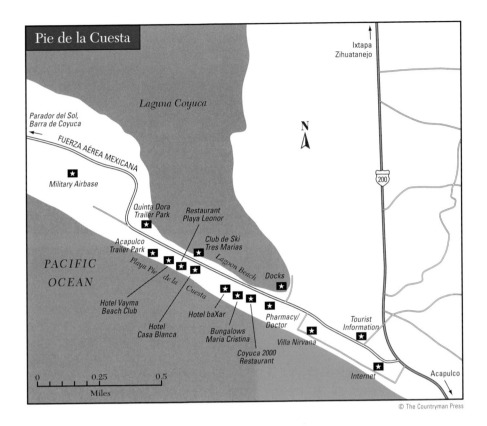

Pie de la Cuesta

Ixtapa
Zihuatanejo

Laguna Coyuca

Parador del Sol,
Barra de Coyuca

FUERZA AÉREA MEXICANA

N

200

Military Airbase

Quinta Dora
Trailer Park

Restaurant
Playa Leonor

Club de Ski
Tres Marias

Acapulco
Trailer Park

Lagoon Beach

Docks

PACIFIC
OCEAN

Playa Pie de la Cuesta

Hotel Vayma
Beach Club

Pharmacy/
Doctor

Tourist
Information

Hotel baXar

Hotel
Casa Blanca

Bungalows
Maria Cristina

Villa Nirvana

Coyuca 2000
Restaurant

Acapulco

Internet

0   0.25   0.5
Miles

© The Countryman Press

are an excellent swimmer. As in many of Acapulco's beaches, the waves here break near the shoreline and recede with a powerful undertow. Generally speaking, they are hazardously rough, powerful, and unsuitable for surfing from March through October. However, from November through February, they tend to settle into a cleaner cycle. Farther afield, the Costa Grande is dotted with beaches and mangroves. Many of these beaches are ideal for beach camping, with unlikely beachfront restaurants set up miles from the next town.

✳ To Do

↬ **BEACH Barra de Coyuca Lagoon** This natural freshwater lagoon sits on the northern side of the narrow Pie de la Cuesta isthmus. It covers 28 square miles and is a haven for water skiers, birdwatchers, and eco-tourists alike. In fact, this area is home to more than 250 species of birds. This sandy-bottomed lagoon is fed by the waters of the Río Coyuca and is lined with mangroves. During the rainy season, this lagoon fills and opens to the ocean. Waterskiing clubs and restaurants line the plumy shore, serving the people who have come here to get away from the bustle of Acapulco. These restaurants feature hammocks, seafood, cold *cerveza,* and even an occasional swimming pool. Many also feature launches where you can put a boat in the water for around $15. Boat traffic is generally confined to the center of the lagoon, so it's safe to dawn your bathing suit and jump in just about anywhere along the shoreline. The weekends tend to bring crowds, so get here during the week if you can.

✳ Lodging

Pie de la Cuesta is a village of simple resorts that offers a respite from the large resorts of Acapulco. Most of the hotels you find out here are relatively shabby places with meager amenities. If it's five-star service you're looking for, it's best to look for it on either side of this coast.

⨍ ⌁ **Baxar Hotel y Club de Playa** (744-460-2502; www.baxarhotel

PIE DE LA CUESTA IS FAMOUS FOR ITS BEAUTIFUL SUNSETS.

acapulco.net), Avenida Fuerza Aerea #356, Pie de la Cuesta, GRO 39900. $$; MC, V. Located in Pie de la Cuesta just 20 minutes from Acapulco, this hotel offers an ecologically friendly alternative to the hustle and bustle of the large resort towns. The specialty here is peace and quiet, so this is not the place to come if you are looking for a party. It offers 21 rooms with handmade Mexican tile, colorful living areas, and either one king-size or two double beds. Some have terraces with woven hammocks and handcrafted chairs. The hotel grounds feature narrow walkways lined with tropical plants. There is a small patio area that opens onto the beach. It is dominated by a modest swimming pool and several chairs for lounging. The beach, which offers club membership, has several *palapa* lean-tos that provide shade for hammocks, beds, beds, and fabric craft chairs. There is also a small bar here that serves up fresh tropical drinks. The hotel restaurant, open daily 7 AM–11 PM, serves traditional Mexican cuisine, as well as several international selections. Just off the beach, you can dine either in the indoor dining room or on a shaded pier that extends all the way to the water.

⨍ ⌁ **Hacienda Vayma Beach Club** (744-460-2892; www.vayma.com.mx), Playa del Sol #378, Pie de la Cuesta, GRO 39900. $$; MC, V. This Mediterranean-style beach resort is located at Pie de la Cuesta on a narrow strip of land between the Pacific Ocean and the Coyuca Lagoon. It offers 25 whitewashed suites decorated in a simple European style and furnished with king-size beds. Many of these beds are canopied and some rooms also have kitchenettes and private Jacuzzis. Guests pass their time surfing the waves on the Pacific, horseback riding on the beach, waterskiing on the lagoon, or just lounging on a hammock. The hotel grounds feature a large swimming pool with a swim-up bar and several islands topped with chaise longues. This hotel also has an open-air bar and grill, open daily 8 AM–10 PM, which specializes in wood-fired pizza and a variety of shrimp, lobster, chicken, and beef dishes. Enjoy dinner right on the beach accompanied by soft jazz, candlelight, and tiki torches.

Hotel Resort Villas San Luis (742-427-0282; www.villassanluis.com .mx), Carretera Nacional Acapulco-Zihuatanejo Km. 142.5, San Luis, GRO 40906. $. Located on kilometer 142.5 on Highway 200, almost halfway between Acapulco and Ixtapa, this hotel offers 43 attractively furnished rooms. Each room has two double beds. The rooms are in long buildings set in the heart of a palm tree and mango plantation. The property is meticulously groomed and has a large patio area shaded by coconut palms. There is a large swimming pool lined with chaise longues and patio furniture. Adjacent to the pool, down a long walkway and over a small arched bridge is the hotel's **La Cabaña Restaurant,** open daily 7:30

AM–11 PM, which serves a selection of fresh tropical drinks as well as traditional Mexican and international cuisine.

Parador del Sol Acapulco (744-444-4050; www.paradordelsol .com.mx), Carretera Pie De La Cuesta A Barra De Coyuca, Km. 5, Acapulco, GRO 39430. $$. MC; V. This all-inclusive resort is located a bit off the beaten path. In Acapulco, this can be a good thing, particularly if you are looking to avoid the crowds. It is several miles northwest of the hotel zone, near La Quebrada and offers a total of 150 villas spread over a 330,000-square-foot property. Of these, 86 are along the ocean and 64 are along a lagoon. All the villas contain two double or a king-size bed, and air-conditioning. These bungalows are simply furnished tiny houses, each with a private terrace and a hammock. The property has two large pools, one located along the ocean and the other along the lagoon. There is also a kid's club, which provides supervised activities and babysitting. Among the activities available to the hotel's adult guests are kayaking on the lagoon, mini golf, an outdoor *palapa* gym, and tennis at the hotel tennis courts. The property also has a barbecue pit that is ideal for outdoor cookouts. If you didn't happen to catch dinner, the hotel's **Delfines Restaurant,** open daily for breakfast 7–11, lunch 1–4, and dinner 7–10, offers buffet-style Mexican dining in an outdoor *palapa* setting.

Ixtapa-Zihuatanejo

2

IXTAPA

ZIHUATANEJO

TRONCONES

BARRA DE POTOSÍ

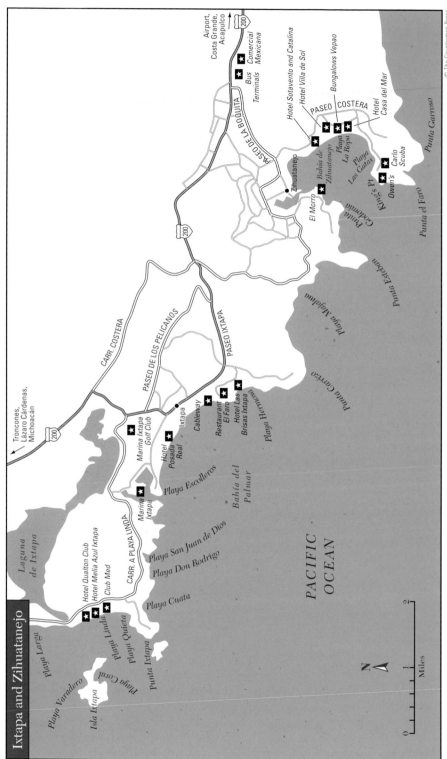

Ixtapa and Zihuatanejo

Airport,
Costa Grande,
Acapulco
200

Bus Commercial
Terminals Mexicana

Hotel Villa de Sol
Hotel Sotavento and Catalina

Bungalows Vepao
PASEO COSTERA
Hotel
Casa del Mar

Punta Garroso

Bahía de Zihuatanejo
Playa La Ropa
Playa Las Gatas

Carlo Scuba
Owen's
Nina's Pt.

Zihuatanejo

El Morro

Punta el Faro

PASEO DE LA BOQUITA

200

Punta Calidonia

Playa Magdalena

Punta Estaban

CARR. COSTERA

PASEO DE LOS PELICANOS

PASEO IXTAPA

Punta Carrizo

Restaurant El Faro
Cableway
Hotel Las Brisas Ixtapa

Playa Hermosa

Bahía del Palmar

Marina Ixtapa Golf Club

Ixtapa

Hotel Posada Real

Playa Escolleros

Marina Ixtapa

PACIFIC OCEAN

Troncones,
Lázaro Cárdenas,
Michoacán
200

CARR. A PLAYA LINDA

Hotel Qualton Club
Hotel Melía Azul Ixtapa
Club Med

Playa San Juan de Dios

Playa Don Rodrigo

Playa Cuata

Laguna de Ixtapa

Playa Linda

Playa Quieta

Punta Ixtapa

Playa Larga

Playa Coral

Isla Ixtapa

Playa Varadero

N

0   1   2
Miles

© The Countryman Press

INTRODUCTION

The twin cities of Ixtapa and Zihuatanejo provide two very distinct experiences. Despite the development of a tourist industry over the last thirty years, Zihuatanejo continues to be a fishing village at heart. The town is built around the picturesque Bahía de Zihuatanejo. The downtown area sits toward the northern end of this bay while most of the hotels sit along the bay to the southeast. Beyond that lie a beautiful long beach and the Sierra foothills. Unlike most Mexican towns, Zihuatanejo does not have a *zócalo*. Rather, the *malecón* waterfront walkway is the heart of town, running along the municipal beach all the way east to Playa Madera. This walkway is lit at night. The town has many distinct beaches scattered along its 12-mile coastline. For this reason, most hotels are not within walking distance of the downtown area, though taxis are easily available and relatively cheap. The downtown area has the feel of the mid-size Mexican beach town that it is. There you will find several restaurants and handicraft markets along and around Avenida 5 de Mayo and Avenida Álvarez.

On the other hand, you will be under no illusion that you are in an old Mexican fishing village while hanging out in downtown Ixtapa. In fact, other than a collection of luxury condominiums, there is really no community of Ixtapa or such a thing as downtown Ixtapa. Ixtapa is really just a collection of resort accommodations and a core commercial center made up of a collection of shopping plazas. This *centro comercial* is located along Paseo Ixtapa across the street from the resort hotels that line Playa del Palmar and is within walking distance from just about all of Ixtapa's resorts and provides plenty of restaurants, convenience stores, and clothing stores. If you are staying in one of the more outlying resorts such as Las Brisas, the *centro comercial* is about a 20-minute walk along the sidewalk that lines Paseo Ixtapa. That can seem awfully far on a particularly hot day. However, the price of a short cab ride is well-worth it to escape the exorbitant prices at the resort restaurants.

Ixtapa and Zihuatanejo have some of the most beautiful beaches in Mexico. These beaches also provide a diverse range of experiences. Several are wide open with a heavy surf and strong undertow, whereas others lie in protected coves and provide excellent snorkeling. For the most part, you will find these beaches to be very clean and well-maintained. The only exception might be Playa la Ropa in Zihuatanejo, which can on occasion have some trash lying around. However, even this beach is kept relatively clean compared to other high-traffic beaches in Mexico. Other beaches, such as Playa Coral on Isla Ixtapa, are kept amazingly clean for the amount of visitors they receive.

For travelers looking for a more down-to-earth vacation, Zihuatanejo and Troncones have many boutique hotels where you can surround yourself with a more traditional sort of elegance. These hotels are generally on the smaller side and feature rooms with unique décor, and are generally within walking distance to the many bars and restaurants. Whatever you choose, this long stretch of beaches along the west coast of Mexico has the facilities and service to meet your desires.

GETTING THERE *By air:* **Ixtapa-Zihuatanejo International Airport** (airport code ZIH) is located about 10 miles south of Zihuatanejo and 15 miles south of Ixtapa. This airport is served by several American airlines, including Alaska Airlines out of Los Angeles and San Francisco, Delta out of Los Angeles, Continental out of Houston, Frontier out of Denver, and U.S. Airways out of Phoenix. As in Acapulco, several major car rental companies have booths in this airport. If you plan on taking a taxi to your destination, be sure to make those arrangements at the booth near the arrival exit. Passage via a compact taxi will run between $28 and $40, depending on the distance whereas a *colectivo* will cost about $12 per person. If you plan on renting a taxi all the way to Troncones, this will cost you around $75.

By bus: Bus service from Mexico City to Ixtapa-Zihuatanejo takes around 9 hours.

By car: Driving north to Ixtapa-Zihuatanejo along Highway 200, from the airport south of town, you will roll along the coast providing many beautiful ocean vistas and fairly easy access to long, secluded beaches.

The drive from Mexico City to Ixtapa-Zihuatanejo takes about 8 hours. You can take Highway 15 to Toluca, then Highway 130/134 the rest of the way. Be sure to gas up because there are fewer gas stations as you get closer to the coast. Another option is to take Highway 95D to Iguala, then hop on Highway 51 west to Highway 134. From Morelia, Michoacán, take the Highway 37 toll road. If you find yourself in Ixtapa-Zihuatanejo with a hankering for experiencing Mexico's colonial side, your best bet is to take Highway 37 into the Michoacán cities of Morelia and Urúapan. Upland Guerrero towns such as Taxco and Chilpancingo are not accessible from the northwest. To get to these towns, you have to go all the way down the Costa Grande and access them through Acapulco.

GETTING AROUND *By bus:* Ixtapa-Zihuatanejo has three long-distance bus terminals, all of which are located next to each other along Highway 200 on the east side of Zihuatanejo. The largest of these is the Central de Autobús operated by the Estrella del Blanca bus company. This station provides daily first-class and second-class service to Acapulco, which then will connect you to Mexico City to the east or Oaxaca to the south. From Zihuatanejo, you must go to Acapulco to get to Taxco. Service to destinations to the north or east from Zihuatanejo, such as Guanajuato or Guadalajara go through Morelia or Urúapan in Michoacán.

The bus carrier Estrella de Oro operates out of a separate station just to the west of Central de Autobús. This station offers first-class connections to the south and southeast through Acapulco and north and northeast through Michoacán. Just to the west of this station is one is serviced by several other bus companies that provide first-class and luxury class service to points throughout Mexico. These lines include La Linea Plus, Autovias, Omnibus de Mexico, and Premier Plus.

Car rental: If you plan on exploring the nearby environs, car rental booths are available at the airport or at the larger resorts. The road between Ixtapa and Zihuatanejo is a four-lane highway, making the journey between the two cities quick and convenient. Keep in mind that both locations have an area called Zona Hotelera. Therefore, if you are staying in Ixtapa, don't follow the signs to the Zona Hotelera if you are still in Zihuatanejo. On the other hand, if you plan on staying in and around Ixtapa-Zihuatanejo, there is little point of spending the money on a rental car as public transportation is more than sufficient. **Advantage Rent-A-Car** (755-553-0033; www.aracmexico.com), Paseo de las Garzas s/n, Zihuatanejo, Guerrero, 40884. Open Mon.–Sat. 7:30 AM–9 PM and Sun. 8 AM–8 PM. Additional locations: Airport (755-553-7205); Hotel Brisas (755-553-2121 ext. 3478), Ixtapa; Hotel Presidente Intercontinental (755-553-0018 ext. 7990), Ixtapa. **Budget Car Rental** (755-553-0397; www.budget.com.mx), Paseo Ixtapa s/n 10, Ixtapa, Guerrero, 40880. Open Mon.–Fri. 8 AM–7 PM, Sat. 9 AM–7 PM, and Sun. 9 AM–4 PM. Additional location: Airport (755-554-4837). **Europcar** (555-207-5572; www.europcar.com.mx), Hotel Melia, Azul, Paseo Ixtapa Lote 2, Ixtapa, Guerrero, 40880. Open daily 9 AM–7 PM. Additional location: Airport (755-553-7158). **Hertz Car Rental** (U.S. 1-800-709-5000; www.hertz.com.mx), Nicolas Bravo 13 #10, Zihuatanejo, Guerrero, 40880. Open Mon.–Fri. 9 AM–7 PM and Sat. 9 AM to 2 PM. Additional locations: Airport (755-554-2952); Hotel Emporio (755-553-3338), Ixtapa. **Thrifty Car Rental** (755-553-3019; www .thrifty.com.mx), Hotel Barceló, Paseo Ixtapa s/n, Ixtapa, 04080. Open daily 9 AM–7 PM. Additional location: Airport (755-553-7020).

By shuttle bus: A shuttle bus runs daily between the two towns, several times an hour, 5 AM–11 PM. This shuttle can be a little crowded but at a cost of 20 pesos, it's well worth it. In Zihuatanejo, you can pick up this shuttle at the corner of Morelos and Paseo Zihuatanejo, a few blocks north of the main market. In Ixtapa, you can hop on at numerous stops along Paseo Ixtapa.

By taxi: Fortunately, taxi drivers here tend to be much more low-key than in Acapulco. In Zihuatanejo, you shouldn't have a problem with their pushing timeshare tours or bugging you to take a ride you don't need. However, you may encounter a bit of this walking along the main thoroughfare in Ixtapa, but nothing like in Acapulco. Taxis are not metered, so settle on a price before you get in. Knowing a lit-

USEFUL PHONE NUMBERS
Emergency: 066
Direct-dial prefix, U.S. to Mexico: 011-52
Direct-dial prefix, Mexico to U.S.: 001
Highway Patrol 755-554-0090
Municipal Police 755-554-2040
Tourist Police 755-554-2207
Fire Department: 755-554-7551
U.S. Embassy: 755-553-2100
Red Cross: 755-554-2009

tle Spanish may allow you to get a better price, but in general the ride between Ixtapa and Zihuatanejo runs around $5. The fare within Zihuatanejo runs about $3, and is between $3 and $5 in Ixtapa. Rates go up after midnight. Taxi services include: **Seguro Mutual APAAZ** (755-544-6545), **UTAAZ AC** (755-554-3900), and **UTZI** (755-554-4763).

MEDICAL ASSISTANCE *Hospitals:* **Hospital General** (755-554-3965), Calle Morelos s/n, Zihuatanejo, GRO 40880; **Hospital de Especialidades** (755-554-6808), Avenida la Parota #1, Zihuatanejo, GRO 40880. *Pharmacies:* **Farmacia Poco Loco** (755-553-1454), Paseo Ixtapa #2, Ixtapa, GRO 40880. Open daily 8 AM–10 PM. **Farmacias Similares** (755-553-3673), Calle la Puerta #9, Zihuatanejo, GRO 40884. Open daily 7 AM–11 PM.

BANKS Banamex (755-553-0405), Paseo la Golondrinas s/n, Ixtapa, GRO 40880. Open Mon.–Fri. 9 AM–4 PM, Sat. 10 AM–2 PM. **Bancomer** (755-553-0603), Calle la Puerta #777, Ixtapa, GRO 40880. Open Mon.–Fri. 8:30 AM–4 PM. **Banco Santander** (755-553-2336), Boulevard Iztapalapa #6, Zihuatanejo, GRO 40880. Open Mon.–Fri. 9 AM–3 PM.

INTERNET CAFÉS Dolfy's Internet Café (755-553-1177), Centro Comercial los Patios #108, Ixtapa, GRO 40880. Open daily 8 AM–9 PM. This cybercafé is located in Los Patios shopping center in Ixtapa. They have several computers for general use but their prices, which convert to around $6.50 an hour, are pretty steep. **Xtapa Conexxion** (755-553-2253), Centro Commercial Ixtapa Plaza #15, Ixtapa, GRO 40880. Open daily 10:30 AM–9:30 PM. This café serves up some good coffee and has several computers available for general use. A bit pricey, similar to Dolfy's.

LAUNDRY SERVICE Lavamatic (755-554-1690), Calle Morelos #87, Zihuatanejo, GRO 40880. Open Mon.–Fri. 9 AM–8 PM. **Tintoreria y Lavanderia Express** (755-554-4393), Calle Cuauhtémoc #37, Zihuatanejo, GRO 40880. Open Mon.–Fri. 9 AM–8 PM.

IXTAPA

✳ To Do

Ixtapa is a playground that straddles the Pacific Ocean, providing activities that take advantage of the areas magnificent climate and its beautiful sandy beaches. The city is well on its way toward establishing itself as a world-class golfing destination with its two championship golf courses, while all along the coast you'll find wonderful opportunities for snorkeling and diving, as well as surfing. Unlike Acapulco, which has Pie de la Cuesta, there are not too many spots here that are great for kayaking, though certain spots at Isla Ixtapa do suffice. If you're into biking, there are several paths in the area, including a bike path that runs from the marina in Ixtapa out to Playa Linda. You can rent bicycles at either end.

BEACHES Playa Linda, about 5 miles north of the main Zona Hotelera, is probably best known as the place you come to catch the water taxi to Isla Ixtapa. For this reason, tourists mostly pass this beach by on their way to spend the day basking in the sun at Playa Coral. However, Playa Linda really does live up to its name, which means "pretty beach." It is a long, wide strip of sand lined with coconut palms that rolls off toward the north, with an estuary, populated with many species of birds, iguanas, turtles, as well as crocodiles, which is largely neglected by beach-goers, making this a great place to take a long walk on the beach. There is also a good surfing spot toward the north end of the beach where a river empties into the ocean. Or, you can rent horses and take a tour of the area. Guides are on hand to take you down the nearby trails for about $10 an hour. At the entrance of the beach,

BANANA BOAT RIDES ARE A POPULAR FORM OF RECREATION AT THE REGION'S TOURIST BEACHES.

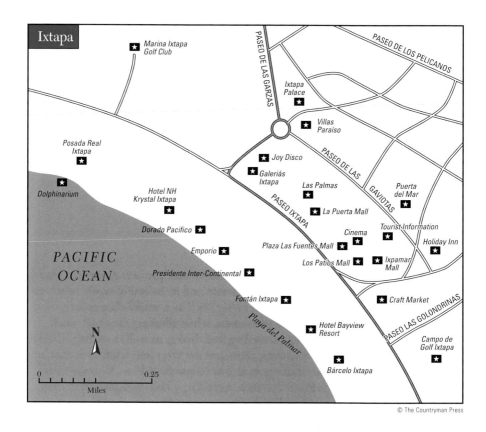

a bazaar of stalls caters to the tourists headed over to the island. Here, you can pick up beach clothing, snorkels, cheap plastic beach toys, and other souvenirs before you disembark. There are also tour companies here that organize banana boat rides and Jet Ski rentals. Several *palapa* restaurants serve fish tacos and beer for very reasonable prices. You can get to Playa Linda by bus or taxi. By car, take Highway 200 north and follow the signs.

Playa del Palmar provides the setting for the major hotels along the strip in Ixtapa. It has beautiful fine sand and water that is clear and warm. The beach is about 2 miles long and has small waves that break right up against the shore. This makes it a tricky place to swim, since these waves can get tough and there are sometimes strong currents. If you are traveling with children, be sure to

STALLS AT PLAYA LINDA OFFER EVERYTHING NEEDED FOR A DAY AT THE BEACH.

PLAYA LINDA IS LINED WITH COCONUT PALMS AND HAS AN ESTUARY.

keep an eye on them when they are playing in the water. However, if you are an experienced swimmer, this is a great place to grab a boogie board and head out to have some fun. The hotels offer their guests shaded seating along the sand. If you happen to be staying at a hotel that is not located on the beach, simply ask one of the waiters if you can take one of their spots. The staff won't mind as long as you buy some snacks and beverages.

Unlike more public beaches in places like Zihuatanejo, only licensed guides are allowed to solicit along this beach; you will not be pestered by freelance vendors. You will know the guides by their white uniforms as they cruise up and down the beach arranging banana boat rides and other diversions. Banana boat rides run about $20 for a group of four for 15 minutes; Jet Skis go for around $40 for a half an hour; and parasail trips cost about $25 for a 10-minute ride. If you're more in the mood for a massage, head for one of the white tents set up along the beach.

Playa Quieta. With a name like "Quiet Beach," could this small strip of sand be anything but tranquil? Located on the north side of the Punta Ixtapa Peninsula, this beach is a sheltered ribbon of fine yellow sand tucked beneath a lush hillside. Clear water laps against the shore, making it an ideal location for snorkeling, sailing, and windsurfing. At the south end, the beach wraps around an inlet where Club Med keeps a regatta of kayaks and sailboats. The rest of this picturesque cove is open. There is a collection of picnic tables that you can rent for a small fee. There is also

JET SKIS ARE JUST ONE OF THE DIVERSIONS AVAILABLE AT PLAYA DEL PALMAR.

PLAYA QUIETA IS A SMALL, TRANQUIL BEACH NORTH OF THE IXTAPA HOTEL ZONE.

a seafood restaurant that sells reasonably priced fish tacos. Climb down to the beach by way of the north end access stairway from the parking lot. You will see a sign marked "Playa Quieta Access Público."

Playa Vista Hermosa. This beautiful beach is several hundred yards of immaculate golden sand tucked between the Pacific Ocean and the lush hillside of the upscale Las Brisas Resort. The hotel elevator provides a convenient way to access the beach or you can walk along the hotel's tropical walkway that leads you out toward the beach club before the switchback brings you down to the beach. There is good snorkeling along the shoals at either end of the beach. Gear is available for rental up at the beach club. The waves can get rough here, so be careful when going into the water. And remember, there are no lifeguards on duty in case you find yourself in trouble.

BUS TOURS Bus Tours I-Z, Autovías (755-112-1002; www.hdp.com.mx). Although this bus line goes through Zihuatanejo, they generally limit their routes

RED FLAGS WARN SWIMMERS TO STAY OUT OF THE WATER ON DAYS WITH STRONG CURRENTS.

to central Mexico in places such as Jalisco, Michoacán, and Querétaro. See their Web site for specific destinations. They offer either Servicios Ordinarios (ordinary services) or Servicio de Primera, which includes bathrooms, television, and air-conditioning. Servicio de Primera is not available with all destinations.

Estrella Blanca (755-554-3477; www.estrellablanca.com.mx). This is one of the largest bus companies in Mexico and they provide service from the border down into Veracruz and Oaxaca. They have by far the biggest footprint in the state of Guerrero. This company operates many different bus lines with varying levels of service.

BEACH ETIQUETTE

All the beaches in Guerrero—in fact, all the beaches throughout Mexico—are federal property. Therefore, no hotel or homeowner can restrict access to the beach from the water or make their own guidelines as to what you can do on the beach. However, hotels can restrict you from crossing their property to get to the beach and they often set up private areas with *palapas* and tables for their guests. That being said, many people have no problem waltzing through the lobby of a beachfront resort as if they were a guest to get to a choice spot on the beach. Whether you choose to do so is entirely dependent on what you feel comfortable with.

Another aspect of Guerrero beaches is the amount of clothing that you're required to wear (or not wear) when playing along this beautiful coast. Mexico as a whole is a pretty conservative and traditional place, and decency laws prohibit going nude or even topless in public. Also, if you do find yourself on a deserted beach, resist the temptation to drive your vehicle along the shoreline. It is illegal to drive on the beaches in Mexico and doing so can result in stiff fines.

Estrella de Oro (755-554-2175; www.estrelladeoro.com.mx) offers routes to various destinations with a concentration on points throughout south-central Mexico, though their biggest presence is in Guerrero. Their Servicio Diamante buses have a twenty-four-seat capacity that leaves plenty of room to stretch out. This service includes refreshment, separate bathrooms for men and women, air-conditioning, movies, and nonstop transportation.

PEOPLE COME FROM ALL OVER THE WORLD TO ENJOY MEXICO'S BEACHES.

ISLA IXTAPA OFFERS SOME OF THE AREA'S BEST SNORKELING.

ISLA IXTAPA

Water taxis to Isla Ixtapa leave daily from Playa Linda, every few minutes, 9 AM–5 PM. To catch a water taxi, walk straight through the bazaar of stalls just off the parking lot and continue out to the pier. If you get here in the morning, you may be approached by friendly locals asking if you need any assistance. These are typically waiters headed over to the island for their shift, and they are being friendly because they are drumming up business. They will find you a spot on the beach near their restaurant and take care of you for the day. However, if you don't want a guide or you find them to be pushy, simply tell them that you know where you're going and that you're not interested in their services. If you happen to be on the island late in the day, make sure you catch the last water taxi to the mainland, or you will find yourself paying a little extra to get back to your hotel. Water taxi fare is 35 pesos.

In any case, you are certain to enjoy your time on the island, which features several beaches within walking distance as well as several restaurants serving up fresh Mexican seafood. The people of Ixtapa have done a wonderful job of preserving the beaches, forests, and waters of this beautiful island. Every day, trash is collected and sent back to the mainland, keeping the island pristine. As a result, you will find the best snorkeling in Ixtapa here, with many kinds of tropical fish swimming in the underwater gardens that surround the island. A net is set up offshore to keep away larger animals, such as dolphins and sharks. During the winter, gray whales are often seen just offshore.

The most popular beach on the island is **Playa Cuachalatate,** named for a tree bark used in medicines of indigenous Mexicans. This beach is located on the island's sheltered inner shore and is where you step off when you arrive. Small ripples lap upon the shore here, making it a great beach for families. The beach is lined with restaurants that provide rows of beach umbrellas and *palapas*. Find a place to sit and stay all day. At the north end of the beach, you will find water sport equipment rental and guides offering diving excursions. You can rent Jet Skis here for about $50 an hour or take a banana boat ride for about $5. If you're in the mood for something a little more relaxing, you can also rent a kayak for about $5 an hour. Just a few yards away, on the island's west side, you will find **Playa Varadero** hugging a rocky cove, and nearby **Playa Coral** with calm crystal-clear waters. Like Playa Cuachalatate, these beaches are lined with *palapas* and beach chairs, where you can get restaurant and drink service. The water is calm and peppered with coral and rocks at each end of the cove that make it a great place to go snorkeling or scuba diving. You can rent snorkel gear for about $12 a day. From Playa Cuachalatate, you can take a boat to the island's smallest and least developed beach, Playa **Carey**. It is located on the southern end of the island and is relatively isolated; it has no services. There is a small lighthouse here where you can enjoy a nice view of the main land. There is also a fenced-off area of this beach used for hatching sea turtles.

PLAYA CUACHALATATE IS THE MOST POPULAR BEACH ON ISLA IXTAPA.

SNORKELERS WALKING ALONG THE BEACH AT ISLA IXTAPA.

Omnibus de Mexico (755-112-1948; www.odm.com.mx). This bus company offers service from Sonora and Chihuahua in the north to Guerrero and Veracruz in the south and just about all points in between. Their Servicio Plus includes movies, air-conditioning, and bathrooms.

TuriStar (755-553-2623; www.turistar.com.mx). Except for a few regions such as Baja California and the Yucatán Peninsula, this bus company covers almost all of Mexico. Their service includes snacks, cafeteria service, plasma televisions, bathrooms, and headphones.

DIVING **Ixtapa Aqua Paradise** (755-553-1510; www.ixtapaaquaparadise.com), Centro Comercial Los Patios, Local 137, Ixtapa, GRO 40880. This PADI-certified tour company and dive school can bring you to several locations, including Caleta de Chon and Morros de Potosí. They also offer PADI diving classes of between two and 10 days, as well as diving classes for children of at least 10 years of age.

GOLF With two excellent and very different golf courses, Ixtapa is quickly becoming known as an excellent spot for golfing vacations. Both courses are located within walking distance of the city's Zona Hotelera and offer challenges to golfers of all levels.

✔ **Campo de Golf Ixtapa** (755-553-1062), Paseo Ixtapa s/n, Ixtapa, GRO 40880. Open every day of the year. This 18-hole, par-72 golf course was designed by Robert Trent Jones Jr. in the early 1970s as part of Ixtapa's original development. At 6,898 yards, it ranks as one of Mexico's finest golf courses, providing a divers assortment of challenges through a course that wanders along a series of lagoons, jungle hilltops, and the sands of Playa Palmar. It is carved through a dense jungle for which it was named. It features long fairways, thick Bermuda grass greens, and closely cropped rough. This course also doubles as a wildlife preserve. If you play here and happen to lose your ball in one of the lagoon lakes, do not try to retrieve it because crocodiles tend to rest just under the water. The facilities here include a practice putting green, a driving range, a large pool, and four tennis courts.

*✦ **Club de Marina Ixtapa** (755-553-1489), Calle Darsena #8, Ixtapa, GRO 40880. Open every day of the year. This 18-hole, par-72 golf course is the newer of Ixtapa's golf courses. It was designed by Robert von Hagge in 1994 and plays at around 6,781 yards. This unique course rolls along a series of saltwater canals, allowing water to come into play on 14 of the holes. It also features dune-style topography with expansive sand traps and undulating greens that require accuracy for both departure and approach. However, there are four departure positions at each hole, making this course enjoyable for all skill levels. The facilities include a driving range, a putting green, two lighted tennis courts, and a swimming pool.

HORSEBACK RIDING Ixtapa has a climate and natural beauty that makes it an ideal place to go for a horseback along the beach and through natural reserves where you will observe wildlife and scenic wonders. These cities have many beachfront resorts that are equipped with horseback riding facilities on the beach and through back trails. The best beach in Ixtapa for enjoying a horseback excursion is Playa Linda, a long, open beach with wide swaths of sand. It is not as frequented as many of the area's other beaches, making it a great place to break into a gallop through the surf. Behind Playa Linda, you will find trails through an estuary wildlife preserve populated with iguanas, many bird species, and even crocodiles.

SPORT FISHING Recent years have seen Ixtapa-Zihuatanejo develop a reputation as a mecca for sport fishermen and today it is recognized as one of the top sport fishing destinations in the world. Because the waters offshore quickly reach

PLAYA LARGA IS A POPULAR PLACE TO GO FOR A HORSEBACK EXCURSION.

A FISHING BOAT OFF THE COAST OF ZIHUATANEJO AT NIGHT.

a depth of over a thousand fathoms, opportunities for hooking big fish begin not long after leaving port. However, the most consistent waters lay between 5 and 15 miles offshore. In these abundant waters, the primary catch is Pacific sailfish, which can weigh up to 175 pounds. There are also dorado and large schools of yellowfin tuna, some weighing 300 pounds. Additionally, marlins of the black and blue variety migrate through these waters in the spring. These fish generally weigh between 275 and 400 pounds, though much larger specimens have been hooked. Closer to shore, you will find high-flying roosterfish, Spanish mackerel, and barracuda.

Mar y Tierra Sport Fishing (755-553-8055; www.sportfishing-ixtapa.com), Ixtapa, GRO 40880. This sport fishing charter company has a small fleet of covered *pangas* and cruisers, all completely fitted with U.S. Coast Guard approved safety equipment. A standard day of fishing begins at 6:30 AM and ends around 2 PM with your fish cleaned and packed or ready for cooking. Your fishing license is included in the price of the trip.

Vamonos Fleet Sport Fishing (755-102-8664; www.sportfishingvamonos.com), Ixtapa, GRO 40880. This sport fishing charter group has a large fleet of *pangas* of varying sizes. These boats can accommodate from six to 10 fishermen and are captained by experienced anglers who know the waters off of Ixtapa well.

MARLIN ARE AMONG THE FISH TO BE HAD IN THE WATERS OFF OF ZIHUATANEJO.

SURFING No matter what your skill level, the Ixtapa-Zihuatanejo area offers some of the best surfing on Mexico's Pacific Coast. It features consistent, uniform surf with a wide variety of breaks. Besides spots right in town, such as Playa las Gatas and Escolleras on Playa del Palmar, there are other popular surfing spots within an hour's drive, such as La Saladita, Troncones, and La Barrita. Perhaps the most popular break in the immediate area is at Playa Linda on the north side of Ixtapa. And don't bother with your wetsuit. The water is warm enough year-round to leave it at home.

TOURING ↬ **Adventours** (755-553-3584; www.ixtapa-adventours.com), Ixtapa, GRO 40880. This company offers a wide variety of guided eco-adventures throughout the region. Tours include excursions such as mountain biking on the outskirts of Ixtapa, kayaking through the Barra de Potosí, and bird and crocodile watching off Playa Linda. These excursions rotate throughout the week and last between 5 and 6 hours.

✔ **WATER PARKS Delfiniti** (755-553-2736; www.delfiniti.com), Zona Hotelera #1, Ixtapa, GRO 40880. Open daily 10 AM–12 PM and 4 PM–7 PM. This park offers you the chance to interact with dolphins, in a variety of experiences. One package is a 45-minute swim with the dolphins during which you will hold their pectoral fins at full speed through the pool. This package is for age 8 and up and require a brief period of instruction. Another package is specifically designed for children between 3 and 7 years old, and there is another designed for babies and toddlers. Children must be accompanied by an adult at all times. Prices vary according to package.

✔ **Magic World Aquatic Park** (755-553-1359), Boulevard de las Garzas s/n, Ixtapa, GRO 40880. Open daily 10:30 AM–5:30 PM. Just in case you don't get enough fun in the sun between your hotel pool, the beach, and your daily excursions, Ixtapa has its very own water park to provide you with yet another opportunity to work on your sunburn. The park is geared mainly toward families. There is a kid's area shaped like a pirate ship, equipped with six water slides of various shapes flowing into a 2-foot kids' pool. There are also two high-speed water slides for older kids and adults, which are open noon–2 and 4–5 every afternoon. A series of canals for toboggan rides and a wave pool are open daily 3 PM–4 PM. There are plenty of shaded lounge chairs perfect for relaxing while the kids have fun. The park offers party packages for groups up to 20 people that include entrance fees and food discounts. $7 admission, children under age 3 free.

JET SKIS ARE JUST ONE OF THE DIVERSIONS AVAILABLE AT PLAYA DEL PALMAR.

✴ Lodging

Despite the fact that this small "town" offers more than 5,000 hotel rooms, Ixtapa offers a secluded experience. This is because the hotels are the entire reason Ixtapa exists and everything else at this site is there to support them. Unlike Zihuatanejo or even Acapulco, Ixtapa is not so much a community as it is a resort destination. Playa Ixtapa is lined with resort hotels, and, for the most part, most of these resorts are designed to allow guests to fly into town, never leave the hotel grounds during their stay, and fly out. Many of them are glorious in scale and luxurious in atmosphere. The pampered experience provided at these large resorts can be not only expensive but overwhelming, as well.

However, if you are looking for a place where you can get away from it all and lose yourself in relaxation, Ixtapa is the place for you. The downside to this is that the town really has no heart and soul. Don't expect to come away from Ixtapa feeling that you have had an authentic Mexican experience because that doesn't exist here. Most hotels here are of the large resort-style with hundreds of rooms and self-sufficient infrastructures. They have their own restaurants, shops, dance clubs, spas, tour guides, entertainment specialists, and on and on. Many of the larger resorts offer all-inclusive packages in which all of your meals, snacks, and beverages are included in the price of your room. If you do not have an all-inclusive package, you may want cross the street to one of Ixtapa's shopping areas for your meals because the options at the resorts, even the buffet, can be very pricy. At the north end of the Zona Hotelera, you will find a charming marina with a cluster of pedestrian-only streets and upscale seafood restaurants.

✦ ✦ **Barceló Ixtapa Beach Resort** (755-553-1558; www.barceloixtapa.com), Paseo Ixtapa s/n, Ixtapa, GRO 40880. $$. AE; MC; V. This grand hotel is located on Playa el Palmar and sits adjacent to an 18-hole golf course. It has 397 suites with an all-inclusive format. Therefore, all meals, domestic beverages, nonmotorized water sports, taxes, and gratuities are included in the room rate. The resort offers a wide array of room options, from the regular suite to the executive villa. Whatever you choose, you will find your accommodations spacious and well appointed. Rooms are furnished with double, queen, or king-size beds, plasma television sets, living rooms, and private terraces. Among the resort's many amenities are four restaurants, two bars, a fitness center, tennis courts, and a large pool area right in front of the beach. For any parents traveling with small children hoping to get a night to themselves, the Barceló Beach Resort also provides babysitting services. This should be booked in advance and it's a good idea to plan ahead of time which nights you'll need it, so you make sure you get a spot. During the day, the hotel also offers a kid's club that provides children ages 5–12 with a program of supervised activities, including pool games, video games and use of the children's play area. Travelers of all ages may want to pursue sporting activities in and around the resort. Pool volleyball, water aerobics, and pool toys are available free of charge at the hotel pool, as well as introductory scuba diving lessons. Guests may also enjoy cooking and arts lessons. For those looking to scuba dive in the ocean, scuba diving equipment may be rented at the hotel's dive shop. Scuba diving tours for beginners and divers that are more experienced may be booked here as well.

✦ ⟨ʷ⟩ **Las Brisas Ixtapa** (755-553-2121; www.brisashotelonline.com/brisas/ixtapa), Playa Vistahermosa s/n, Ixtapa, GRO 40880. $$$. AE; MC; V. This amazing hotel is designed to resemble an Aztec pyramid built into a cliff overlooking Playa Vista Hermosa. It has more than 400 suites, each with a private terrace with hammocks overlooking the Pacific. These rooms are spacious, elegant, and feature modern décor with either a king-size or two double beds. Some rooms are equipped with private Jacuzzis, pillow-top beds, and even private swimming pools. Bring some comfortable shoes because getting around this sprawling resort requires some walking; for example, the beach club is located at the base of the hotel down a long walkway. Here you will find a couple of gorgeous pools, a Jacuzzi, and several tennis courts set in the middle of a lush jungle setting. In fact, the entire hotel is surrounded by native greenery as well as tropical birds and iguanas and offers plenty of open space. Other amenities include private white-sand beach that is accessed through a shrub-lined path near the beach club, a beach club, and a gym. There are five restaurants and three bars. Among these is the **Bellavista Restaurant,** open daily 7 AM–10 PM, which provides a sumptuous buffet for breakfast, lunch, and dinner. Nearby, you will find **Restaurante el Mexicano,** open daily for dinner 6–11:30, which serves haute

THE LOBBY OF THE BARCELÓ IXTAPA BEACH RESORT.

Mexican cuisine in a refined colonial hacienda atmosphere. Reservations are required. You will find Italian cuisine in an intimate atmosphere at **Portofino Ristorante,** open daily for dinner 6–11:30; reservations are required. All of these restaurants are very pricy (even the buffet), but they're well worth trying at least once during your visit. However, you can save yourself a bunch of cash by spending $5 on the cab ride into the Ixtapa commercial zone and selecting from many restaurants there.

✦ ✦ **Dorado Pacifico Hotel** (755-553-2025; www.doradopacifico.com/), Paseo Ixtapa s/n Lote 3-A, Ixtapa, GRO 40880. $$. AE; MC; V. This is just another one of Ixtapa's gorgeous resorts that sits along the beach at Playa del Palmar. It offers 285 rooms and suites in a modern high-rise. The regular rooms are furnished with two double beds and have sitting areas, satellite television, and private ter-

OVERLOOKING PLAYA VISTA HERMOSA FROM THE LAS BRISAS IXTAPA.

races overlooking the ocean. Junior suites are a bit roomier and are furnished with a king-size bed as well as a sofa and love seat, plus a private terrace overlooking the ocean. Master suites are much roomier with a full living room, two bathrooms, and a kitchenette. The hotel grounds are well manicured, with tropical plants and bright walkways. The hotel courtyard is dominated by a sprawling pool with two water slides, lined with an ample amount of beach chairs and umbrellas. A children's pool and playground are nearby for the younger guests. If you need a little help relaxing, the hotel offers a spa and massage center under private white tents down by the beach. Amenities include tennis courts, a babysitting service, and a doctor on call. This resort has five restaurants for you to choose from. Perhaps the most interesting is the **Coco-La Palm Restaurant,** open daily 11 AM–midnight, located poolside under a large *palapa*, which serves regional and international cuisine. **La Cascada Café** provides a large buffet breakfast 7 AM–noon. For

a more romantic atmosphere, don your beach formal attire and head over to **Terraza del Mar,** open daily for dinner 6–midnight for fresh seafood and international specialties. It features live music every night.

((ŋ)) ∮ **Emporio Ixtapa** (755-553-1066; www.hotelesemporio.com), Paseo Ixtapa s/n, Ixtapa, GRO 40880. $$. AE; D; DC; MC; V. With just over 200 rooms and suites, this is one of the *smaller* hotels in Ixtapa. However, this resort is certainly not short on amenities. The rooms are decorated in a relaxing contemporary style with either two double beds or one king-size, topped with high-quality linens. Wooden folding doors open to private terraces overlooking Playa del Palmar. The hotel grounds are spacious, well tended, and provide easy access to the beach. The pool area is located in a large courtyard just in front of the beach. It is lined with palm trees and has ample beach chairs and umbrellas so that you don't have to worry about finding a spot. There is a laundry/dry cleaning service, tennis courts, and a gym. The hotel also has three restaurants and two bars. For more casual fare, check out the surf-and-turf buffet at the **Sunset Grill,** open daily for lunch and dinner 1–10. This restaurant is located down by the beach and features fresh seafood and steak as well as a nice salad bar. The **Condimento Restaurant,** open daily 7 AM–10:30 PM, provides a lavish buffet as well as Mexican and international dishes for lunch and dinner. And for a more formal meal, the open-air **Arrecife Restaurant** serves dinner daily 6–11 under the stars as you hear the water lapping on the shore nearby.

✂ ⨍ ((ᵖ)) **Fontan Ixtapa Hotel** (755-553-1666; www.hotelfontanixtapa.com), Paseo Ixtapa, s/n, Ixtapa, GRO 40880. $$. AE; MC; V. This triple-towered resort hotel, with 472 rooms and suites, is right in front of Playa del Palmar. The rooms are simply appointed in a comfortable and colorful manner and come in two types. Standard rooms are furnished with a king-size bed; double standard rooms are a bit larger and come with two double beds. All rooms feature air-conditioning, satellite television, and a private terrace. However, not all terraces overlook the ocean, so be sure to request an ocean view when making your reservation if this is important to you. Animals are prohibited in this hotel, so you will have to look elsewhere if you are bringing your pet. There is a rectangular pool that dominates a large courtyard that opens onto the beach. A kid's pool is located nearby. There is also a gym, laundry service, and a babysitting service. Two restaurants are open year-round, three during the high season. The **Real Palapa Restaurant** provides a buffet daily 7 AM–10:30 PM. The **Miramar Restaurant,** open daily 1 PM–5 PM, offers Mexican and international dishes à la carte for lunch and early dinner. For a more formal meal, **La Hacienda Restaurant,** open for dinner 6–10 during the high season, features Mexican cuisine and fresh seafood. There is also a sports bar.

⨍ **Intercontinental Presidente Ixtapa** (755-553-0018; www.InterContinental.com), Paseo Ixtapa s/n, Ixtapa, GRO 40880. $$. AE; D; DC; MC; V. The 400 rooms and suites of this luxurious resort are decorated in contemporary style. Standard rooms have a garden view and are furnished with either a king-size or two double beds. Suites are also furnished with either a king-size or two double beds, and feature a small living area and a sofa bed, as well as two full bathrooms. Not all suites have terraces, so you may want to request one when making your reservation. On the premises are a gym, massage services, and yoga classes. This hotel's six

IXTAPA'S RESORTS FEATURE MANY AMENITIES.

restaurants provide a fairly wide variety of cuisine. A large, winding pool dominates a garden courtyard that faces the beach. Across the pool bridge, you will find the family-friendly **La Isla Restaurant,** open daily 8 AM–10 PM. This restaurant faces the beach and serves buffet meals with 15 different themes, including Italian, Chinese, seafood, and Mexican cuisine. For a romantic dinner, leave the kids in the room and visit **La Terraza,** open 6 PM–11 PM, which features international cuisine on an open-air poolside terrace. Or you can really switch gears and go to the **Sushi & Martini Lounge,** open 6 PM–11 PM, where you can dine on fresh fish and apple martinis.

NH Krystal Ixtapa (755-553-0333; www.nh-hotels.com), Paseo Ixtapa, s/n 4 y 4A, Ixtapa, GRO 40880. $$. AE; MC; V. Located right in front of the beach at Playa del Palmar, this hotel has 255 rooms and suites decorated in a modern minimalist style. Widely regarded as one of the best deals in Ixtapa, it towers over a lush garden compound with rooms that come with either a king-size or two double beds. These rooms are spacious, particularly the suites, which include a full living room and a dinette. All rooms have balconies with ocean views. A large, winding swimming pool featuring a suspended bridge and a faux desert island dominates a lush courtyard that opens onto the beach. This pool has its own waterslide as well as a waterfall. It is lined with sun chairs and there are rows of *palapas* on the beach to provide shade, so you should have no trouble finding somewhere to park for the day. There are also tennis and racquetball courts, and a gym, The hotel's open-air **Aquamarina**

Restaurant, open daily 8 AM–10 PM, is located on the beach and serves a nice buffet breakfast with seasonal fresh fruits and a large variety of fruits. For lunch and dinner, the restaurant offers a variety of Mexican and international dishes.

🐾 🏌 **Pacifica Resort Ixtapa** (755-555-2500; ww.pacifica.com.mx/pacificaresort/eng/), Paseo de la Colina s/n Colonia Vista Hermosa, Ixtapa, GRO 40880. $$. MC; V. This hotel is located on a hill above Palmar Bay and provides beautiful views of Ixtapa's Zona Hotelera. Its 200 suites have a variety of layouts. For example, the Senior Golf Suite is a ground-floor, 187 square-foot apartment with a queen-size bed plus and two double sofa beds in the living room. The Sands Suite is an 883-square-foot apartment that also has a queen-size bed plus and two double sofa beds in the living room. It also features a private Jacuzzi and a private grill, as well as a private beach-facing terrace with a hammock and shaded sitting area. The Master Sands Suite is a 492-square-foot two-bedroom apartment with a king-size bed in one room and two queen-size in the other. This suite also has an ocean-facing terrace and a private swimming pool. See their Web site for other options. This sprawling resort has a professional 18-hole golf course and a kid's club with a variety of activities for the resort's younger guests. The resort has three fine restaurants. **El Faro Restaurante,** open daily for breakfast 8–noon and dinner 6–11, is situated at the highest point of the entire hotel to offer a stunning view of the Ixtapa shoreline. This restaurant offers international cuisine in an intimate setting on five terraces, two of which are under *palapa* thatched roofs and three are open-air. If you would rather dine at the beach, **Tulipanes Restaurant,** open daily 8 AM–11 PM, is located in the beach club of the Pacifica Beach Resort and serves Mexican and international dishes. For a romantic candle-lit dinner featuring authentic Italian cuisine, **Bugambilias Restaurant** is open 7 PM–11 PM.

🔥 (𝕨) **Park Royal Ixtapa** (755-555-0550; www.parkroyalixtaparesort.com), Paseo Ixtapa Lote 5-A, Ixtapa, GRO 40880. $$. AE; D; MC; V. This all-inclusive luxury resort at the north end of Ixtapa's Zona Hotelera has 281 rooms and suites. The spacious and comfortable rooms, decorated in Mediterranean style, are furnished with either a king-size or two double beds. Bathrooms are equipped with a shower or a full bathtub. Suites also come with a living room and dinette set. These rooms also have a private terrace overlooking the ocean. There is a lush courtyard behind the hotel that leads to the beach. This courtyard is dominated by a large swimming pool with ample seating so you will always find a spot. Beyond that, you will find a large expanse of beach with plenty of room to allow for privacy. There is also a gym on site. Being that this is an all-inclusive resort, all of your meals, snacks, nonalcoholic beverages, and selected domestic and imported beers are included in the price of your room. Toward that end, this hotel has three restaurants, including **La Veranda Restaurant,** which serves an open-air buffet breakfast 8 AM–noon and lunch and dinner until 10 PM. For fresh seafood, sample the cuisine at **El Pescador Restaurant Bar,** open daily 4 PM–11

PM. For a romantic candle-lit dinner, **El Italiano Restaurant Bar** serves authentic Italian cuisine 7–11.

✎ 🔥 **Puerta del Mar** (755-553-0025; www.hotelpuertadelmar.com.mx), Paseo de las Gaviotas s/n, Ixtapa, GRO 40880. $$. MC; V. With only 45 suites, this is practically a boutique hotel by Ixtapa standards. It is located in a six-story stucco building with interesting architecture. The hotel does not sit on the beach, as do most others in Ixtapa; however, the beach is only a 5-minute walk away. The apartment-style rooms are clean and spacious and decorated with handmade Mexican furniture. These terraces open onto the pool area where you will see two circular pools that dominate a large tropical garden area. One

IXTAPA EXISTS IN A LUSH TROPICAL LANDSCAPE.

of these pools has a water slide and a swim-up pool under a large *palapa.* This bar also serves ice cream to the younger guests, so be prepared to share the bar with the kids. However, the drink prices make it worth the trouble with dollar beers all day. The grounds also feature a beach volleyball court, a playground, and several outdoor Ping-Pong tables. Amenities include laundry/dry-cleaning service. This hotel is certainly not as fancy as the beach hotels of Ixtapa. However, it is a good option for travelers on a budget. However, be aware that the staff here speaks only limited English. You may want to brush up on your Spanish before staying here.

♂ ∱ (⋅⋅) **Qualton Club Ixtapa** (755-552-0080; www.qualton.com), Carretera Escénica #14, Ixtapa, GRO 40880. $$. AE; MC; V. This hotel has 152 rooms and suites in ten low-rise buildings surrounded by a lush garden property. It is not quite as luxurious as many of the other Ixtapa hotels but it is clean and provides good service. The rooms are simply furnished in a rustic style and come with either a king-size or two double beds. The hotel is located at beautiful Playa Linda and offers plenty of beach chairs under *palapas,* where you can get oceanfront drink and snack service. You can also get drinks by the pool as the hotel has a large pool area with plenty of seating and palm trees for shade. There is also an adults-only pool where you will find Benny's Bar, which serves drinks daily 10 AM–5 PM. There are tennis courts, a game room, and a babysitting service. This is an all-inclusive resort and therefore all of your meals, snacks, nonalcoholic beverages, and selected domestic and imported beers are included in the price of your room. There are two restaurants and four bars. The **Villalinda Restaurant,** located next to the reception area, serves a buffet breakfast 7–11, lunch 1–4, and dinner 7–11, and is the primary place to come to satisfy your hunger. Snacks are available here all day. **Jalapeño Restaurant,** down by the beach, offers Mexican specialties noon–6 PM.

♂ ∱ **Tesoro Ixtapa** (755-553-1175; www.tesororesorts.com), Paseo Ixtapa s/n Lote 5, Ixtapa, GRO 40880. $$. AE; MC; V. There are 200 rooms and suites in this elegant hotel across the street from Ixtapa's golf course. The décor is modern Mexican style. The spacious rooms are furnished with either a king-size or two double beds and feature balconies that open onto a grand pool area and the Pacific Ocean. There are also small studios with one double bed and windows facing the garden area. The pool, a large, oddly shaped area in the center of the courtyard, is actually divided into several pools, including a circular children's pool. Other amenities include a gym, aerobics classes, laundry service, and babysitting service. In addition to the traditional room rate, this resort offers an all-inclusive room rate. Under this rate, all of your meals, snacks, nonalcoholic beverages, wine, and selected domestic and imported beers are included in the price of your room. There are three restaurants and three bars, including one bar that is open 24/7. **La Mar Restaurant,** which overlooks the Pacific Ocean, serves breakfast 7–11, lunch 1–4:30, and dinner 6:30–10:45, all in buffet style. For small, quick meals such as nachos and sandwiches, visit the hotel's **Arrecifes Restaurant,** open daily noon–6. And for a more elegant dining experience, visit **El Mesón Restaurant,** open daily for dinner 7–10:45, which serves Mexican and international cuisine; reservations are required.

⚡ **Tres Puertas** (755-553-0194; www .ixtapa-zihuatanejo.net/trespuertas), Colina de las Palomas #325, Ixtapa, GRO 40880. $$. MC; V. The Tres Puertas Hotel—meaning "Three Doors Hotel"—offers a bit more than the name would suggest. In fact, this boutique hotel has four villa-style suites in a beautiful Mexican colonial-style building. Because this is such a small hotel, you can expect very personal service and excellent hospitality while staying here. The units here accommodate up to four people each and are furnished with a king-size and two single beds. They are also equipped with a kitchen, a sitting area, and a terrace that opens onto the pool area. The swimming pool is relatively small by Ixtapa standards but certainly large enough for a hotel of this size. It is surrounded by a small tropical garden area that is perfect for relaxing in the late afternoon. The hotel is located close to the golf course and the beach.

⚡ ((ᵗ)) **Villas Paraiso** (755-553-0194; www.villasparaisoixtapa.com), Paseo del Rincón Lote 1 Manzana 3 Súper-manzana III C.P., Ixtapa, GRO 40880. $$. AE; MC; V. This 89-suite hotel is near the *centro comercial.* The rooms are roomy and simply appointed in modern Mexican style. Standard suites have one bedroom and are furnished with two double beds as well as a double sofa bed. These rooms can accommodate up to four adults and two children. The hotel also has two master suites, which each have two bedrooms; one bedroom is fur-

nished with a king-size bed while the second room has two double beds. The living area also has two double beds. These rooms can accommodate up to eight adults and two children. Keep in mind that if you wish to keep the air-conditioning on all day (and during the summer this may be a good idea), this will accrue an additional $10 per night. The hotel also has a garden pool area with tropical plants and plenty of shade. Here you will find a relatively large swimming pool and a wading pool for children. There is also a restaurant on site that servers Mexican specialties daily 8 AM–10 PM. The hotel, which has its own on-site convenience store, is located close to the shopping center and the beach.

✳ Where to Eat

Now that these twin cities are developing into a world-class resort destination, you can now find a fairly good variety of food, both in type and

BEACH ACCESS

In Ixtapa, getting to the beach can be a problem if you're not staying at a hotel that is actually on the beach. This is because you have to go through the large resorts to get to the beach and despite the fact that it is illegal for them to restrict your access to the beach, they are certainly not accommodating to nonguests, either. Rather than ask permission to pass through, it's best to go into the resorts as if you are there to check in or rent a car, and just continue walking until you get to the beach.

RELAXING IN A HAMMOCK

There's nothing quite like relaxing in a beachside hammock with a cool beer in your hand, listening to the waves lap against the shore. However, for the inexperienced hammock sitter, you're likely to wonder what the big deal is all about if you don't know what you're doing. After straddling the hammock in the center and then lifting up your legs, with your head up on one end and your butt sagging toward the ground in the middle, you'll probably be there only a minute or two before realizing that it's actually not all that comfortable.

But it's easy to fix this back-wrenching posture. By lying in the hammock diagonally, with your head as far to one side as you can get it, the center of your body going across the center of the hammock, and your feet either at the edge or hanging off the other side, you will find that your weight is spread out across the hammock webbing more evenly instead of being concentrated at your butt. Suddenly you will find yourself comfortably lost in contemplation, drifting away in a hang-loose haze.

THERE'S NOTHING QUITE LIKE SPENDING AN AFTERNOON RELAXING IN A HAMMOCK.

quality. In Ixtapa, the resorts feature restaurants that serve everything from buffets to meals prepared by gourmet chefs. Both can be extremely expensive. If you cross the street to shopping centers along Paseo Ixtapa, you will find less expensive options that mostly serve up standard bar-room favorites such as tacos and hamburgers. To the north around the marina, you will find options that are both more interesting and more elegant.

DINING OUT Beccofino (755-553-1770), Valeros #6, Ixtapa, GRO 40880. $$–$$$. AE; MC; V. Open daily for breakfast, lunch, and dinner 9 AM–midnight. This excellent Italian

SHRIMP AND COCKTAILS MAKE A NICE
TREAT WHEN RELAXING AT THE BEACH.

restaurant is located right on the
beautiful marina in Ixtapa. The menu
features a selection of northern Italian
and seafood specialties, including
calamari, shrimp, clams, mussels, and
crayfish. There are also soups, salads,
and an excellent wine list to accentuate your meal perfectly. Owner Ange-
lo Rolly Pavia hails from San Remo,
Italy, and has more than 30 years'
experience in restaurants in Europe
and Mexico. This is a good choice for
a romantic dinner and also a popular
place to have breakfast. The breezy
terrace tends to get loud when it is
crowded during the high season.

Frank's Bar & Grill (755-553-2777),
Plaza Ixpamar Lote 26, Ixtapa, GRO
40880. $$. MC; V. Open daily for
lunch and dinner 11 AM–midnight.
This bar and grill is tucked away in
the southeast corner of Plaza Ixpamar.
It features a spacious outdoor patio
featuring traditional Mexican favorites
as well as dishes that are famous
north of the border, such as lobster,
wood-fired pizza, Alaskan king crab,
and baby back ribs. All of this is
served up in a casual atmosphere with

the Pacific breeze to provide the air-
conditioning. This restaurant also has
an extensive bar that can create just
about any concoction that suites your
fancy. There are also several television
sets set up around the bar where you
can see all major sporting events.

Lili Cipriani Restaurant Bar (755-
120-0404, Playa Coral, Isla Ixtapa,
Ixtapa, GRO 40880. $$. MC; V. Open
daily for lunch and dinner 9 AM–5 PM.
Situated right on the beach in Isla
Ixtapa, this restaurant provides waterfront service under beach umbrellas
on one of the areas prettiest beaches.
So dig your feet in the sand and order
up a *cerveza* and some chips and guacamole, because it's going to be a
good day when you're here. They
offer a wide selection of tropical
mixed drinks, tequilas, and Mexican
beers, as well as soft drinks. The
menu also features several shrimp and
fresh seafood dishes. Waiters here will
also arrange for the rental of snorkeling gear, massages, as well as any
other diversions that are available on
the island.

Señor Frog's (755-553-0692), Paseo
de Ixtapa, Centro Comercial Lote 5,

LILI CIPRIANI RESTAURANT AT ISLA
IXTAPA.

Ixtapa, GRO 40880. $$. AE; MC; V. Open daily for dinner 6 PM–3 AM. This bar and grill is famous throughout Mexico for catering to young party crowds. The long menu lists all types of bar-style food such as fajitas, burgers, and barbecue. They also have a full bar that will make you just about any drink you can think of and several that you've never heard of. But the real reason for coming to Señor Frog's is the atmosphere, which is party hard all the time. It's hard to have a meal here without seeing someone dancing on a table nearby. And don't be surprised if you suddenly find yourself in the grip of a waiter pouring a tequila shooter down your throat while blowing on a whistle to the cheers of onlookers. This restaurant has a distinctly loose ambience with its own dance club, making it an essential part of the nightlife in Ixtapa. The restaurant closes at 1 AM but the club stays open later.

Señor-Itto (755-553-0272), Centro Comercial la Puerta, Ixtapa, GRO 40880. $. MC; V Open daily for lunch and dinner 5 PM–midnight. This friendly Japanese restaurant is located next door to Señor Frog's in La Puerta Mall. It has a fun atmosphere and specializes in delicious sushi. There are also such Japanese specialties as tempura, *yakimeshi*, and *teppanyaki*. All are prepared in the traditional Japanese manner right at your table.

Villa de la Selva (755-553-0362), Paseo de la Roca Lote D, Ixtapa, GRO 40884. $$$. AE; MC; V. Open daily for dinner 6–11. If you are looking for somewhere to have a romantic dinner with a stunning view and delicious cuisine, bypass Señor Frog's and come to this gorgeous restaurant. It is perched on a cliff overlooking the Pacific Ocean with white linen and candle-lit tables on several terraces so that every table has an incredible view. That said, tables on the lower terrace provide the most amazing ones. Palm and mango trees, also decorated with hanging candles, complete the romantic atmosphere. Hidden speakers provide ambient music that makes you feel like you're about to experience something special. And you are. Diners here are treated to international

SEÑOR FROG'S IS LOCATED ACROSS THE STREET FROM THE BEACH IN IXTAPA.

seafood works of art made from the freshest shrimp, lobster, and fish. There is also a nice wine list to provide just the right wine to accentuate your meal, as well as desserts that are equally attractive and satisfying. Reservations are recommended during the high tourist season.

EATING OUT Carlos 'N Charlie's (755-553-0085), Playa del Palmar s/n, Ixtapa, GRO 40880. $$. AE; MC; V. Open daily for lunch, dinner, and snacks 1 PM–1 AM. The theme of this restaurant is all about having a good time. And isn't that what being in Ixtapa is all about? Located in the heart of the city's Zona Hotelera, this restaurant provides a lively crowd and a fun atmosphere in a laid-back casual setting. The menu features mostly Mexican bar food, with items like fajitas, quesadillas, and fish tacos. However, there are also several steak dishes as well as a small selection of hamburgers. Be prepared to party when you're here, as guests are encouraged to cut loose among the comical skit performances, singing, and dancing on the chairs done by the staff. This restaurant also has a beachfront disco with raised platforms, making it an important part of the Ixtapa nightlife scene as well. The dance floor gets packed with young patrons bumping to international beats during high tourist season.

The Golden Cookie (755-553-0310; www.goldencookieshop.com.mx), Los Patios Center, Ixtapa, GRO 40880. $. Open daily for breakfast and lunch 8–3. This popular bakery and deli serves freshly baked goods and coffee drinks, which can be hard to come by in Ixtapa. They also have nutritional cookies, pastries, and cakes, as well as vegetarian and low-carb items, fruit

smoothies, yogurt, Mexican and American-style breakfasts, as well as sandwiches for lunch. The Golden Cookie can be a bit tricky to find. Look for it upstairs in Los Patios shopping center.

Los Mandiles (755-553-0379), Punta Carrizos s/n, Ixtapa, GRO 40880. $. MC; V. Open daily for lunch and dinner noon–midnight. This Mexican restaurant is an energetic establishment that provides a one-stop shop for the night's entertainment. It has an informal atmosphere accentuated by the colorful tiles and sombreros that decorate the walls. The menu here features such favorites as shrimp and chicken fajitas, enchiladas, and fish tacos. They also have barbecue chicken and salads. Chase that down with a jumbo margarita from the bar and your night is off to a good start. The bar also has a good selection of beer and tequila, if that's more of what you're in the mood for. After dinner, head upstairs to the disco where you will find a giant-screen television and a dance floor.

NIGHTLIFE Ixtapa-Zihuatanejo has a small but dependable nightlife during the high season of November through April. However, if you happen to be here during the off season, the nightlife is pretty hit-or-miss. Even during the high season, the nightlife here does not really compare to what you will find in Acapulco. For the most part, it gets going early by Mexican standards and dies down early. There are a few exceptions, particularly in the Zona Hotelera of Ixtapa. Furthermore, there are relatively few chic nightclubs in the area. Most bars that cater to adults tend to have casual atmospheres consistent with the laid-back attitude of the region. Keep in mind that the drinking age in Mexico is 18.

Christine's (755-553-0456), Paseo Ixtapa, #4, Ixtapa, GRO 40880. Open Thu.–Sat. 10:30 PM–5 AM during high season. Hours vary during off season. Ixtapa's most elegant nightclub, this has a large dance floor surrounded by several tiers of tables. The music is loud, and is a mixture of English language and Latin dance tunes. There is also a light show at midnight. Dress to impress when you come to this club; no flip-flops or tennis shoes are allowed. The crowd here tends to be in their 20s and 30s, though not exclusively. The cover here varies from free to $20, depending on the season. Sometimes, this cover is said to cover drinks. However, be careful because there have been instances in which patrons have reported that they were told later in they owed money because the open bar had ended at a certain hour.

Cohiiba Video Bar (755-553-1738), Andador Petatlán Lote 9, Ixtapa, GRO. Open daily 8 PM–4 AM. This lively Mexican bar and grill is located in the heart of the Ixtapa commercial district by the Flamingo Cinema movie theater. It's a small establishment but offers a laid-back atmosphere and plenty of cheap drinks. There is a pretty good selection of beers here and the food satisfies after a long day of touring around. The crowd here is a good mix between regulars and tourists, all out for a good time.

EL Bar (755-553-0383), Plaza Ixtapa, Ixtapa, GRO 40880. Open daily 7 PM–2 AM. This is a warm and inviting establishment with a laid-back ambience. The crowd here is a little older, largely because they play music from the '70s and '80s. This bar also features live music by local artists and special out-of-town guests. It is fairly spacious and has a dance floor in case the mood takes you. It is popular with tourists and locals alike not only for the music but for the drinks as well.

Le Rouge (755-553-5832), Plaza Ixsol, Ixtapa, GRO 40880. Open Thu.–Sat. 11 PM–5 AM. This large club has a sizeable dance floor in front of a stage, as well as several comfortable spaces off to the side. The décor is modern but spare, with iron railings surrounding the dance floor and stage. Add lights and confetti and . . . well, you get the picture. The music here is mostly Latin dance tunes and they sometimes feature concerts well-known acts. Again, the crowd tends to skew young.

Varuna After Hours (755-553-3138), Paseo Ixtapa s/n, Ixtapa, GRO 40880. Open Thu.–Sat. 1 AM–8 AM. This animated nightclub is located in front of the Hotel Barceló and is the kind of place that you can hear a half mile down the street. They often feature guest DJs and play a variety of dance and techno music, laying heavy on the bass. The lights are kept low but the bar is lit by fluorescent lights so you always know where you're going. The crowd here is mostly very young.

✳ Selected Shopping

Ixtapa offers a variety of shopping options for accessories jewelry, and handcrafted items inspired by Mexico's rich culture. Shopping centers are conveniently located on the east side of Paseo Ixtapa, right across the street from the major hotels. Most stores break for lunch followed by "siesta time." Generally speaking, business

FOOD AND WATER

Getting used to the food in Mexico can sometimes take a period of adjust-
ment, particularly if you are not used to the spices. A little common sense
will go a long way toward making sure you don't get sick while you're enjoying yourself with sun and fun. Spend the first few days of your trip taking it
easy. Many people go on vacation, suddenly find themselves free of the
workaday hours and the social mores of home—and sometimes tend to cut
loose and overdo it. Resist this urge—at least for a little bit. Give yourself
time to adjust to jetlag, new cuisine, and the other strains traveling to a new
place puts on your body.

Some hotels have purified water systems, and others generally offer
complimentary bottled water. Try to carry bottled water wherever you go so
that you have it on hand to keep yourself hydrated. Be sure to brush your
teeth with bottled water if you're staying at a hotel without a purified system
(if the hotel has one it will be advertised). Restaurants serve ice made of
purified water, so it's fine to have ice in your Coke. You may see street
venders selling flavored *aguas frescas* (fresh waters) with flavors such as
sandía (watermelon), *limón* (lemonade), *melón* (cantaloupe), and *fresa*
(strawberry). These are delicious and can be quite refreshing—but there is
no guarantee that they are made with purified water. It's a good idea to ask
just to be sure, though the answer is likely to be yes either way. The bottom
line is that by consuming these refreshments, you are taking a calculated
risk, and you need to be aware of that.

In fact, any time you consume peeled, raw fruits and vegetables, or eat
from a small "locals"
restaurant or street ven-
dor, you are taking a risk
of getting sick. You can
help to prepare your body
for these risks by eating
plenty of yogurt for several weeks prior to your trip.
Scientific studies have
shown that the live active
cultures in yogurt have
properties that protect the
intestinal tract from gas-
trointestinal infection.

A TRIP TO MEXICO PROVIDES AN OPPORTUNITY TO
SAMPLE A VARIETY OF REGIONAL CUISINE.

hours are Mon.–Sat. 9 AM–2 PM and resume 4 PM–8 PM. However, during the high tourist season many shops extend their business hours and are open on Sundays. Depending on your taste, shopping excursions can include perusing national and international chains for the basics as well as stops at boutiques and independent shops for more unique purchases.

Cielito Lindo (755-553-2714) Centro Comercial Los Patios #26, Ixtapa, GRO 40880. Open Mon.–Sat. 9 AM–8 PM. This shop specializes in silver pieces, unique jewelry designs, and handmade leather goods. The jewelry is made with 0.925, 0.950, and 0.999 silver from the mines of Taxco. Other silver pieces they have include a selection of animal figurines. They also have a small selection of 14k gold pieces. The leather goods are mostly wallets and purses.

La Fuente (755-553-0812), Centro Comercial Los Patios, Ixtapa, GRO 40880. Open daily 9 AM–10 PM high season 10 AM–2 PM and 5 PM–9 PM low season. This shop stands out among the many of Ixtapa that tend to be a bit soulless. It carries a wide selection of regional crafts from around Mexico, including gorgeously designed *talavera* pottery from Puebla, hand-embroidered indigenous clothing from Chiapas, intricately painted *alebrije* wooden animal figures from Oaxaca, and of course ceremonial masks from Guerrero. They also have a selection of other items, including hand-blown glassware, papier-mâché figures, and even wooden furniture. If you're looking for Mexican handicrafts, this is not a bad place to start.

Paseo Ixtapa market, open weekdays 10 AM–9 PM, is just across the street from Hotel Barceló. Because there is a ban on street vendors and beach entrepreneurs in Ixtapa, this is really the only place to do some traditional Mexican shopping without heading over to Zihuatanejo. This market has about 150 stalls.

PASEO IXTAPA IS LINED WITH LARGE RESORTS AND SHOPPING CENTERS.

ZIHUATANEJO

T he town of Zihuatanejo has managed to maintain an amazing balance. It has managed to garner a reputation as a resort destination while preserving itself as a fishing village nestled along a beautiful bay on the Pacific Ocean. This balance is, no doubt, the result of the construction of Ixtapa, which has served as an outlet which has kept all of the large resorts out of Zihuatanejo. The result is that these two locations, set only 5 miles apart, offer two completely different experiences.

✴ To See

This area does not have the rich cultural sites that you will find around Acapulco and Taxco. This is largely due to the fact that this area largely fell into obscurity when the Spanish crown decided that Acapulco would be the Spain's exclusive port of entry on the Pacific in 1561. The region has only begun to be widely known in the last several decades. Despite the construction of Ixtapa in the early 1970s, this area has not gained a household recognition the way other Pacific Mexican destinations have, such as Cabo San Lucas, Mazatlan, Puerto Vallarta, and of course Acapulco. Interestingly, it wasn't until Morgan Freeman spoke the name of Zihuatanejo at the end of the movie *The Shawshank Redemption* that many people had ever heard of it. Today, that is still the first thing people think of when they hear the name, though that seems to be changing rapidly.

Museo Arqueología de la Costa Grande (755-554-7552), Paseo del Pescador #7, Zihuatanejo, GRO 40880. Open Tue.–Sun. 10 AM–6 PM. This small museum was established in 1992 and is located at the east side of the municipal beach, just south of the downtown area where the *malecón*

HOTEL POOLS LINE THE BEACH AT PLAYA LA ROPA.

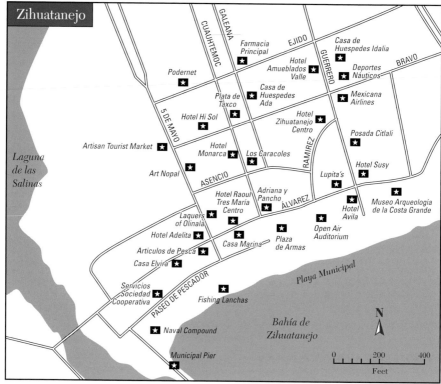

© The Countryman Press

ends. In its six exhibit rooms are pieces that illustrate the historical and cultural development of the Costa Grande. A permanent collection of pre-Hispanic pottery, murals, maps, and archaeological pieces traces this history from tribes that subsisted by hunting and gathering through the incursions of the Olmec, Teotihuacans, Tarascans, and Aztecs, culminating in the Spanish conquest and colonization. In addition to many items that have been recovered locally, the museum also spotlights other ancient cultures from around Mexico, including the Aztec civilization. Beyond the museum, a footpath cut into the rocks leads to Playa Madera. 12 pesos admission.

Soledad de Maciel Archaeological Zone, Highway 200 Km 214, Soledad de Maciel, GRO, is an archaeological site in the making, about 19 miles east of Zihuatanejo. At kilometer 214 of Highway 200, take a well-marked dirt road south for about 5 miles. This road is narrow and not well maintained and leads along a grove of coconut palms. The turnoff to the site is on the left. If you enter the actual village of Soledad de Maciel, you've gone too far.

This site is a classic-era settlement from around AD 300. It covers a territory of almost 2 square miles around the current village of Soledad de Maciel and includes several ceremonial mounds and courtyards, a ball court, and three unexcavated pyramids. It was first identified by the INAH (National Institute of Archaeology and History) in 1925. Since then, periodic excavations have uncovered many artifacts such as pottery, monoliths, and two stone ball rings used in an indigenous ball game. Sometime in the next decade, archaeologists expect to have this site completely excavated. Once this is accomplished, planners intend to have a visitor center here with a small artifact museum. There isn't much to see yet; however, visitors to the present site are allowed to have a quick gander of the archaeologists digging in the dirt. Free admission.

✳ To Do

BEACHES In Zihuatanejo, several distinctive beaches offer various activities as well as clear waters. Playa las Gatas and Playa Madera provide great surfing.

Playa Contramar, located at the northwestern end of Zihuatanejo Bay, is a tiny beach covered with small stones polished by the surf. It is not a sand beach. It provides a beautiful setting for an afternoon of snorkeling but there are no services here, so bring lunch. The best way to get here is by water taxi.

Playa las Gatas. The calm clear water off this secluded beach makes it the place for snorkeling in Zihuatanejo. It lies beneath the southern end of Punta El Faro escarpment. This beach is accessible by a rocky mile-long footpath along the coast from the south end of Playa la Ropa, or you can take a water taxi (35 pesos roundtrip) from Zihuatanejo's municipal pier. Boats make this trip across the bay every few minutes 8 AM–5 PM. Be sure to hold on to your ticket for that return trip. There is a reef here that, according to legend, are the remains of private bathing pool that a Tarascan ruler named Caltzontzín had built for his family and friends. However, archaeological investigations have shown this reef to be a natural formation. One certainty, though, is that marine life along this reef is plentiful. You will find sea urchins, damselfish, angelfish, pipefish, eels, and even an occasional sea turtle. Look for beachside booths that rent snorkeling equipment, as well as a professional dive shop right on the beach. If you plan on

THE ROAD TO SOLEDAD DE MACIEL.

Parroquia de Cristo Jesús, 20 de Noviembre s/n, Petatlán, GRO 40800. About 23 miles south of Zihuatanejo, you will come upon the sleepy little village of Petatlán, famous for its church and its gold market. Both are located at the center of town. The gold market is filled with friendly vendors that sell jewelry by the gram. This is a great place to practice your bartering skills. Directly across from this market sits the modern church of Cristo Jesús surrounded by lush trees adjoining the town square. Although it is not a historic church or in the colonial style, people travel here from all over the world in search of miracles. Inside the church, in a glass case above the altar, sits a wooden effigy of Jesus robed in white and gold, bent to his knees under the weight of a wooden cross. This statue is known as Padre Jesús de Petatlán, and there are three legends for how it came to be here.

All of the legends take place around the late 16th century, when the population around Petatlán was a collection of unfortunate indigenous tribes that had been ravaged by smallpox and the injustices of the Spanish conquistadors. At the time, there was a kind village priest who managed a modest chapel. Each year at Easter, he would parade a tattered statue of Saint Anthony in place of Jesus as he did the Stations of the Cross. Determined to replace this statue with a proper visage of Christ, he took up a collection and prepared to travel to Puebla in time to return before Holy Week. Here is where the three stories begin to diverge.

In one version, a peasant was working his parcel early one morning when he heard someone moaning. Believing that it was a wounded person, he went toward where the sounds were coming from and came upon the statue of Jesus on his knees from the weight of the cross. He informed the priest, who later built a small church on the site where the statue was found, which today is the site of the modern church and the center of the entire town.

In the second version, the priest was praying for guidance the night

snorkeling, try to get here in the morning when the water is a little clearer. A paved walkway off the southern end of the beach leads to a lighthouse that provides a spectacular view of the coastline. There are over a dozen seafood restaurants here. Pick one that looks good and grab a seat for the day.

Playa Larga, a wave-swept beach about 6 miles south of Zihuatanejo, just before the airport, is a long, wide stretch of sand that goes on for nearly 10 miles. It is bordered by large groves of coconut palms and swampy lagoons that give way to lush hillsides. Guides take horseback excursions through trails that wind through this area and let out onto the open sand. This beach is generally uncrowded, though a few boutique hotels and beachfront restaurants are located before he set out for Puebla, knowing that his meager collection could never purchase a statue fit for an Easter celebration. At that moment, there was a heavy knock at the door. The visitor was a pirate captain whose ship had been washed ashore at Bahía de Potosí during a great storm. The pirates had taken the statue as booty and had prayed to it as their ship was going down and had vowed to donate it to the nearest town if they were saved.

In the third, and perhaps most widely believed version, the priest opened his door to find a ragged vagabond standing there. The man appeared to be a peasant but claimed to be a sculptor and promised to create the sculpture himself in time for the Easter celebration, less than two weeks away. The priest thanked him but dismissed his promise. Nevertheless, a storm hit that prevented the priest from making the trip to Puebla. Easter morning came and the priest prepared to deliver his homily. At that moment, a man burst into the church and told the congregation that Jesus had appeared to him. The crowd followed the man to a stream where they found the statue of Padre Jesús sitting under a tree. The people joyfully carried it back to Petatlán, where it remains to this day.

THE STATUE OF PADRE JESÚS AT THE PARROQUIA DE CRISTO JESÚS IN PETATLÁN.

here. The big waves and strong undertow make it a dangerous place to get in the water if you are not a strong swimmer. Get here from downtown Zihuatanejo by taking the *combi* marked "Coacoyul." Tell the driver you want to get to Playa Larga. He will drop you at a spot where you can catch another *combi* that will take you to the beach. For a much simpler experience, take a taxi.

Playa la Ropa got its name, meaning "Clothing Beach," during the days of the Manila galleons, when a ship laden with silks and other fabrics spilled its cargo and the textiles washed upon the sand here. Today, it is Zihuatanejo's main tourist beach, lined with boutique hotels and larger resorts as well as a host of seafood restaurants. It is a milelong crescent of yellow sand with relatively gentle

PLAYA LARGA IS A LONG STRETCH OF OPEN BEACH SOUTH OF ZIHUATANEJO.

surf and a nice view of the bay. It's a popular place for swimming and basking in the sun as parasailors drift overhead. This is also a great place to go for a jog in the evening as the sun dips into the Pacific. Vendors roam the beach selling shell necklaces, velvet paintings, and other tchotchkes. Wave them off if you're not interested and be prepared for a lot of attention if you express any interest in what they're selling. Concessionaires rent Jet Skis for around $40 for a half an hour and Hobie Cats can be had for about $50 an hour. All this traffic means the beach is occasionally less than pristine, though the hotel and restaurant workers do their best to keep the trash picked up. These hotels and restaurants provide *palapas*, beach chairs, and umbrellas. Order some chips and guacamole and stay a while. This beach is a 20-minute walk from Playa Madera or a short taxi ride from town. There's public parking located at the south end of the beach.

PLAYA LA ROPA PROVIDES BEAUTIFUL VIEWS OF ZIHUATANEJO BAY.

Playa Madera, a relatively small beach, got its name, meaning "Wood Beach," because the Spanish used it as a loading dock for cedar, oak, mahogany, and pine cut from the nearby forests. Reach this beach by walking along the footpath east from Playa Municipal. This walkway continues south toward Playa la Ropa. Playa Madera is a relatively quiet beach that is mostly only used by the few hotels that line the shore here. It has dark sand and gentle waves that lap against the shore with little undertow, making it a good place for families to come swimming. Not a lot of shade is to be found here, so be sure to wear sunscreen.

Playa Municipal, located next to the pier right in front of Zihuatanejo's downtown area, is also known as Playa Principal. This isn't a good beach for swimming because of the fishing boats that operate nearby and the drainage from the pluvial canal. Definitely stay out of the water here during the rainy season. This beach is lined with shopping and restaurants and the boats just off shore provide a picturesque view. Go to the pier to catch the water taxi to Playa las Gatas, or take a short walk down the beach to Playa Madera for some good swimming.

BUS TOURS TuriStar (755-553-2623; www.turistar.com.mx). Except for a few regions such as Baja California and the Yucatán Peninsula, this bus company covers almost all of Mexico. Their service includes snacks, cafeteria service, plasma televisions, bathrooms, and headphones.

DIVING AND SNORKELING The region around Zihuatanejo has the kind of underwater treasures that will leave the most experienced professional diver or even marine biologist in awe. Whether you're snorkeling in a 10-foot coral cove or scuba diving through a 100-foot canyon, there is something here for you. In the waters off this beautiful coast, two ocean currents—the Humboldt and the Equatorial Counter Current—converge creating an extraordinarily rich atmos-

MUSICIANS WALKING ALONG THE BEACH NEAR DOWNTOWN ZIHUATANEJO.

phere for marine biodiversity. Everything from the tiniest sea horse to giant humpback whales can be found in these waters. Other common sights are various species of angelfish, striped Mexican goatfish, crabs crawling on the sandy seafloor, multicolored octopus, and even the enormous whale shark. If you happen to be here between June and October, you may even see sea turtles returning to the nearby beaches to lay their eggs. These waters have relatively mild currents, especially when compared to other locations such as the Caribbean. There are dozens of sites that provide fascinating exploration, from shallow corals to jagged underwater ravines. There are even sunken ships hundreds of years old. These sites include Playa Manzanillo just south of Zihuatanejo Bay. It is accessible only by boat and provides vivid corals with abundant sea life at 10 to 20 feet. Another is Caleta de Chon, a relatively shallow coral reef outside of Zihuatanejo Bay, which provides good scuba diving.

Adventure Divers (755-554-9191; www.adventuredivers.com.mx), Calle Adelita #68, Zihuatanejo, GRO 40880. This PADI-certified diving company provides many excursions around the Ixtapa-Zihuatanejo area, suitable for all experience levels. They offer instruction, from classes for beginners to certification courses for more advanced divers.

Carlo Scuba (755-554-6003; www.carloscuba.com), Playa las Gatas, Zihuatanejo, GRO 40880. This PADI-certified diving company gives excursions to well over a dozen sites in the Ixtapa-Zihuatanejo area. These include double-dives, night dives, snorkeling, and special trips for more advanced divers. They also offer a variety of classes.

Nautilus Divers (755-554-9191; www.nautilus-divers.com), Juan Álvarez #33, Zihuatanejo, GRO 40880. This company provides guided dives at all of the popular diving spots around the Ixtapa-Zihuatanejo area. They also offer 2-hour resort pool instruction for beginners and 4-day NAUI certification courses for more advanced divers. Certified divers can also take night dives, shipwreck dives, and deep-water dives though underwater canyons.

Zihuatanejo Dive Center (755-544-8554; www.zihuatanejodivecenter.com), Avenida la Noria #1, Zihuatanejo, GRO 40880. This PADI-certified diving school and tour company provides trips to a variety of locations at depths ranging from 10 to 120 feet. They also offer classes for children and beginners at Playa las Gatas or even in your hotel pool. Once certified, you will be qualified to dive with an instructor at depths of up to 40 feet.

HORSEBACK RIDING In Zihuatanejo, **Playa Larga** is the place to go for horseback rides. It has jungle trails that lead back through swampy estuaries and hilly groves of coconut palms.

✧ **Beach and Country Tours** (755-559-8884), Playa la Ropa s/n, Zihuatanejo, GRO 40880. This company offers eco-tours by horseback. Your guide, Ignacio Mendiola, will arrange travel from your hotel to Playa Larga, where he will guide you along jungle trails that are typical of what Ixtapa was like before it was developed into the resort location that it is today. The tour ends with a trot along the beach and refreshments at a beachfront restaurant.

SPORT FISHING Zihuatanejo Bay boasts International Game Fish Association world records in fly-fishing. Keep in mind that certain local restaurants are happy to prepare fillets brought in by angler-customers.

Gitana Sportfishing (755-554-7812; www.gitanasportfishing.com), Zihuatanejo, GRO 40880. This company offers sport fishing adventures throughout the Ixtapa-Zihuatanejo region. They provide both conventional and fly-fishing rods. They have a 25- and a 27-foot covered *panga*. Charter includes artificial bait, fishing license, ice, six sodas, six bottles of water, lures, dead baits, and seven hours' fishing time.

Oleaje Sportfishing Charters (755-554-6737), Zihuatanejo, GRO 40880. This sport fishing charter company offers a 24-foot covered *panga* and years of experience fishing in these waters. The boat can accommodate up to four people and trips are about 7 hours long. Fishing license, tackle, bait, and soft drinks are included.

TOURING ⌁ **Julio's Tours** (755-108-9734; www.juliostours.com), Zihuatanejo, GRO 40880. This company offers in-shore and off-shore fishing excursions. They also offer trips that combine fishing and snorkeling, as well as adventure cruises. All trips are for the day and include bait, all tackle, ice chest, water, and sodas.

Picante Sailing Catamaran (755-554-2694; www.picantecruises.com), Zihuatanejo, GRO 40880. This tour company offers a variety of excursions around Ixtapa-Zihuatanejo on their 75-foot catamaran. This includes snorkeling adventures, sunset cruises, and nighttime champagne tours. For a real thrill, hook up to their 2,400 square foot spinnaker and soar above the catamaran as it treads through the water.

✸ Lodging

Although Ixtapa is known for its megaresort hotels, there are only a handful of hotels in Zihuatanejo that offer more than a couple dozen suites. The majority of Zihuatanejo's resorts line Playa Madera and Playa la Ropa, squeezed in between lovely white-sand beaches and steep cliffs. This means that getting around many of the hotels here means walking a lot of stairs. Farther to the south, toward the airport, is Playa Larga, 10 miles of flat, open beach bordered by large groves of coconut palms. In recent years, a string of boutique hotels have popped up here providing basic beach bungalows as well as luxury accommodations. Although this area is somewhat isolated from town, it does offer the kind of seclusion that is perfect for a romantic getaway.

⌁ (ᵠ) **Amuleto** (755-544-6222; www .amuleto.net), Calle Escénica 9, Playa la Ropa, Zihuatanejo, GRO 40880 $$$. AE; D; MC; V. This small boutique hotel, located on a hillside between Playa la Ropa and Playa las Gatas, features highly personal service and a breathtaking atmosphere. Designed to be organically integrated with Zihuatanejo's natural environment, it offers both privacy and open spaces that are perfect for a romantic getaway. This hotel's six uniquely designed suites are positioned around a central *palapa*, each furnished with a king-size bed

HOTELS HUG THE CLIFFS ALONG PLAYA LA ROPA IN ZIHUATANEJO.

and a terrace overlooking Zihuatanejo Bay. These suites are elegantly appointed with handmade furnishings and decorations of stone, ceramic, and wood. The terraces are equipped with lounge chairs and woven hammocks for the ultimate enjoyment of the view. Each suite has its own private infinity-plunge pool. The hotel's open-air restaurant provides gourmet cuisine for breakfast, lunch, and dinner daily 8 AM–9 PM. Reservations are required and a deposit may be required for groups larger than six. Room service is also available. The emphasis at this hotel is on tranquility. Therefore, you will not find any televisions, radios, or Internet access in your room. Additionally, this may not be the best hotel for those travelers who like to be on the go or constantly entertained. The truth is that there is not much to do at this hotel outside relaxing, being pampered, and enjoying the company of your travel mate. Furthermore, there is no direct beach access here. Getting to the beach from this hotel requires a short taxi ride or a brisk walk.

Brisas Del Mar (755-554-2142; www.hotelbrisasdelmar.com) Eva Samano de López Mateos s/n, Playa Madera, Zihuatanejo, GRO 40895. $$. AE; D; MC; V. This hotel sits on Playa Madera at the center of Zihuatanejo Bay and is just a 10-minute walk from downtown Zihuatanejo. It is a terraced structure built into the side of a steep hill and has 30 spacious suites. Gorgeously decorated in traditional Mexican style, they are furnished with either a king-size or two double beds and have terraces that overlook the bay. Be prepared to walk a lot of stairs when you're here, as the hotel is built on a hillside and there are stairs throughout. If you need more exercise than that, there is also a gym, plus a game room. The on-site pool is embedded in a lush hillside and has a waterslide, making it a great place to spend some time with the kids. At the single gourmet restaurant, open daily 8 AM–10 PM, you can dine in a large dining room or an open-air patio that opens onto the beach. It serves everything from authentic wood-fired pizza to crepes to traditional Mexican cuisine. .

✦ **Casa Cuitlateca** (755-554-2448; U.S. 877–541-1234; www.casa cuitlateca.com), Calle Playa la Ropa, Apartado 124, Zihuatanejo, GRO 40880. $$. AE; MC; V. This boutique hotel sits high above Zihuatanejo Bay in a secluded area, providing the kind of privacy, solitude, and serenity that make it perfect for a romantic get-away. It was designed by well-known Mexican architect Carlos Desormaux and takes its name from the region's pre-Hispanic inhabitants. Each of the hotel's five rooms has been specially designed to represent various parts of Mexico and the indigenous people of those respective regions. All rooms are furnished with a king-size bed. One suite has a living room and a sep-arate bedroom, as well as a patio that opens onto a beautiful private garden. Another room has a large private deck offering a dramatic view of Zihuatane-jo Bay. There are two executive suites with private decks overlooking the hotel's lush grounds and Zihuatanejo Bay. The upper level of the original house includes an open-air room that is a perfect spot for private dining or an afternoon siesta. The general gar-den area contains a cobbled swim-ming pool overlooking the city of Zihuatanejo. This pool is designed to appear as if it were pouring right into the bay below and provides probably the best view in the hotel. At night, relax with a dip in this pool and it's backdrop of the city's lights lining the bay. Look for the additional private gardens if you would like to get away from it all.

✦ ((ᵖ)) **Casa Don Francisco Hotel** (755-554-8030; www.hotelcasadon francisco.com), Playa la Ropa S/N,

Zihuatanejo, GRO 40880. $$. AE; D; MC; V. Situated at the south end of Playa la Ropa, this boutique hotel has eight unique suites, each elegantly appointed with private terraces and a king-size bed. However, only five of these suites have views of the ocean, so be sure to request one of these accommodations if that is important to you. Also, four of the suites have private swimming pools; all are sur-rounded by lush tropical gardens. Because of its size, this hotel offers highly personal service and privacy, making it a great choice for a lazy romantic getaway. There is a modest swimming pool in a garden setting with a *palapa* bar. The hotel is plan-ning on implementing a restaurant but for now they do offer free conti-nental breakfast each morning that includes a variety of seasonal tropical fruits, juices, cereals, milk, coffee, and sweet rolls. Dinner won't be much of a problem as the hotel has a good location on Playa la Ropa. Just take a stroll down the beach and take your pick of the several restaurants offer-ing service there each evening.

✦ **Casa Kau Kan** (755-554-6226; www.casakaukan.com), Playa Larga, Zihuatanejo, GRO 40880. $$$. AE; MC; V. This small boutique hotel has 11 suites surrounding a swimming pool and lush garden area right off the expansive Playa Larga in Zihu-atanejo. All suites are air-conditioned, roomy, and decorated in traditional Mexican style, and contain a king-size bed and handmade Mexican furni-ture. Unlike the hotels of Playa la Ropa, which are built into the hillside and require StairMaster training in preparation for your stay, this hotel is basically ground level with the beach; five of the suites actually open onto the beach itself. The other suites have terraces that open onto the pool area and have partial views of the beach. The hotel kitchen is run by a well-known local chef and guests can expect gourmet meals cooked for them each night made from the freshest seafood. Because this hotel is located several miles south of town, it is certainly off the beaten path. Expect to take a taxi if you plan on doing any shopping or sightseeing. However, the location also provides privacy that you won't find at the beaches closer to town.

La Casa Que Canta (755-555-7000; www.lacasaquecanta.com), Camino Escenico a Playa Ropa, Zihuatanejo, GRO 40880. $$$. AE; MC; V. This intimate resort near Playa la Ropa offers excellent service and a wonderful experience. This architecturally striking hotel is perched on a cliff with a panoramic view of Zihuatanejo Bay. The 25 suites come in a wide variety of floor plans and are furnished with a king-size bed. They are decorated in a modern Mexican style that accentuates the surroundings. Some suites are equipped with private plunge pools. All of the suites have terraces equipped with elegantly embroidered hammocks so you can enjoy this gorgeous view in privacy and experience hearing the waves lap against the shore as you lie in bed at night. This hotel has two swimming pools. One is a freshwater pool that is on a promontory overlooking Zihuatanejo Bay and seems to overflow directly into the water below. There is also a saltwater pool with an adjoining Jacuzzi that is tucked into the rocks down by the ocean. Amenities include a gym and yoga classes. The fine dining open-air restaurant, open daily for dinner 6–10, specializes in Mexican food and seafood and has been recognized as one of the best restaurants in Mexico. Please note that children under the age of 16 are not allowed at this hotel.

Catalina Beach Resort (755-554-2137; www.catalina-beach-resort.com), Playa la Ropa S/N, Zihuatanejo, GRO 40880. $–$$. AE; MC; V. This hotel is set among tropical gardens on a hill overlooking Playa la Ropa. Built in 1952, this was the first resort to be built along Zihuatanejo Bay. Since then, it has gone through many upgrades and additions. It now has 46 rooms that vary from spacious to huge, all equipped with private terraces that open onto the Pacific Ocean. These terraces are furnished with two chaise longues, a hammock, and a small table. The rooms, decorated in rustic Mexican style with Mexican tile floors, wrought-iron furniture, and traditional artwork, have a king-size, queen-size, or two double beds. Be ready to walk plenty of stairs while staying at this hotel as you will have to scale the hill to move from the restaurant to your room and farther down to the beach. At the bottom of the hill, you will find a freshwater infinity pool overlooking the beach and the Palapa Bar that serves snacks and drinks while you lounge next to the pool or on the beach. The hotel's **Linda Vista Restaurant,** open daily 7 AM–10 PM, which is perched in the middle of the complex, serves a free continental or American-style breakfast in the morning and Mexican and international dishes in the afternoon for lunch. In the evening, the restaurant offers a variety of steaks and seafood specialties.

⚡ ((ᵗ)) **Cinco Sentidos Hotel** (755-544-8908; www.hotelcincosentidos .com), Calle Escénica 8 Playa la Ropa, Zihuatanejo, GRO 40895. $$$. MC; V. Meaning "Five Senses," the name of this boutique hotel says it all; it has been designed to provide a complete pleasurable experience. With only five suites, the emphasis here is on privacy, a fact that makes this hotel ideal for honeymooners. The rooms here are spacious and designed to provide a romantic atmosphere that is ideal for enjoying the company of your traveling mate. Each room is attractively appointed in a modern, tropical style. These suites are furnished with either a king-size or two double beds and are equipped with a private terrace and a private infinity plunge pool with an ocean view. There is a library on the premises. There is no restaurant or bar on site at this hotel. However, several dining options are within easy walking distance down the beach.

⚡ **Las Palmas Hotel** (755-557-0634; www.hotellaspalmas.net), Lot 5, Playa Blanca, Zihuatanejo, GRO 40895. $$$. AE; D; MC; V. Located off the beaten path along the long stretch of coastline south of Zihuatanejo, this boutique hotel offers an ideal setting for a romantic getaway or wedding. It is nestled among a large palm grove and offers six uniquely designed suites that offer amazing views of the garden and beach. This is not the hotel for travelers looking to party and meet new people. However, if you are looking for seclusion, this hotel offers an ideal experience. The rooms are nicely decorated in modern Mexican style to enhance the tropical feel of the surroundings. They are furnished with a king-size bed, hand-loomed rugs, and original artwork. These suites are located in an attractive *palapa*-roofed building just up from the beach. There is a well-manicured garden area just in front of the beach where you will find a small but attractive

PLAYA LA ROPA IS ZIHUATANEJO'S MOST LIVELY BEACH.

swimming pool lined with chaise longues. The hotel's **Palmeras Restaurant and Bar,** which serves breakfast 8–10, lunch noon–3, and dinner 6–9, offers a relaxed but elegant dining experience in an open-air patio facing the beach. This restaurant specializes in Mexican cuisine and fresh seafood. In-room private dining is also available.

F **La Quinta Troppo** (755-554-3423; www.laquintatroppo.com), Playa la Ropa, Zihuatanejo, GRO 40880. $$$. AE; D; MC; V. This small boutique hotel, located on the beach at Playa la Ropa, has 8 suites. Upon arrival, guests are greeted with complimentary margaritas and have the option to schedule a massage in their room. Each room is decorated individually in styles meant to celebrate Mexican art and artisans, from the elegant Mexican style of a Frida Kahlo–inspired room called El Jardín de Frida to the colorful and indigenous style of the room known as Zihuatlán. All rooms have a private bath, a king-size bed, and either a terrace or sitting area. However, only six of the rooms have views of Zihuatanejo Bay, so be sure to request one of these rooms when making your reservation if the view is important to you. There is a narrow garden patio area that features a long swimming pool and bar. This is an ideal place to enjoy a glass of wine while enjoying the tranquility that surrounds you. Guests of this hotel also have access to tours on a 26-foot twin-hulled power boat that provides a great way to get over to Isla Ixtapa or other excursions such as fishing trips and sunset cruises. Dining at **La Quinta Troppo** is an informal affair daily 1 PM–10 PM. There are tables on the hotel terrace overlooking the ocean where you can enjoy breakfast, lunch, or dinner with a great view of Zihuatanejo Bay. There are no menus. Breakfast is served in the continental style with coffee, juices, pastries, and seasonal fruits. Dinner is a set three-course meal. Advise the staff of any special dietary requirements that you may have and they will accommodate you.

∂ F (ꜛ) **The Tides Zihuatanejo** (755-555-5500; www.tideszihuatanejo .com), Playa la Ropa S/N Zihuatanejo, GRO 40880. $$$. AE; MC; V. With 70 rooms and suites, this is one of the larger hotels in Zihuatanejo. Located at the north end of Playa la Ropa, this hotel has garnered a reputation as a world-class resort. It offers a beautifully manicured property with adobe-inspired rooms that are all uniquely decorated in a modern Mexican style. This includes rustic floor tile and handcrafted wall art. They are furnished with luxuriously soft king-size beds and all rooms feature private terraces with garden or ocean views. Suites also have private outdoor infinity plunge pools. Children are permitted in two-bedroom suites only. The hotel grounds include three general-use swimming pools, including a seaside infinity pool. There is also an on-site health spa, open daily 9 AM–8 PM, were you can enjoy everything from a full-body massage to lava shell therapy and full-body exfoliation. Other amenities include a gym, tennis courts, and a beauty salon. This hotel has two restaurants and one bar. **La Villa Restaurant,** open daily 8 AM–11 PM, features Pacific-Mexican cuisine as well as a variety of fine French and international dishes. **La Marea Restaurant** open daily for lunch and dinner noon–10, serves

Mediterranean and Mexican seafood cuisine. If you are interested in learning to cook the dishes featured on the menu here, the Tides also offers cooking classes with its own executive chef.

 Villa Carolina Hotel (755-554-5612; www.villacarolina.com.mx), Camino Escénico Playa la Ropa s/n, Zihuatanejo, GRO 40880. $$$. AE; MC; V. This boutique hotel offers seven split-level suites under palm-thatched roofs near Playa la Ropa. These suites are all very spacious and equipped with a full kitchen, hand-made Mexican furniture, and a king-size bed. They are decorated in an unexpectedly modern style. The two-bedroom Master Suites have private terraces with hammocks and a private Jacuzzi. The Garden Suites are studios with sitting areas in front of the bed and have garden patios that open onto the pool area. The Grand House is a two-bedroom casita with a spacious kitchen, 42-inch television with a satellite system, as well as a living room and dining room area abutting a private pool. Both bedrooms have full private bathrooms and private terraces facing Zihuatanejo Bay. There is also a general patio area that is dominated by a swimming pool surrounded by plenty of chaise longues and umbrellas. Although this hotel is not actually on the beach, Playa la Ropa is only a short walk away. This is a good place to come in the evening to find a convenient place to dine if you don't feel like cooking.

 Villa Mexicana Hotel (755-55-8472; www.hotelvillamexicana.com.mx), Playa la Ropa, Zihuatanejo, GRO 40880. $$. MC; V. This hotel has 64 warmly appointed rooms in a Mexican hacienda-style building at Playa la Ropa. This is one of the few hotels in Zihuatanejo that expressly tries to accommodate families by providing a kid-friendly experience. The rooms are decorated in a modern style and come furnished with either a king-size or two double beds. There are a few rooms here that are designed to accommodate families, with two double plus a king-size bed. Rooms come with private terraces that open onto Zihuatanejo Bay. There is a patio with a small swimming pool and chaise lounges. This patio opens onto the beach where you can also get beverage service. There is a daycare center here that provides activities for children ages 3 to 9, and babysitting service is available. There is also laundry service. The hotel's **Doña Prudencia Restaurant,** open daily 8 AM–9 PM, specializes in Mexican-style haute cuisine. Meals are served under a *palapa* in full view of the beach. This provides a nice atmosphere to enjoy the sunset.

BATHERS PLAY IN THE WATER OF PLAYA LA ROPA IN THE LATE AFTERNOON.

✳ Where to Eat

Zihuatanejo has many interesting restaurants to choose from. However, they are a bit more spread out here than in Ixtapa. Certainly, you can walk along Playa la Ropa and have your pick of Mexican seafood restaurants offering beachside service. However, the more interesting restaurants are either in town or tucked away high on the cliffs overlooking the bay. Although they take a little more work to get to, you will find that the cuisine and the view are well worth the trouble.

DINING OUT Capricho's Grill (755-554-3019; www.caprichosgrill .com) Cinco de Mayo #4, Zihuatanejo, GRO 40880. $$–$$$. MC; V. Open daily for lunch and dinner 5 –11. This diverse and trendy restaurant has a tranquil dining room and a candle-lit hacienda-style courtyard area with palm trees, fountains, and hanging lanterns. They also have a lounge furnished with velvet chairs. This makes Capricho's a relaxing place to enjoy a cocktail or a selection from their extensive wine list. The unique menu features mesquite-grilled fare inspired by Mediterranean and Latin American culture. Enjoy dishes such as red snapper with lime and guajillo sauce or chicken breast stuffed with spinach and goat cheese, topped with poblano pepper sauce. Follow that up with an espresso drink and a dish of their homemade ice cream. They have live local Latin, bossa nova, and flamenco acts on Thu., Fri., and Sat. nights. Additionally, they occasionally host special events such as the annual guitar festival.

La Casa Vieja (755-554-9770), Josefa Ortíz de Domínguez #7, Zihuatanejo, GRO 40880. $$. MC; V. Open for lunch and dinner Mon.–Sat. noon–11 pm, Sun. 9 am–11 pm. This traditional Mexican restaurant offers a casual but intimate dining experience just a block off Playa Madera. The menu here features delicious seafood and traditional Mexican dishes. Fresh seafood selections include freshly caught tuna, red snapper, and mahimahi prepared any way you like. Nonseafood items include such favorites as *filet a la tampiqueña* (tenderloin steak) and *cochinita pibil* (slow-roasted pork). This savory cuisine is served in a beautiful open-air garden setting among tropical plants and hanging lamps. Ambient music adds to the atmosphere but doesn't stifle conversation. Despite its slightly hidden location, this restaurant is popular with the locals, particularly on Thursday nights when live music is featured and pozole (a pork and hominy soup) is on the menu.

Coconuts (755-554-2518), Augustín Ramírez #1, Zihuatanejo, GRO 40884. $$, MC; V. Open daily for lunch 11:30–4:30 and dinner 6–11; closed June–mid-Oct. This fine dining restaurant is located in the city's oldest building, which has been beautifully restored to create an ambience that is truly captivating. This old house was once used as a way station for coconuts and other goods; today it is festooned with plants and flowers to create a lovely tropical atmosphere. The restaurant's open air patio makes a wonderful place to enjoy a warm Mexican evening; inside you will find a horseshoe-shaped bar stocked with a good selection of wines and other spirits. Dishes include several shrimp and seafood specialties, traditional Mexican favorites with an eclectic twist, as well as other unique dishes such as grilled chicken with goat cheese. For dessert, the banana flambé does not disappoint. Or try one of their many dessert coffees. There is nightly live entertainment featuring local talents playing bossa nova or jazz.

La Gaviota (755-554-3816), Playa la Ropa s/n, Zihuatanejo, GRO 40880. $$. MC; V. Open daily for lunch and dinner 11–10. This beachfront restaurant is located at the southern edge of Playa la Ropa, It features fresh Mexican seafood in the tropical seaside setting that you traveled a long way to enjoy. Sit on their open-air patio and enjoy the breeze coming off the Pacific. It's a great place to enjoy a beer and watch people frolicking on the beach. The seafood is prepared in a variety of ways. The *mahimahi al ajillo* is particularly good and comes with rice and vegetables. Make sure you try their handmade tortillas and fresh salsas. For the freshest fish, get here after 2 pm when the day's catch has been delivered.

La Gula (755-554-8396), Calle Adelita #8, Zihuatanejo, GRO 40880. $$$. MC; V. Open for lunch and dinner Mon.–Sat. 5–12:30; closed Aug.–Oct. This restaurant is located on a hill behind Playa Madera, and though it is on the second floor, the setting is not that extravagant. It is a single dining room with several linen-covered tables and an open balcony overlooking the mountains and the city lights. However, there is all the extravagance you will need is at the other end of the room in the open kitchen. Here is where fresh seafood and select meats are turned into works of art that are presented to you in haute-style small portions. The emphasis here is on

preparation and presentation. Entrées include such imaginative works as rib eye in tarragon sauce with vegetables and hash brown potatoes, beef medallion and shrimp in chocolate mole, and grilled salmon fillet in deviled tamarind sauce with mixed greens. There is a full bar here as well, providing the spirits to accentuate your meal perfectly. Desserts are presented in an equally attractive way and do not disappoint. Reservations are recommended but not required.

Kau Kan (755-554-8446), Carretera Escénica Lote 7, Zihuatanejo, GRO 40884. $$$. AE; MC; V. Open daily for lunch and dinner 5–midnight; closes in late September. Not to be confused with its sister hotel, the Casa Kau Kan, this elegant restaurant is situated above Playa Madera along the scenic highway that leads you to Playa la Ropa. It features a shaded patio dining area that is fantastic for

MANY RESTAURANTS OFFER BEACHSIDE SERVICE AT PLAYA LA ROPA.

enjoying lunch, as well as an upstairs open-air dining area that provides a romantic setting for a candle-lit dinner under the stars. In either case, this restaurant provides an unforgettable view of the Zihuatanejo Bay. Head Chef Ricardo Rodriguez presents small works of seafood art such as shrimp prepared in a basil and garlic, grilled mahimahi in sweet and spicy pineapple sauce, crab and olive tarts, and stingray in black butter sauce. Or, if you're in the mood for something a little simpler, you can always go with the lobster with baked potato. Reservations are recommended but not required. If you're coming for dinner, try to arrive in time to catch the sun set. You'll thank yourself.

La Perla (755-554-2700), Playa la Ropa s/n, Zihuatanejo, GRO 40880. $$–$$$. AE; MC; V. Open daily for breakfast, lunch, and dinner 10 am–11 pm. This enjoyable Mexican restaurant is located right on the sand at Playa la Ropa. Look for the blue umbrellas skirting the sand at the south end of the beach. Just a short walk from many of Zihuatanejo's hotels, this is a popular spot to stake out a spot and hang out all day, sipping beers and watching beach volleyball games. Dig your feet in the sand and order some food. Then sit back and enjoy. They offer a variety of fresh seafood prepared with a Mexican flair. If you're in the mood for a light snack, you can hardly beat their fish or shrimp tacos made with fresh corn tortillas and guacamole. Dinner options include everything from their specialty, the *filete La Perla*, which is fresh fish baked with cheese, to chiles rellenos (stuffed chiles), to broiled lobster. This restaurant also carries a

good selection of wines as well as Cuban cigars. Satellite television is available at the bar for all the big sporting events.

La Sirena Gorda (755-554-2687), Paseo del Pescador #90, Zihuatanejo, GRO 40880. $$. MC; V. Open for breakfast, lunch, and dinner Thu.–Tue. 9 am–11 pm. This restaurant is a good choice at just about any time of the day that you decide you're hungry. They are famous for their breakfasts, which include such lip-smacking favorites as apple walnut pancakes, omelets, fruit with granola and yogurt, as well as French toast. Later on, come back for their super-burgers, blackened red snapper, and even lobster. However, the house specialty is the fish tacos, which come in a variety of seafood and salsas. Whatever you choose, the food here is enjoyable, as is the friendly bohemian atmosphere. Fat mermaids decorate the walls and miniature boats hang from the ceiling, giving the place a distinctly casual atmosphere. Don't be surprised if a passing mariachi band stops to serenade you while you're enjoying your fish tacos. Keep in mind, though, that if you indulge them they will expect a tip.

EATING OUT La Casa Café (755-121-2593), Calle Adelita #7, Zihuatanejo, GRO 40880. $$. MC; V. Open for breakfast and lunch Tue.–Sun. 8–2. If you're someone who needs a good strong cup of coffee to get you going in the morning, you may have some cranky moments if you stick to your hotel cafés. The *café americana* hotels serve tends to be weak and actually kind of bad. So if you're looking for a cup of coffee that is fresh and . . . well, real, this is the place to come. This courtyard restaurant offers a selection of light snacks and sandwiches along with some traditional Mexican specialties. They also offer freshly ground organic coffee for about 50 cents. And that comes with free refills. Additionally, they have real espresso drinks here, which can also be hard to come by in this part of Mexico.

Tamales y Atoles Any (755-554-7373), Calle Vicente Guerrero 38, Zihuatanejo, GRO 48884. $. Open for breakfast and lunch Mon.–Sat. 8–3. When it comes to their specialty, the name kind of says it all. If you're in the mood for some delicious tamales and hot *atole* to wash it down, this is the place to be. However, the menu doesn't stop there. They have a host of other Mexican fare served up in a no-frills homemade style. In fact, this restaurant may be known for its delicious pozole (hominy and pork soup) more than tamales, and that's really saying something. This restaurant will not win points for its elegance, but it is heavy on authenticity. And when it

comes to good food at a reasonable price, you can't go wrong here.

NIGHTLIFE Bandidos (755-553-8072), Cinco de Mayo s/n, Zihuatanejo, GRO 40880. Open daily 11 PM–2 AM. May –Oct.; closed Sun. Located right in the middle of downtown Zihuatanejo, this bar has live music Monday through Saturday nights. Here you will find local artists playing all sorts of tropical rhythms, such as salsa, bossa nova, and meringue music. Bandidos also fancies itself a sports bar, though the music trumps most sporting events. The television may be turned to the big game; however, the sound is usually off and the band is playing. Order up your favorite tropical drink and enjoy the sounds. They also offer a small menu of light food such as fish and shrimp tacos, as well as a few full meals, such as pork chops in mushroom sauce and grilled lobster.

Blue Mamou (755-544-0825), Camino Escénico a Playa la Ropa s/n, Zihuatanejo, GRO 40880. Open

DOWNTOWN ZIHUATANEJO BUSTLES WITH TRAFFIC.

Mon.–Sat. 7 PM–3 AM high season; hours vary during low season. This club specializes in live blues, swing, and jazz. It is located at Playa la Ropa and features guest artists from different Mexico and the United States. It offers a fun and laid-back atmosphere perfect for hanging out in shorts and flip-flops with a drink in your hand. It's also a great place to cut loose and dance in your bare feet. The club also hosts private events if you call ahead and schedule them. Besides all kinds of drinks, this is a great place for barbecued chicken, ribs, and even fish.

La Playa Bar Calle Nicolás Bravo #39, Zihuatanejo, GRO 40880. Open daily 11 AM–1 AM. This tiny sports bar is a hole in the wall is centrally located in downtown Zihuatanejo. With room for just over a dozen people, it has just a few tables and bar stools, with a small bar and a television on the wall. However, this place gets particularly crowded and lively during soccer season. They carry about a dozen Mexican beers along with about as many tequilas, plus several vodkas and brandies, along with a few mixed drinks. All in all, a fun place with a relaxed atmosphere.

Revolución 1910 (755-554-9484), Calle Nicolás Bravo #47, Zihuatanejo, GRO 40880. Open Wed.–Sun. 8 PM–2 AM. This cozy bar is made for kicking back with friends. Located in downtown Zihuatanejo, the theme here is the style of revolutionary Mexico combined with a rock attitude. Toward that end, the music is rock from Mexico and north of the border. The crowd is young and mostly Mexican but you probably won't feel out of place, whatever your age group. That, even if you don't know the lyrics to the songs being belted out by the

band, which most of the patrons do. The crowd's singing only adds to the fun. It has a publike atmosphere, with several small tables with wicker chairs, besides a well-stocked bar. This is a lively place that offers several televisions for sporting events and live music from Thursday through Saturday night.

Rick's Bar (755-554-2535), Avenida Cuauhtémoc #5, Zihuatanejo, GRO 40880. Open Mon.–Sat. 7 PM–midnight. This small bohemian establishment is popular with locals and American expatriates alike. This bar is located in downtown Zihuatanejo, half a block off the Plaza Municipal. Amenities include Internet access, a trading library, and even showers if you happen to wander in off the beach. There is also a kitchen here, offering a selection of light snacks. The small stage area is open to anyone willing to share his or her talents (or lack thereof). Rick's also features live music by local artists, particularly during the high season.

Zihuablue (755-554-4844), Carretera Escénica la Ropa s/n, Zihuatanejo, GRO 40880. Open Nov.–May 8 PM–2 AM. Located on a hillside overlooking Playa la Ropa, this chic Mediterranean lounge is one of Zihuatanejo's more stylish nightlife options. It has an open-air terrace featuring a hookah bar, with a candlelit bar with a small dance floor. You will also find canopied beds and comfy couches, and a fine sand floor. The drinks are strong and the view is amazing. Unlike most options here, the music is not too overpowering for conversation, but is instead ambient and inviting. If you're in the mood for dinner, you can dine in either the indoor fine dining restaurant or the outdoor grill.

The fusion Euro-Asiatic cuisine here is delectable. Dress in your best casual loungewear and leave the shorts and flip-flops in your hotel room. The lounge has no cover, so come on up and take in the view.

Zorro's Sports Bar (755-110-5143), Calle Hermenegildo Galeana #1, Zihuatanejo, GRO 40880. Open daily 10 AM–2 AM. This bar, in downtown Zihuatanejo, is great for enjoying a cold beer day or night. This is the kind of place where you happily strike up a conversation with other patrons. It has a very casual atmosphere and plenty of televisions for all major sporting events, making it the perfect spot to nurse that sunburn. The staff is friendly and the beer is cold and cheap. Check out the list of specials posted by the door.

✴ Selected Shopping

In Zihuatanejo, the best shopping is in and around the downtown historic district.

CERAMICS AND FOLK ART

Arte Mexicano Nopal (755-554-7530), Avenida Cinco de Mayo #56, Zihuatanejo, GRO 40880. Open Mon.–Sat. 10 AM–2:30 PM and 4 PM–8 PM. This shop sells high-quality art, furniture, and crafts. They offer many pieces inspired by the work of Frida Kahlo, such as prints, post cards, and wall hangings. If you are looking for souvenirs for your loved ones back home, there are many small gifts as well as incense. They also have a small selection of jewelry at reasonable prices, and many interesting light fixtures ranging from the rustic to the fancy.

CLOTHING

Lupita's (755-554-2238), Calle Juan Álvarez #5, Zihuatanejo, GRO 40880. Open daily 10 PM–2 PM and 5 PM–8 PM. This boutique sells handmade traditional Mexican clothing from the Mexican states of Guerrero, Oaxaca, Chiapas, and Jalisco, as well as from Guatemala. This embroidered clothing is made of

TALAVERA IS ONE TYPE OF MEXICAN *ARTESENÍA* AVAILABLE AT THE SHOPS IN THIS AREA.

Michael Brady

either cotton broadcloth or satin and ranges from the casual beachwear to elegant pieces suitable for dinner parties. The shop also carries a range of accessories such as handmade hats, purses, and scarves.

FURNITURE Muebleria Cuauhtémoc (755-554-9150), Avenida Morelos #2, Zihuatanejo, GRO 40880. Open Mon.–Sat. 9 PM–8 PM. This shop sells high-quality, handmade Mexican furniture made of solid wood. They have a great selection of cabinets, wall units, bed frames, dining tables, dressers, cribs, as well as other pieces. Their furniture is also made to order if you have a particular design in mind.

Rattan Muebles (755-554-4477), Calle Ejido #17, Zihuatanejo, GRO 40880. Open Mon.–Sat. 9 AM–9 PM. This shop offers a wide selection of rattan and pine furniture, including a variety of handmade tables, chairs, cabinets, and dressers. They also have a small selection of wall hangings and artwork. Additionally, they will make a piece special order if you care to design one yourself.

JEWELRY Alberto's (755-554-2161; www.albertos.com.mx), Calle Cuauhtémoc #15, Zihuatanejo, GRO 40880. Open Mon.–Sat. 9 AM–9 PM. This fine jewelry shop has been in operation since the 1930s. They specialize in exclusive modern and traditional designs made of 0.925 silver and 14K gold. Here, you will find some of the most beautiful rings, necklaces, and bracelets in the region. Some even feature precious stones. They also do custom design work.

SHOPPING CENTERS Casa Marina (755-554-2373) Paseo del Pescador #9, Zihuatanejo, GRO 40880. Open daily 9 AM–9 PM high season, Mon.–Sat. 10 AM–2 PM and 4 PM–8 PM low season. This small shopping arcade is located at waterfront just south of downtown Zihuatanejo. It is home to several specialty shops

THE MERCADO MUNICIPAL IS A LARGE BAZAAR OF SMALL STANDS.

offering an interesting selection of traditional clothing, home items, beachwear, jewelry, and handcrafted folk art from all over Mexico. There is also a coffee-shop bookstore here that sells used books, which is the place to go if you are in need of some fresh reading material.

Mercado de Artesanía Turístico, Calle Cinco de Mayo s/n, Zihuatanejo, 40880. Open Mon.–Sat. 9 AM–7 PM. Between Paseo del Pescador and Avenida Morelos is a market with over 250 stalls selling all manner of Mexican handicraft, artesenía, and jewelry. This is one of the main tourist shopping centers in Ixtapa-Zihuatanejo. Here, you will find a wide variety of handicrafts from all over Guerrero and other nearby regions. For example, vendors sell jewelry embedded with semiprecious stones, shells, and coral, as well as silver jewelry from Taxco. You will also find hand-painted ceramics called *talavera* from Mexi-

co's central valley regions. You can also find anything from woven hammocks to gauzy traditional blouses and even T-shirts.

Mercado Municipal, Avenida Benito Juárez, Zihuatanejo, GRO 40884. Open Mon.–Sat. 8 AM–8 PM. This is the place to come if you want to experience old-world shopping. Located three blocks from the beach in a large, flat building just east of the town center, this is a bazaar of small stands squashed together to create a dark labyrinth. Local shoppers come here to buy fresh vegetables, poultry, meat, and seafood. There are also stalls selling everything from clothes to children's toys and household knickknacks. This place is a jumble of aromas and sights. Come here to pick up some inexpensive shell necklaces, huaraches (leather sandals), and other souvenirs for your loved ones back home.

TRONCONES

This seaside village, 20 miles north of Zihuatanejo, is an idyllic and relatively undeveloped stretch of beach. The population hovers around 600 people, though you can go a day here without seeing more than a dozen. The town has telephone and cell phone service and it is a local call to Ixtapa-Zihuatanejo from here; also, several establishments in town offer Internet access. However, there are no high-rise buildings or wide, multilane streets here. In fact, the main road that runs along the beach is only partially paved.

The rustic dirt road that runs along the shore is lined with gorgeously decorated boutique hotels, a bar, surf camps, and spiritual retreats owned and operated, for the most part, by expatriate Americans. Despite its proximity to Ixtapa, Troncones is a world apart in terms of the experience it offers. This is a simple place where chickens roam the streets and the ocean is the loudest thing for miles. Even in the high season of November through April, you can walk along the beach and not run into anyone. There are a few restaurants as well as a grocery store in town. Señor Frog's won't be opening up here anytime soon, but that's the way this community likes it.

The hotels here are mostly open-air villas with bungalows and private pools that open onto the beach. The beach itself is a long, wide stretch of sand that goes on for 3 miles and is populated by seagulls and not much else. The white sand is interspersed with the occasional rock outcropping. These rock formations harbor tide pools teeming with sea life. It is a wonderful place if you're looking for seclusion. If you are looking for a setting for a romantic getaway, you will

PLAYA TRONCONES IS LINED WITH SMALL, BOUTIQUE HOTELS.

TRONCONES HAS A GROWING COMMUNITY OF AMERICAN EXPATRIATES.

have to look hard to beat Troncones. Days here consist of hours of beachcombing, horseback riding, swimming, snorkeling, kayaking, and a lot of relaxation of the hammock variety. And, of course there is surfing. The best surfing spots are to the north at Troncones Point and just beyond at Manzanillo Bay. The waves here tend to be gentler and better suited for long boards. Peak season is from May to November, when waves can get as high as 115 feet. Many of the hotels here offer surfing classes.

GETTING THERE You can get here by taxi or bus and the village has its own taxi service for getting back to civilization. *By car:* Take Highway 200 north for about 16 miles past Ixtapa. Just past the small village of Buenavista, right around Km 31, there is a sign for Troncones. Traveling north, the turnoff will be on your left. The turnoff is marked on both sides of the highway. Take this road straight to the ocean. When you hit a dead end, you are in Troncones. Most of the hotels are off to the right. If you're hungry, the Burro Borracho Restaurant just off to the left is rustic but tasty.

BEACHES At Troncones, the best surfing is found at the north end of the 3-mile beach at Troncones Point and Manzanillo Bay just beyond. Longboarders will be in heaven just a few miles north of that at secluded La Saladita, which has perhaps the best longboard waves in all of Mexico.

Majahua. This slender stretch of beach will give you a good idea of what Troncones was like before it was discovered by the gringos—although that development does seem to be on its way here too. The rustic village of Majahua has hardly anything that might be considered an amenity, though there are several small food vendors that sell seafood along the beach. Their stalls are equipped with hammocks so you can nap away your food coma after you eat. Camping is welcomed here, though space is limited. And, although water is available, you

MAJAHUA IS A SECLUDED BEACH THAT IS A POPULAR SURF SPOT.

should bring your own water or have water purification tablets on hand so that you know the water you're drinking is safe to drink. Or, just have a beer instead. To get to Majahua, take the beach road from Troncones or take Highway 200 for about 20 miles north of Zihuatanejo and take the signed turnoff around Km 33. Then, continue west for about 2.9 miles to get to the beach.

La Saladita, a tiny seaside village, used to be a collection of oyster divers. Today, those oysters have been all fished out and this beach has been become a popular surf spot. The beach is level with smooth, rolling waves that are good not only for surfing, but swimming and boogie boarding as well. However, swimmers and particularly surfers should beware of rip currents and rocks. The beach is spread over several hundred yards and is a popular camping spot during Christmas and around Easter, but if you show up at other times you are just as likely to have the entire beach to yourself. Be sure to bring your own water, though there are a few seaside restaurants and small stores along the highway where you can pick up supplies as well. To get here, take Highway 200 about 25 miles north of Zihuatanejo and turn off at the village of Los Llanos around Km 40. Then turn right at the village church and continue for another 3 miles to the beach.

SURFING CAMP ✪ **Instructional Surf Adventures** (755-558-3821; www .isamexico.com), Troncones, GRO 40880. This company offers a five-day progressive surf camp in the isolated splendor of Troncones. The program is designed for young and old alike and classes are kept small, with no more than four participants. It is recommended that participants arrive a day or two prior to the beginning of class.

✳ Lodging

The hotels in Troncones are a world away from what you will find along the beach at Ixtapa. Most of the accommodations are brightly painted open-air bungalows with palm-thatched roofs. All hotels are clean, well maintained, and relatively new.

🐾 🐾 (📶) **Casa Ki** (755-553-2815; www.casa-ki.com), Calle Troncones, Troncones, GRO 40880. $–$$. This lovely boutique hotel located about a mile north of the road leading into Troncones and offers four colorful private bungalows and a main house. Each of the bungalows is uniquely decorated with bright colors and tile floors, and is furnished with a canopied king-size bed and a small refrigerator, as well as a private bathroom with hot water. Each also has a small patio with a hammock and a sitting table, perfect for hanging out in the evening. If necessary, a single bed can be added. The main house has two large bedrooms with en-suite bathrooms and a full kitchen and dining area. On the west side of the house, there is a garden porch that opens onto the Pacific Ocean. Laundry and babysitting services are available. Guests enjoy a simple breakfast of coffee, tea, juice, yogurt, granola and fresh fruit. There is a well-stocked library with board games as well as a communal dining area and a kitchen that is fully equipped with spices and utensils for guests staying in the bungalows.

🐾 **Casa Luciernaga** (U.S. 415-602-4320; www.casafirefly.com), Calle Troncones, Troncones, GRO 40880. $–$$. This is one of the newer hotels in Troncones. It is located about a mile and a half north of the road into town and offers a large, beachfront cottage and two bungalows. The cottage is a two-story open-air structure facing the beach, with three bedrooms and three bathrooms. The bottom floor has a living room with a kitchen and dining area. There is also a bedroom with an ocean view and a queen-size bed. Upstairs, there is another living area in a room with a fantastic view of the ocean. The master bedroom has a queen-size bed and a balcony overlooking the beach. Behind the house, two charming bungalows have queen-size beds and private bathrooms. They are decorated in modern Mexican style, with stained-wood French doors opening onto a small patio with a hammock. These accommodations have a shared kitchen and dining area. In front of

A *PALAPA* BUNGALOW AT CASA LUCIERNAGA.

the house is a small circular pool with a lap lane. Beyond that, the beach beckons—you will find hammocks and *palapa* lean-tos in front of the property.

✦ ⒮ **Casa de la Sirena** (916-425-1258; www.casadelasirena.net), Calle Troncones, Troncones, GRO 40880. $$–$$$. This luxurious beachfront resort is located about a mile north of the road leading into Troncones. Right on the beach, it has eight gorgeous lodgings that can accommodate between two and 20 people. This includes a three-bedroom villa with its own private swimming pool. The spacious master suite is furnished with a king-size bed and is appointed in a warm modern Mexican style with *talevera* tile and unique arts and crafts. It is located on the second floor and opens onto an open-air dining room with a full kitchen that provides dramatic ocean views. Downstairs, two smaller suites are furnished with king-size beds and mini fridges. Each of these rooms has its own poolside patio entrances. The pool area has a gas grill and several chaise longues and opens onto the wide beach at Troncones. There are also three one-bedroom mini-villas spread among a three-story building. They are furnished with a king-size bed and an open-air dining room, with a full kitchen decorated in the same modern Mexican style. The two-story bungalows are furnished with a queen-size bed and a sitting area. On the third floor is a communal kitchen with a stunning view of the beach. Just in front of the beach is a swimming pool with a swim-up bar that is a wonderful place to catch the sunset.

✦ ⒮ **Inn at Manzanillo Bay** (755-553-2884; www.troncones.com.mx/manzanillo), Calle Troncones, Troncones, GRO 40880. $$. This hotel is located several miles north of the road leading into Troncones, beyond the fork in the road that leads to Manzanillo Bay. With eight beachside bungalows, this is one of the larger hotels in Troncones. These bungalows have palm-thatched roofs, ceiling fans, and *talavera* tile floors, and are furnished with canopied king-size beds. They are clustered around a swimming pool and a tropical garden that abuts the beach. Each bungalow has a poolside patio with colorful patio furniture and a hammock for afternoon dozing. The hotel also offers access to a variety of outdoor activities, including horseback riding, tide pooling, snorkeling, mountain biking, and sea kayaking. Additionally, there is a sports shop here that rents and sells surf boards and boogie boards. The hotel's **Garden Patio Beachfront Bar and Grill,** open daily 8 AM–10 PM, offers Mexican and international specialties. This restaurant is located in an attractive open-air *palapa* that provides the perfect atmosphere. The master chef here is a graduate of the California Culinary Academy in San Francisco and has succeeded in provided one of the best dining experiences to be found in Troncones.

✦ **Mi Casa Es Su Casa** (755-553-2910; www.micasasucasa.ws), Calle Troncones, Troncones, GRO 40880. $–$$. MC; V. This air-conditioned hotel is located just north of the road into town and offers 10 comfortable rooms, each uniquely decorated in a modern style and featuring handmade Mexican furniture. Deluxe King Suites, located on the second floor, feature a king-size bed, full kitchen, dining area, and a private balcony overlooking the beach. The two-bedroom suite on the ground floor has a full kitchen and dining area as well as a private patio. One bedroom is furnished with a king-size bed and the other has two double beds. The family suite is also located on the ground floor, with a private patio, and comes with a king-size bed and three double beds. The deluxe family suite offers a full kitchen and dining area, a private patio, one king-size bed and one double bed. There are also poolside bungalows with one king-size bed and a private patio with a hammock. The hotel's **Troncones Steakhouse,** open daily 8 AM–10 PM, offers Mexican and American specialties.

Present Moment Retreat (755-103-0011; U.S. 916–580–3418; www .presentmomentretreat.com), Calle Troncones, Troncones, GRO 40880. $$. AE, DIS, MC, V. This health spa is located north of the road into Troncones just beyond Casa de la Sirena. It specializes in physical, spiritual, and mental rejuvenation through the healing arts of yoga, meditation, Qigong, as well as drumming and dancing. Its 10 beachside bungalows are individually dedicated to such spiritual values as compassion, tranquility, harmony, peace, and serenity. They have *palapa* roofs and are furnished with pillow-top queen-size beds topped with 400-count sheets and a linen canopy. This retreat is centered around an open-air yoga pavilion with a hand-woven canopy suspended on stilts above the beach. This area is large enough to accommodate 26 people. Thus, the calming atmosphere of Playa Troncones provides the backdrop for either group or private instruction. This hotel also has a spa that offers a

variety of massage therapies, including Thai, Balinese, Lomi Lomi, Champassage, and Sukothai. Each session includes a cooling footbath, an outdoor garden shower, and a refreshing herbal drink. Guests also enjoy gourmet cuisine made from fresh seafood and organic vegetables from local growers.

⨍ (ɢᵖ) **Regalo del Mar** (755-553-2865; www.regalodelmar.com), Calle Troncones, Troncones, GRO 40880. $–$$. AE; MC; V. This bed-and-breakfast is located a couple of miles north of the road into Troncones and offers five beach-front bungalows. These bungalows are rustic huts with wooded floors and *palapa* roofs. They are nicely decorated in bright, modern Mexican style and furnished with king-size beds. Farthest back from the beach, you will find the Garden Room and Balcony Suite in a two-story adobe building. On the ground floor, the Garden Suite has a private patio with a garden view while upstairs the Balcony Suite offers a covered deck with a sitting area and lounge. At the center of the property, the Casita Redonda Suite offers a lounge area and a partial ocean view. Just to the west, the Casa Grande offers a large living room and a full ocean view. The hotel also offers a private villa with a living area and a private garden area overlooking the ocean. In front of the beach, you will find a large swimming pool surrounded by tropical gardens. South of the pool, you will find a covered out-door dining area surrounded by palm trees. Next to this, there is a large communal kitchen with a microwave, propane stove, and a dishwasher. Despite its rustic appearance, this hotel has free long-distance calling to the U.S. and Canada, and satellite TV.

BARRA DE POTOSÍ

This small fishing village sits on the southern side of Bahía de Potosí. The bayside beach here, a crescent of pristine sand that sits behind a sheltering headland, is an idyllic setting for tranquil relaxation and a perfect place to unwind in the rippling water. A paved road runs along the beach, providing stunning vistas. A nearby lagoon is home to several beachside seafood restaurants complete with *palapa* roofs and hammocks hanging invitingly in the sea breeze. Have a fish taco, lean back in the hammock, and be entertained by nearby pelicans nose-diving for their meals. Kayaks are available for rental and can be used in either the lagoon or the bay. You can also take a horse ride along the beach or through nearby jungle trails.

COSTA GRANDE'S BEACHES PROVIDE PLENTY OF SOLITUDE FOR ANYONE LOOKING TO ESCAPE THE RESORT CROWDS.

GETTING THERE *By car:* Take Highway 200 about 9 miles south of Zihuatanejo and turn off the road at the signed turnoff at Km 225. Continue along the well-maintained road for about 5 miles. *By bus:* Take the Estrella Blanca bus bound for Petatlán and ask the driver to let you off at the turnoff to Barra de Potosí. Then wait for the Barra de Potosí–bound covered pickup trucks that come along about every half hour during the day.

✳ To Do

BEACHES Playa Arroyo Seco At Km 183, you will find a long stretch of open, wind-swept beach tucked between a sparse grove of coconut palms and incessant waves tumbling on the seashore. There is a wide park-

174

A SUN BATHER WADES INTO THE WATER AT PLAYA ARROYO SECO.

ing area that is sufficient for RV parking and a rustic seafood restaurant where the proprietor, Rita, will serve you fresh handmade corn tortillas and succulent shrimp while you lounge in a hammock. The restaurant, La Esmeralda, is named after her first granddaughter who lives in the United States. This beach is ideal for camping, but be careful when entering the water. The tide can get rough with a strong undertow.

Playa el Calvario Further south along the Costa Grande, past the town of Petatlán, Highway 200 twists over headlands that create cliffs overlooking long stretch of beaches. The many seafood restaurants perched on these cliffs offer rustic fare to road weary travelers. At around Km 185, you will see the turnoff to this beach down a steep dirt road. This beach is a beautiful wide swath of dark sand behind a grove of coconut palms. It is well frequented by pelicans and locals from Petatlán and other nearby communities. It provides a good surfing spot but is not a good place for camping not only because of the access road is slightly treacherous, but also because this flat beach is prone to flooding.

PLAYA EL CALVARIO IS A WIDE STRETCH OF BEACH ALONG THE COSTA GRANDE.

KAYAKING NEAR ZIHUATANEJO.

KAYAK TOURS Zoe Kayak Tours (755-558-8564; www.zoekayaktours.com). This company offers kayak tours through the lagoons of the Barra de Potosí. The routes take are customized by your interests. The longest routes are designed for birdwatchers and adventurous kayakers while the shorter routes have mountain and headland vistas with plenty of bird-watching at a slower pace.

SNORKELING AND SCUBA DIVING Morros de Potosí, located off the coast of Barra de Potosí, has huge islets made of solid granite that rise 90 feet out of the sea. However, of more interest to divers is that they sink to depths of over 100 feet, creating underwater caverns and valleys with huge patches of coral. Most of the diving companies located in nearby Zihuatanejo offer excursions to this location.

Taxco 3

TAXCO

CHILPANCINGO

IGUALA

Michael Brady

Acapulco and Taxco

MÉXICO

MORELOS

PUEBLA

GUERRERO

Cuernavaca

Ixtapan de la Sal
Xochicalco
Miacatlán
Cuautla

*Grutas de
Cacahuamilpa
National Park*
Acuitlapan
Jojutla
Taxco
Tehuixtla

Ixcapuzalco
Ixcateopan

Acapetlahuaya

Teloloapan
Jolalpan

Iguala
Huitzuco

Tepeacuilco

Oxtitlán
Cocula
Atenango
del Río
Temalac

Apaxtla
Copalillo
Ixcamilpa

Balsas

Tlacotepec
Xochipala

Apango

Chichihualco
Acatlán
Atlaca
Chilapa

Corral de Bravo
Atlixtac
Tlaca de
Comonfort

Chilpancingo
Mochitlán

Jaleaca de
Catalán
Colotipa
Zapotitlán
Tablas

Acahuizotla

Tlacuapa

El Ocotito

Ixtapa-
Zihuatanejo
Tierra Colorado

Bajos
del Ejido
Xaltianguis

Pie de
la Cuesta
Ayutla
Tecuanapa

Acapulco

Puerto Marqués
San Marcos
Acatlán

Barra Vieja
Cruz Grande

Puerto Excondido,
Oaxaca

**PACIFIC
OCEAN**

N

0   25   50
Miles

© The Countryman Press

TAXCO

The first thing you will notice about Taxco is the fact that it is built on rugged terrain. Near the city center, narrow streets wind along steep hills leading to the *zócalo*, known as Plaza Borda. This square is dominated by Santa Prisca Parish Church and shaded by manicured Indian laurel trees. Life in Taxco seems to center around this plaza and, therefore, you will want to spend a good amount of time here.

Generally speaking, the people of Taxco are a religious people, which is obvious from the number of churches and shrines around the town. Church bells day and night, marking the time, calling parishioners to attend religious services, and even to knell news of a death. Many people maintain private shrines in their homes that are constantly adorned with fresh-cut flowers. Although it seems strange now, the Mexican government once outlawed religious processions in an effort to curb the power of the Catholic Church. However, today these processions occur routinely in the streets of Taxco. Sometimes, believers make their way from nearby villages to place a religious icon in one of Taxco's churches for a time before returning it to its home village in yet another procession. Taxco is world-famous for its Easter Week processions of penitents. These individuals participate anonymously, their faces covered with hoods, and their motivation to seek penitence is never revealed. These processions are not joyous affairs, nor are they easy to watch. Yet, Taxco is never fails to be full of spectators during Holy Week, there to witness this medieval expression of religious fervor. Whenever you happen to be in Taxco, you will find that the town's churches and religious monuments are wondrous sights unto themselves.

TAXCO'S RUGGED LANDSCAPE PROVIDES MANY BEAUTIFUL VISTAS.

SANTA PRISCA'S FAÇADE DEPICTS THE BAPTISM OF CHRIST.

Taxco's rich culture is easy to spot. A walk along the cobblestone streets in the city center will reveal a hodgepodge of storefronts that have based their livelihood on the attraction of silver. It is what motivated people to settle in this hearty environment in the first place, what built the town's impressive churches, and ultimately what pulled it from obscurity to make it one of the most visited colonial cities in Mexico. This strange mix of commerce based on the silver trade and deeply held religious beliefs has made this a must-see destination for decades. However, travelers have the opportunity to delve even deeper into the regions past by visiting the nearby archaeological sites. From the ruins of a city that was contemporaneous with the Olmec to the final resting place of the last Aztec emperor, the region around Taxco has plenty to interest you.

GUIDANCE For information about local attractions, as well as guided tours, there is a tourist information booth located at the west side of the *zócalo* (Plaza Borda), open daily 9 AM–7 PM. Two other booths with similar hours are located at the north end of town next to the north-end PEMEX gas station and to the south about a quarter mile past the south-end PEMEX gas station; or call 762-622-0542 for tourist information. For a reliable travel agent visit or call the Hotel Posada de la Misión (762-622-1125), where you can arrange tours as well.

GETTING THERE *By bus:* Because of its location between Mexico City and Acapulco, several lines provide regular daily connections to Taxco. The town has

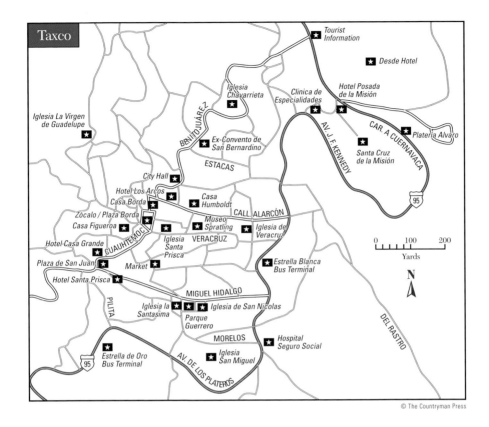

Taxco

Tourist Information

Desde Hotel

Iglesia Chavarrieta

Clínica de Especialidades

Hotel Posada de la Misión

Iglesia La Virgen de Guadelupe

BENITO JUÁREZ

Ex-Convento de San Bernardino

ESTACAS

Platería Alvaro

CAR. A CUERNAVACA

AV. J.F. KENNEDY

Santa Cruz de la Misión

City Hall

Hotel Los Arcos

Casa Borda

Casa Humboldt

CALL ALARCÓN

Zócalo / Plaza Borda

Casa Figueroa

CUAUHTÉMOC

Museo Spratling

VERACRUZ

Iglesia de Veracruz

Hotel Casa Grande

Iglesia Santa Prisca

Plaza de San Juan

Market

Estrella Blanca Bus Terminal

Hotel Santa Prisca

MIGUEL HIDALGO

PILITA

Iglesia la Santasima

Iglesia de San Nicolás

Parque Guerrero

MORELOS

Hospital Seguro Social

DEL RASTRO

Estrella de Oro Bus Terminal

AV. DE LOS PLATEROS

Iglesia San Miguel

0   100   200
Yards

N

one bus terminal operated by Estrella Blanca on the east side of town just below the historic center. Though it is not far, the streets are too steep and narrow to make walking into town a good option.

GETTING AROUND Walking is probably the best option for getting around Taxco once you've gotten your bearings. The cobblestone streets here are narrow and often steep and certainly not intended for cars. Also, they can get congested due to foot traffic. This is particularly true in the early afternoon when children get out of school or in the evening between 7 and 8, when everyone is trying to get home from work. On the other hand,

TAXCO IS A MAZE OF STEEP ALLEYWAYS AND NARROW COBBLESTONE STREETS.

SEMANA SANTA IN TAXCO

Many of us think of Holy Week as that warm and fuzzy pastel period of Peeps and jelly beans, cute bunnies, and prettified eggs. This is not the case in Taxco. The festivities here are as relentless as they are shocking. But one thing is for certain: It's not for everybody.

Taxco's elaborate Holy Week processions and ceremonies have garnered international attention for this small colonial city. During the week between Palm Sunday and Easter, devout Catholics carry out 10 major processions the streets of Taxco. They are each about a mile and a half and last about 2 hours. These ceremonies date back to 1598 when they were carried out in the atrium of the Church of the Ex Monastery of San Bernadino de Siena.

The week begins with the festiveness that is common in traditional Mexican celebrations. Ceremonies begin on Palm Sunday, when people from the countryside stream into town and set up shop around the Santa Prisca Parish Church selling cruci-

THESE 8-FOOT BRONZE STATUES COMMEMORATE TAXCO'S *COFRADIAS.*

fixes made of intricately woven palm leaves. The first procession begins with a parade of children riding bicycles decorated with palm leaves. This is followed by barefooted marchers dressed as the Apostles, priests dousing the crowd with holy water, and a sculpture of Christ under a canopy of flowers. Every day there is another procession through

you will find that this picturesque mountain village provides beautiful views around every corner.

By taxi: Volkswagen beetle taxis and Volkswagen buses known as *combis* provide efficient public transportation in and around Taxco. *Combis* follow a set route and charge a fare of around 50 cents. Keep in mind that most of these minibuses have been modified to fit up to 14 passengers along with the driver. They carry town, and they grow more somber as the week goes on. The celebratory mood disappears altogether during processions are performed by *cofradias*, religious brotherhoods known as the Animas, the Encruzados, and the Flagelentes. For the members of these organizations, Holy Week is a time for penance and, because these are secret brotherhoods, they parade through the streets wearing dark robes cinched with horsehair rope and hoods that show only their eyes. The penance they pay is a mix between the bloody self-atonement practiced in Spain at the time of the Spanish Inquisition and the demonstration of devotion exhibited in indigenous blood rituals.

The Animas are the only *cofradias* to allow women into their organization. Members of this group rattle through the street with chains attached to their ankles and carry small crosses or lighted candles. They are guided by attendants because they stoop at a 90-degree angle as they walk. Members of the Encruzados also perform their procession carrying lit candles. However, they do it with bundles of thorny blackberry branches tied across their bare back and outstretched arms. These bundles typically weigh 100 pounds or more. However, perhaps the most gruesome procession to watch is that of the Flagelentes. Each member of this group carries a large wooden cross, typically weighing over 100 pounds, held aloft in front of them in the crooks of their arms. They stop their procession at predesignated points along the way. However, this is not to allow them to rest. Instead, they hand the cross to an attendant and proceed to flagellate themselves by whipping their back with a rosary with special pointed tips. Alternating from side to side, they quickly develop bloody open sores below each shoulder blade. And because they do this every night of the week, the sores get worse as the week wears on.

Other types of *penitentes* are carried out over the course of the week, including marchers bearing large wooden statues and a person dressed as Judas Iscariot roaming town while rattling 30 pieces of silver. On Friday, mock Roman soldiers reenact the Crucifixion and, on Saturday after mass, these same soldiers fall to their knees after receiving word of the Resurrection. Most people spend Easter Sunday at home with their families and, perhaps, beginning their recovery.

people in and around Taxco beginning around 7 AM and continuing until around 9 PM. *Combis* with "Zócalo" painted on the windshield loop through town from the *zócalo* down to Avenida de los Plateros and up again. This loop will give you a good sense of how the town is laid out. The full circuit will take only about a half hour, or tell the driver where you are trying to get to and he will drop you at the nearest point along the route and tell you how to get there. Taxis are also very inexpensive here. No trip within the town should cost you more than a couple of dollars during the day and $3 at night. Call **Oficina Visitantes Taxi** (762-622-5073).

MEDICAL ASSISTANCE *Hospital:* **Centro de Salud** (762-622-4564), Calle Juan Bautista s/n, Taxco, GRO 40200. *Pharmacy:* **Issste Farmacia [COMP: Note spelling is correct]** (762-622-4747), Calle Pajaritos #14, Taxco, GRO 40200. Open Mon.–Fri. 8 AM–7:30 PM, Sat. 8:30 AM–7:30 PM, Sun. 8:30 AM–3 PM.

BANKS Banamex (762-622-4455), Calle Estacadas #19, Taxco, GRO 40200. Open Mon.–Fri. 8:30 AM–4 PM. **Bancomer** (762-622-8363), Avenida los Plateros #174, Taxco, GRO 40200. Open Mon.–Fri. 8:30 AM–4 PM.

INTERNET CAFÉ X Net Café (762-622-1721), Delicias #4, Taxco, GRO. Open daily 10:30 AM–11 PM. This cybercafé is located near the center of town and offers about eight computers for general use, as well as a printer and a scanner.

USEFUL PHONE NUMBERS
Emergency: 060
Direct-dial prefix, U.S. to Mexico: 011-52
Direct-dial prefix, Mexico to U.S.: 001
Municipal Police 762-622-1017
Red Cross: 762-622-3232

TAXCO'S STREETS WERE NOT DESIGNED FOR AUTOMOBILE TRAFFIC.

LAUNDRY SERVICE Josepha Hernandez Flores (762-622-5100). By appointment only.

✳ To See

Cuetlajuchitlán Archaeological Site Autopista Cuernavaca Km. 188, Cuetlajuchitlán, GRO. Open Tue.–Sun. 10 AM–5 PM. Cuetlajuchitlán (kooay-tlah-hoo-chee-TLAN) is a partially restored archaeological site about 2 miles southeast of the Guerrero village of Paso Morelos, about an hour by car (2 hours by bus) east of Iguala. It was saved from destruction in 1991 during the construction of Cuernavaca-Acapulco Highway 95. Engineers had to adapt this project by constructing the Los Querendes expressway tunnel under the archaeological zone to avoid preserve this archaeological site. The zone itself covers about 90 acres and was once one of the most important pre-Hispanic population centers in the Balsas River Basin. Its development occurred between 800 BC and AD 300. Although the site continues to be excavated, archaeologists have determined that the site developed in three stages. Between 800 and 600 BC, a small Mezcala population erected limestone structures. The placement of these buildings suggests that this population had ties to the Olmec civilization that dominated Mexico's east coast at the time. Between 200 BC and AD 2 00, Cuetlajuchitlán continued to develop. Archaeologists have recovered an abundance of ceramic objects dating from this period, as well as several sculptures and carved cylinders and blocks quarried for the construction of columns and walls. After AD 200, inhabitants began reusing construction materials from previous generations, and by AD 300 the city had been abandoned.

Archaeologists believe that this settlement was once an influential trading hub due to the fact that the type of cylindrical monoliths common to Cuetlajuchitlán can be found throughout the region. The highlight of this site is the Recinto Ceremonial, a 100 by 60-foot enclosure at the center of the ruins, where you will find many stone cylinders as well as ceremonial baths, probably for purification rituals. About 30 yards to the south of this, you will see where the stone cylinders were probably carved. Here, a large number of cylindrical monoliths lie about apparently, amazingly carved but unused. Free admission.

To get to Cuetlajuchitlán by bus from the main bus station in Taxco, take the bus to Huitzuco, a trip that takes about an hour and a half. From here, transfer to the local bus which takes you to Paso Morelos, east of the Cuernavaca-Acapulco Highway 95. From Paso Morelos, walk or take a taxi to the archeological zone (ask for directions). By car from Chilpancingo, take Cuernavaca Acapulco Highway 95D north for about 40 miles to the eastbound turnoff to Paso Morelos. By car from Taxco, take Highway 95 to about 6 miles south of Iguala and take the eastbound turnoff to Huitzuco. Continue on this road for about 25 miles past Huitzuco to Cuernavaca-Acapulco Highway 95D and Paso Morelos. From Paso Morelos, ask for directions to the site.

Casa Borda (762-622-6617), Plaza Borda #1, Taxco, GRO 40200. Open daily 10 AM–7 PM; gallery Tue.–Sat. 10AM–5PM. This town house was

VEHICLES AND FOOT TRAFFIC SEEM TO WEAVE TOGETHER ON TAXCO'S COBBLESTONE STREETS.

originally the 18th-century family home of José de la Borda, who set off Taxco's second silver boom. Today, the house is the Taxco **Casa de Cultura.** It features exhibits by local artists and artisans in the upstairs gallery. The house was built at the same time as the nearby Santa Prisca Cathedral (which Borda also commissioned) and is a good example of the baroque colonial style. The city's irregular terrain gives the house a unique architecture that allows for more floors than are apparent by looking at the building's façade. The interior layout has parallel stairways that lead to sunken patios below street level. There are balconies whose forged- iron handrails are imprinted with anagrams of Jesus, Mary, and Joseph in the mortar. Through the centuries, the house was well maintained by the Borda family and the town of Taxco. In 1981 the governor of Guerrero, Raúl Figueroa Figueroa, designated the house an architectural and historic treasure. Free admission.

Casa Humboldt (762-622-5501), Calle Juan Ruiz de Alarcón #12, Taxco, GRO 40200. Open Tue.–Sat. 10 AM–6 PM, Sun. 10 AM–2 PM. Located near the Spratling Museum, Casa Humboldt is a restored colonial house named for the celebrated German geographer and explorer Alexander von Humboldt, who is said to have spent the night here during his travels through the Spanish colonies in 1803. Over the years, this fine home has been used as a hospital during the Mexican Revolution, as the city's first movie theater and as a hotel. Today, the house is home to Taxco's **Museum of Viceregal Art,** devoted to religious art from the colonial period. This includes displays of religious sculptures and paintings, mostly from the churches of Taxco. $3 admission.

THE CRISTO MONUMENTAL TOWERS OVER TAXCO.

Cristo Monumental, Cristo del Monte Park, Cerro del Atache, Taxco, GRO 40200. Not all of Taxco's religious monuments are centuries old. On the west side of town, high above the *zócalo*, an almost 10-foot statue (including the base) of Christ towers over the city with his arms outstretched. This statue was commissioned by the town's municipal government and erected in 2002 at one of the city's highest points. It presents visitors with a stunning panoramic view of Taxco and the nearby countryside, though getting to it requires some fairly serious uphill

EX CONVENTO DE SAN BERNARDINO DE SIENA IS THE OLDEST BUILDING IN TAXCO.

lo along Calle Cuauhtémoc. After about 2 miles, veer to the right at the Huixteco sign and continue for about 200 yards to the dirt driveway to Cristo del Monte Park. Or save yourself from the grueling walk and take a taxi for about $2.50.

Ex Convento de San Bernardino de Siena, Benito Juárez s/n, Taxco, GRO 40200. This neoclassical structure is considered to be the oldest building in Taxco. It was constructed by Friar Francisco de Torantos and his Franciscan monks in 1592 to be one of the first monasteries in the Americas. In 1598, it was the site of the first Holy Week penitence, which has become an annual tradition in Taxco. This building was originally made completely of adobe. However, it was destroyed by fire and was refurbished with quarry and rubblework in 1804. Shortly thereafter, this church was used by Agustín de Iturbide in negotiations for unifying insurgent forces with the hopes of winning Mexico's independence. Inside, you will find the two important paintings, *Christ of the Silversmiths* and *Gentleman of Santo Entierro*.

Iglesia de Santa Maria de la Asunción, *Zócalo*, Ixcateopan, GRO. Church open Mon.–Sat. 9 AM–3 PM and 4 PM–5 PM, Sun. 9 AM–3 PM; archaeological site open Wed.–Sunday 10 AM–5 PM. Ixcateopan (eeks-kah-tay-OH-pan) is a picturesque village located 28 miles east of Taxco in rugged, pine-forested mountains. Although the town is admired for its furniture makers, it is best known as the final resting place of the last Aztec emperor, Cuauhtémoc. His remains were rediscovered here in 1949 by archaeologist Eulalia Guzmán, who found them under the parish church. This church has since been converted into a museum that displays several pre-Hispanic artifacts as well as the shattered remains of Cuauhtémoc himself. This glass sarcophagus lies over the very spot where he was buried more than 400 years ago. Next door, there is a small museum dedicated to Cuauhtémoc and his defense of Tenochtitlán, the Aztec capital. This whitewashed church borders the town plaza, where you will find a monument to the Aztec emperor. Down the hill 3 blocks along Calle Guerrero is an archaeological site that was once a ceremonial complex. Free admission. To get here from Taxco, take the *colectivo* van labeled "Ixcateopan" from the main bus station.

Museo Guillermo Spratling (762-622-1660), Calle Porfirio A. Delgado #1, Taxco, GRO 40200. Open Tue.–Sun. 9 AM–5 PM. Located just off Plaza Borda behind the cathedral, this was the house that belonged to the American architect and writer William G. Spratling. He arrived here from New Orleans in the 1930s and was enchanted by Taxco. He set up a silver jewelry shop specializing in designs that combined indigenous motifs and art deco styles. Many of these designs have become iconic with Taxco's silversmiths and inspired Mexican artisans to create pieces that were not tethered to traditional European forms. Spratling's appreciation and patronage of the Taxco brought about an economic revival that continues to this day. The museum features works of indigenous-style art from Spratling's private collection, as well as some fine examples of his signature jewelry, tableware, and other decorative pieces. Because of his influence, Spratling has been called "the father of Mexican silver." $3 admission.

Museo Platería (762-622-0658), Plaza Borda, Taxco, GRO 40200. Open daily 10 AM–6 PM. This museum is located near Taxco's town square, on the third floor of a building known as the Patio de las Artesanías. It was created by the famous Taxco silversmith Antonio Pineda and was inaugurated in 1988 during a national celebration of Mexican silver. This museum illustrates the history of the Taxco silversmithing industry. On display, you will find a number of prize-winning pieces by well-various Taxco artists, including a few by William Spratling, regarded as the creator of the Taxco silversmith tradition. $3 admission.

Museo Regional de Chilpancingo (747-472-8088), Plaza Civica Primer Congreso de Anahuac s/n, Chilpancingo, GRO 39000. Open Tue.–Sun. 9 AM–6 PM. Located at the center of the city, this museum illustrates the natural and cultural history of the state of Guerrero. One of the main attractions is the faded but still impressive mural by Roberto Cueva del Río and Luis Arenal, which depicts the history of Guerrero and wraps around the entire inner patio. The building that houses the museum dates back to 1902, when the president Porfirio Díaz was attempting to modernize Mexico by commissioning works inspired by French and Italian architectural models. The museum has six rooms, including one that is a panoramic depiction of the local ecology. Other exhibits depict important Guerrero historical events. $2 admission.

Parroquia de la Preciosa Sangre de Cristo en Chavarrieta (762-622-1581), Plazuela de Chavarrieta s/n, Taxco, GRO 40200. This pretty little church, which is located several blocks north of Plaza Borda, is the epitome of a small Mexican puebla church. Dating from 1923, it has a fairly straightforward neoclassical façade that features twin bell towers. The entire exterior is painted white with brick red accents. It is located inside its own little plaza cobbled with stone masonry. Inside the church, the main altar features a golden arch held aloft by polished marble columns, under which is the image of the crucifixion. This is encircled by the words *Dios Es Amor* (God Is Love). Flanking the altar is a series of arches of various sizes.

Parroquia de Santa Prisca (762-622-0184), Plaza Borda, Taxco, GRO 40200. This beautiful baroque church is a masterpiece of Churrigueresque architecture located in the heart of Taxco. The façade is composed of pink quarry and is intricately decorated with representations of saints surrounded by cherubs, arches, and spiraled columns that accentuate its vertical grandeur. At the center of all of this is a medallion depicting the baptism of Christ. Above is a small chancel window with a rounded gable. Its twin bell towers are some of the most profusely ornamented examples of the baroque style in all of Mexico. The church's arched door is flanked on each side by a pair of Corinthian columns that enclose

PARROQUIA DE LA PRECIOSA SANGRE DE CRISTO EN CHAVARRIETA.

THE PARROQUIA DE SANTA PRISCA CAN BE SEEN FROM ALMOST ANYWHERE IN TAXCO.

sculptures. The interior of the church is superbly carved, gilded, and painted with many depictions of angels and saints. There are 13 gilded altarpieces and many paintings. The main altar is made of intricately embossed woodwork covered with gold leaf. There is also an impressive pipe organ that arrived from Germany by ship in Veracruz in 1751 and was then shipped overland by mule pack.

This church was designed and built by the architects Diego Durán and Juan Caballero between 1751 and 1758. This church was paid for by José de la Borda to express his gratitude for the fortune in silver he unearthed in the hills around Taxco. His brother, Manuel de la Borda, was the church's first priest. Portraits of the two men, along with a portrait of Pope Benedict XIV, who sanctioned the church, hang in a somber gallery just off the main chamber.

Santuario del Señor de la Santa Veracruz (762-622-7676), Domicilio Conocido, Taxco, GRO 40200. This charming little church is located about four blocks east of Plaza Borda, behind Santa Prisca past the Spratling Museum. It has a neoclassical design with twin bell towers and a clock built into the façade. Perhaps the most impressive thing about this clock is the fact that it actually works. The church was constructed in 1847 and is best known for housing a carved figure known affectionately as "The General." This figure is an image of Christ that is carried at the front of the town's famous Holy Week processions.

Xochicalco (777-312-3108), Zona Arqueológica, Xochicalco, Morelos, 62790. Open daily 10 AM–5 PM. Located about 2 hours' driving time north of Taxco,

SANTUARIO DEL SEÑOR DE LA SANTA VERACRUZ.

Xochicalco (zoe-chi-CAL-co) is one of Mexico's best-restored archaeological sites. In Nahuatl, the name means "In the House of Flowers." The apex of Xochicalco culture came after the fall of Teotihuacan, a mysterious ancient site north of Mexico City. Some archaeologists have speculated that Xochicalco may have played a part in the fall of the empire. The first descriptions of this site were published in 1777 by explorer José Antonio Alzate. Mexican archaeologist Leopoldo Batres restored the Temple of the Feathered Serpent in 1910. Several other major archaeological excavations and further restorations were done between 1940 and 1970. In the mid-1970s, archaeologists from Penn State mapped the entire site and conducted excavations of houses and obsidian workshops.

The main ceremonial center sits atop a hill, with remains of mostly unexca-

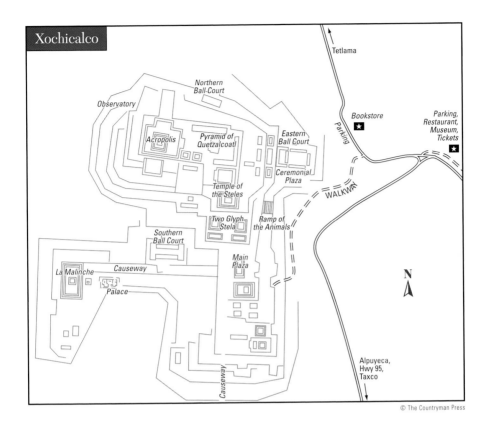

vated residential structures covering the slopes. This hill has been modified in order to improve the defense of the city. The site was first occupied around 200 BC but did not develop into an urban center until sometime around AD 700. Nearly all the standing architecture at the site was built during this period. At its peak, the city may have had up to 20,000 residents. At some point around AD 900, the city was destroyed. A number of the excavated structures show evidence of this destruction. However, in these devastated structures, archaeologists found many objects undisturbed, as if the site was destroyed and abandoned quickly. Around AD 1200, the site was resettled by the Nahuatl-speaking people, ancestors to the Nahuatl-speaking population that continues to live in the area to this day.

Perhaps the most impressive feature of the site is sculptured reliefs on the sides of some buildings. For example, the Temple of the Feathered Serpent has stylized depictions of Quetzalcoatl, the feathered serpent god. Due to the fact that depictions of this deity can be found elsewhere, it has been speculated that Xochicalco may have had a community of artists from other parts of Mesoamerica. Other monuments at the site include several step-pyramids, ball courts, sweat-baths, and free-standing sculptured stelae. There is also an observatory in a cave that allowed these people to study of the movement of the sun. The cave was covered with stucco and fixed with a chimney with a small opening that allows the sun's rays to be projected on the floor of the cave. In mid-May and late July, the sun shines directly through the chimney onto an image of the sun on the floor of the cave. Visitors are allowed to enter this observatory in the afternoon. $5 admission.

You can get to Xochicalco by taxi or through local tour companies. To drive here, take old Highway 95 north out of Taxco for about 50 miles to the town of Alpuyeca. Then take the road west toward Miacatlán for about 10 miles. Watch for the signs to Xochicalco.

✳ To Do

If you are looking for outdoor recreation during your time in Taxco, there is plenty of beautiful scenery to be had on the outskirts of town. Just 6 miles away, you will find the Alexander von Humboldt National Park, which offers an abundance of pine and oak forests ideal for enjoying a long walk through a wooded trail. For a long walk underground, the Grutas de Cacahuamilpa should not be missed. This amazing cave structure is a little further afield but well worth the trouble of getting there. If you are without a car, buses to these caves leave regularly from the main bus station.

CABLE CAR **Teleférico Cableway** Paseo de los Plateros and Avenida Lomas de Taxco s/n, Taxco, GRO 40210. Open daily 8 AM–7 PM. This cable car runs 800 meters from the Paseo de los Plateros up to one of the highest points in the city. Along the way, it reaches heights above the city of more than 550 feet. From the suspended cable car, you can take in the panoramic view and observe the haphazard layout of the city and the lush hills of the surrounding countryside. The entire trip lasts about 5 minutes and ends at the Hotel Monte Taxco, where you can go for a swim in the hotel pool, go horseback riding, play some tennis, or just have lunch with a beautiful view of the city. 30 pesos per roundtrip.

COUNTRY CLUB **Monte Taxco Country Club** (762-622-1300), Avenida Lomas de Taxco s/n, Taxco, GRO 40210. Open daily 9 AM–7 PM. Visitors to this country club located at the Hotel Monte Taxco can rent horses for around $15 per hour to go for a horseback ride along the pine tree–lined trails around the hotel. If you're itching to hit the links, there is a nine-hole golf course available to nonguests of the hotel for around $50 per person. There are also some good tennis courts here that can be had for around $14 per hour. Call or visit the country club sports desk located on the hotel grounds.

HIKING **Alejandro Humboldt National Park** This natural reserve is located 6 miles northwest of Taxco, off State Highway 55. It is comprised of 2,667 acres of tick pine and oak forests that offer stunning natural scenery and vigorous hiking. There are many nature trails as well as camp sites available.

Cascada de Cacalotenango A good hiking spot known as the Cerro el Cedro, or Cedar Hill, lies 8 miles northwest of Taxco, off State Highway 55. This area features a thick coniferous forest with several miles of trails. Along the way, the forest occasionally opens up into open fields that make a beautiful spot to stop for a breather. Follow these trails along a stream called the Plan de Campos, which leads to a 264-foot freefalling waterfall known as the Cascada de Cacalotenango. The top of this waterfall offers a panoramic view of the entire area. It is best to hire a guide to bring you to this spot. Be sure to bring water and appropriate clothing.

Grutas de Cacahuamilpa National Park (721-104-0155; http://cacahuamilpa .conanp.gob.mx), Municipio de Pilcaya, GRO 40391. Open daily 10 AM–7:30 PM. This park is located 32 miles northeast of Taxco via Federal Highway 166. Despite the fact that this site is a bit out of the way, it truly is a must see if you have any interest in geology. The Grutas de Cacahuamilpa (cah-cah-wah-MIL-pah) is one of the largest cave systems in the world, and well worth the trouble of getting to them, evidenced by the 350,000 people who visit the park annually. This live cave system continues to filter groundwater causing the rock formations to continue to grow. Inside, the cave system that stretches for more than a mile is open to the public, there is a series of large caverns separated by large natural rock walls and connected to one another via a well-lit central gallery. There are many more miles of this cave system that have yet to be fully explored. These caverns average about 130 feet in width and range in height from about 65 and to 265 feet. In one cavern, a permanent auditorium has been erected and can be rented out for events. In another cavern toward the end of the tour is the gravesite of an Englishman who got lost while exploring with his dog and eventually died of starvation. He sent the dog to get aid. However, when no one paid any attention to it, the dog returned to the cave to be with its master. Their remains were found together and they were buried in the cave under a simple cross.

THE GRUTAS DE CACAHUAMILPA ARE A VAST CAVE SYSTEM WELL WORTH A VISIT.

Sections of this cave system have been known for centuries and some have been used since pre-Hispanic times. Excavations in the caverns have produced fragments of Olmec and Chontal pottery, suggesting that these tribes used the caves for ceremonial purposes. Indigenous people called these caves Salachi, though the current name, Cacahuamilpa, means "peanut field" and refers to a location near the cave entrance. Indigenous people kept the caves hidden from their Spanish conquerors. In 1834, a man by the name of Manuel Saénz de la Peña used the caves to hide from authorities. This prompted a thorough search of the area and thus, the caves were "discovered." The caves were opened to the public in the 1920s. The first scientific expedition of the caves was done in 1935 and the national park was established in 1936 by President Lázaro Cárdenas.

Cave tours run every hour and last about 2 hours. These tours involve a roundtrip walk of about 3 miles and they are conducted in Spanish. However, even if your Spanish is very limited, the caves are impressive enough to be appreciated without the benefit of an explanation. The majority of this tour is over a flat, paved surface, though at the deepest point open to the public, the terrain gets a bit rough and is not recommended for older visitors. During the tour, the guide lights each cavern as you enter. However, on your way out of the caves, the only light comes from small lamps lighting the pathway out. There are a number of natural wonders in Mexico that have been poorly cared for and suffer from the litter and negligence left behind by previous visitors—unfortunately, Isla Roqueta off the coast of Acapulco comes to mind. This is not the case at the Grutas de Cacahuamilpa. This park is well maintained and clean. It has two underground rivers called Chontalcoatlán, which is 5 miles long, and San Jeronimo, which is more than 7 miles long. These rivers continue to cut away at the rock little by little. Both have sandy underground beaches that sit in complete darkness. They reemerge above ground and join to form the Amacuazac River, which is a tributary of the Balsas River. The park is also home to Limontitla Botanical Garden, which features the native flora that exists in the subtropical, deciduous forest that surrounds the cave entrance. You can tour the garden alone or with a guide. The best time to visit the garden is between October and June during the rainy season when everything is green and in full bloom. 30 pesos admission.

Buses to the site leave hourly from the main bus station in Taxco beginning at 8:30. Look for the word "Grutas" written on the windshield. The fare is about $2 each way. Be sure to tell the driver where you want to get off and pay attention to make sure you don't miss it. By car, take Highway 95 north from Taxco and continue for about 10 miles. When the road forks, stay left onto Highway 55 toward Toluca and continue for another 5 miles until you see the sign for the Grutas de Cacahuamilpa. The turnoff is to the right.

RAFTING Mezcala River Rafting Located 77 miles southeast of Taxco, this river presents a challenge for rafting enthusiasts. As you make your way down the river, choose among various routes that offer rapids of varying difficulty levels. The river was once the starting point for the Balsas River Nautical Marathon.

THE MEZCALA RIVER IS A TRIBUTARY OF THE BALSAS RIVER.

Z O O ✏ **Zoofari** (751-351-9001; www.zoofari.com.mx), Km 55 Carretera Federal Cuernavaca-Taxco, Teacalco, MOR, 62320. Open daily 9 AM–5 PM. Just a 40-minute drive from Taxco, this zoological park opened in May 1984 with the goal of providing visitors with the opportunity to observe various animal species up close or from the comfort of your car. The park is now home to 1,200 animals of 150 different species. Visitors tour the grounds mostly by car along on safari-like roads that take you through the animal paddocks where you are able to observe them in a somewhat natural environment. Many of the animals are endangered and have managed to reproduce successfully at the park. And, just in case you're wondering, yes, visitors are occasionally witness to the animals engaging in this as well (beware of frisky zebras). Visitors are able to get surprisingly close to some animals, such as the hippos, which are kept in fenced enclosures. Some visitors are also given the opportunity to feed some animals, such as the giraffes, ostriches, camels, and antelopes. The park tends to be lusher between the months of June and December. This is also the period when many of the animals are birthing. To get here, take Highway 95 North toward Cuernavaca. The park is located at Km. 55. Look for the signs when you cross into Morelos. 130 pesos adults, 110 pesos children.

✳ Lodging

Because of where Taxco is located, you should be prepared to walk up a lot of stairs and steep grades during your stay. Most of the more interesting hotels are located in buildings that are at least a century old and do not have elevators. Furthermore, the city is located on the side of a mountain and several of the hotels are actually built into the side of it. Although you'll undoubtedly see local women wearing them, this is not a town that has been constructed with high heels in mind. Be sure to pack some comfortable walking shoes.

Lodging here is generally less

expensive than what you will find along the coast. You can usually find inexpensive accommodations for less than $75 per night, and it's certainly not unheard-of to find adequate lodging for $50 per night or less even at the city center if you don't mind a no-frills room. Rates tend to go up a bit during the high tourist season of December 15 to April 1, when days are sunny and clear and nights are crisp and cool. However, during festivals such as Semana Santa, prices go up rather dramatically. Lodging in the other towns of the Guerrero upcountry are usually very basic and generally meant for business travelers rather than tourists. Most hotels in the upcountry fall in the inexpensive range of under $100 a night. There are some moderate hotels in Taxco with rates up to $175 a night.

Although there are several adequate hotels on the outskirts of town, it makes more sense to stay closer to the city center, particularly if you are without a car. The hotels near the *zócalo* tend to be smaller and offer fewer amenities, but what these establishments do have—besides convenience—is authentic colonial Mexican ambience. Here there are several inviting boutique hotels in well-maintained colonial buildings. They invariably have lovely patios or terraces that often provide and fine view of the city and are always a good place to sit back and relax. However, if you happen to be in town during a festival, it is a good idea to request a room away from the busiest streets. Noise can be a serious problem if your window happens to open onto throngs of people laughing and speaking loudly late into the night.

𝄡 (ᵒ) **Agua Escondida** (762-622-0726), Plaza Borda #4, Taxco, GRO 40200. $. Situated right on the *zócalo*, this hotel has a fantastic location for getting to know and exploring Taxco. Its 50 rooms, spread out among three floors, are simply but adequately appointed in Mexican colonial style and furnished with two double beds. At Agua Escondido (Hidden Waters), the hotel earns its name with its swimming pool, located on the roof toward the back of the building. In fact, the entire layout of the hotel is an interesting multilevel maze leading to hidden patios and a rooftop terrace that provides a great view of the *zócalo* and the nearby mountains. Here you will find **La Terraza Bar,** open daily noon–11, a great place to relax after a long day of touring around. The hotel also has a small restaurant, open daily 7:30 AM–10:30 PM, decorated with handmade Mexican chairs and tables, which serves Mexican cuisine.

(ᵒ) **Los Arcos Hotel** (762-622-1836; www.hotellosarcos.net), Calle Juan Ruiz de Alarcon #4, Taxco, GRO 40200. $. Just a short walk from the town's main plaza, this hotel occupies a converted monastery built in 1620. Its 21 rooms are decorated in colorful Mexican colonial style with woven blankets and carved headboards. There are also natural tile floors, original artwork, and handmade wooden furniture. These rooms are intimate and relatively spacious. The hotel also has an attractive stone fountain in a central courtyard complete with handmade pottery and rustic furnishings, surrounded completely by the three vine-draped levels of the guest rooms. Guests enter this courtyard under a series of brick arches held aloft by carved columns. This area is worth a visit just for its 17th-century authenticity. The hotel also boasts an elevated terrace that offers a spectacular view of the town, which seems to rise up on all sides with colonial beauty.

((ŋ)) **Emilia Castillo Hotel** (762-622-6717; www.hotelemiliacastillo.com, Juan Ruiz de Alarcon #7, Taxco, GRO 40200. $. AE; DC; MC; V. Only one block off the main plaza, this hotel has 14 rooms handsomely appointed in colonial Mexican style, with carved doors, handmade wood furniture, oil paintings, stone sculptures, and tiled bathrooms. The rooms are fairly small but comfortable and furnished two double beds. If you are visiting during a festival, be sure to request an interior room, infinitely quieter than those facing the street, which can sound like the party is in bed with you. All of the rooms open onto a central courtyard, adding to the hacienda feeling of the place. Inside, you will find a small wine bar that makes a great place for sharing an intimate conversation. Guests are provided with a free continental breakfast upon request.

((ŋ)) **Hotel Casa Grande** (762-622–0969; www.hotelcasagrande .com.mx), Plazuela de San Juan #7, Taxco, GRO 40200. $. This hotel is located on Plazuela de San Juan, which is right off Plaza Borda. This means not only do the rooms have lovely views of the city, but also the hotel is conveniently located near all of Taxco's main attractions. The downside is that the ancillary noise from the street can make it hard to sleep at night. In fact, some of the loudest noises come from La Concha Nostra nightclub, which is located right in the hotel itself. This is only a problem

on the weekends and during festivals. However, if a good night's sleep is important to you, you may want to think twice about this hotel. That said, the hotel's 12 rooms are basic but very clean, featuring bright fabrics and hand-made Mexican furniture. They are simply furnished with double beds and can accommodate one to five people.

((ŋ)) **Hotel Monte Taxco** (762-622-1301; www.montetaxco.com.mx), Avenida Lomas de Taxco s/n, Taxco, GRO 40210. $$. AE; MC; V. This 170-room hotel offers plenty of country-club amenities that are relatively rare in Taxco. It is located on the city outskirts, away from most of the main attractions. However, if you happen to be in Taxco during a festival, staying at this hotel you will not have to deal with the street noise the way would if you were to stay in town. The hotel is accessible by cable car from the edge of town, or you can take a fairly short and inexpensive cab ride into town. The rooms here are fairly standard, fully carpeted but otherwise decorated in Mexican colonial style. On site are three restaurants that serve Mexican and international cuisine. The hotel also boasts a swimming pool, a gym, a 9-hole golf course, and a tennis court.

✦ **Hostal Villa San Francisco** (762-622-7458), Estaciadas #2, Taxco, GRO 40200. $. This pretty little, family-run, hacienda-style hotel is a short walking distance from the city center. Its 10 rooms are decorated in a sparse but authentic colonial Mexican style. These rooms are furnished with two double beds as well as carved doors and wooden furniture. The property has a gorgeous little interior courtyard with carved statues and there is also a small pool on the property that is straddled by an arched walkway. It helps to know a little Spanish if you are going to stay here.

❧ ✿ **Loma Linda Hotel** (762-622-0206; www.hotellomalinda.com), Avenida de los Plateros #52, Taxco, GRO 40200. $. AE; MC; V. This hotel is perched on a hillside that overlooks a long valley. Its 70 rooms open onto a terrace that provide nice views of the valley as well as a nearby hacienda. These rooms are appointed in a simple, neocolonial style and are furnished with wooden Mexican furniture. Standard rooms have either a single or double bed. There is also a central courtyard with a small heated swimming pool. A playground is located on the property. Loma Linda is a bit out of the way, so you may need to get a taxi to get where you need to go. Next to the hotel, you will find **Café Balbas,** open daily 7:30 AM–10 PM, which serves traditional Mexican fare.

Hotel Mi Casita (762-627-1777; www.hotelmicasita.com), Altos de Redondo #1, Taxco, GRO 40200. $. AE; DIS; MC; V (PayPal in advance). Once the workshop of an apprentice of William Spratling, this is the only bed & breakfast in Taxco and is located in a large colonial house in the heart of Taxco. Its 12 uniquely appointed rooms, distributed among three floors, are furnished with queen-size or double beds. They are decorated in Mexican colonial style with carved wooden doors, handmade furniture, and antique *talavera* tile. These rooms open onto a terrace that overlooks the town. In the morning, you will wake to gourmet a breakfast served in a charming and intimate dining room. If you happen to be driving through Taxco, gated parking is available at the hotel for a small fee. The hotel also features a lending library.

THE HOTEL MI CASITA IS TYPICAL OF TAXCO ARCHITECTURE.

Posada de la Misión (762-622-5519; www.posadamision.com), Cerro de la Misión #32, Taxco, GRO 40200. $$–$$$. AE; MC; V. This hotel has 90 comfortable rooms and suites in a beautiful brick and stone colonial building near downtown Taxco. The accommodations vary widely depending on the size of the room; for the most part, the rooms are smallish but nicely decorated in neocolonial style with stained-wood furniture and arched windows; some even have fireplaces. Be aware that those rooms facing the street can be noisy during festivals. The hotel terrace is a lovely place to sit and enjoy the day in full view of the Santa Prisca Parish Church that dominates the Taxco scenery. The hotel also has an art gallery, as well as a small but attractive swimming pool and an adjoining bar where you can lounge and enjoy a wide variety of drinks. In addition to the poolside bar, there is also a piano bar and a coffee shop, as well as the hotel's **El Mural Restaurant,** open daily 8 AM–10 PM, which serves traditional Mexican fare.

✦ **Posada de San Javier** (762-622-0231), Calle Estacadas #32, Taxco, GRO 40200. $. This hotel is located near enough to the central plaza to be convenient but far enough to provide a little seclusion. Its 18 rooms and 7 suites are nicely appointed in Mexican colonial style. The rooms are furnished with two double beds, whereas the suites have one bedroom apiece and are equipped with living rooms and kitchenettes. These accommodations are decorated individually, and they are simple yet comfortable. They are arranged haphazardly around a large, lush garden with a modest-size swimming pool and an attractive

stone wishing well. This area is adorned with a mural by noted Mexican artist Juan O'Gorman, with a silver workshop and boutique that sells silver jewelry. There is also a restaurant on the property called **Café del Convento,** open daily 7:30 AM–9 PM, which serves traditional Mexican cuisine. Staying at this hotel will give you a sense of what life was like in Taxco in years past.

((ᵠ)) **Santa Prisca** (762-622-0080), Cenaobscuras #1, Taxco, GRO 40200. $. AE; MC; V. This hotel, one of the oldest in the city, is well maintained and has a great location right in the heart of Taxco. However, this location is both a blessing and a curse, as there is a nearby disco that tends to play its music loud enough to be heard in certain rooms late at night on some weekends. If you will be in town

THE SANTA PRISCA PARISH CHURCH AT NIGHT.

during a festival or a holiday, be sure to mention this when making your reservation and get assurances that you will not be placed in one of these rooms. The 32 small rooms are nicely furnished with two double beds and feature tile floors, wooden beams overhead, and an authentic colonial atmosphere. Some rooms also have terraces and fireplaces. These rooms are certainly not luxurious but you will find that they are comfortable and very clean. There is a reading area in an upstairs salon that overlooks the town, as well as a nice garden patio complete with stone fountains. An on-site restaurant, open mornings only, 7 –11, serves a nice Mexican-style breakfast.

✳ Where to Eat

In the 1986 movie *Three Amigos,* Chevy Chase can't figure out how to eat the food given to him by his hosts in a small Mexican pueblo, so he looks at them and delivers the deadpan line, "You got anything besides Mexican food?" In Taxco, the answer to that question is definitely yes. In fact, nearly all of the restaurants in Taxco offer traditional Mexican specialties such as mole, tortilla soup, and enchiladas. However, they tend to combine their menus with selections from a variety of other types of cuisines. Many carry pizza and pasta, or classics from north of the border such as club sandwiches and burgers. However, some offer completely unexpected dishes such as French onion soup, chow mein, and even

A FEW WORDS ABOUT BATHROOMS AND TOILET PAPER

One of the less delicate issues that you will quickly face when you are traveling in Mexico, particularly in less tourist-centered areas, is the differences in bathroom etiquette. Toilet paper tends to clog most Mexican plumbing and septic systems to the point where it sometimes even requires digging up the pipes to clear them. Therefore, it is necessary to deposit used paper into the wastebasket that is invariably placed next to the toilet. Many moderate and expensive hotels understand that this is more than a minor culture shock to their American guests and have gone to the trouble to equip rooms with plumbing that can handle toilet paper. However, you shouldn't assume this is the case unless there is a sign posted in the bathroom directing you to flush toilet paper. Part of the draw of small hotels in places like Taxco and Zihuatanejo is the architecture and many of these old buildings simply have not been brought up to the standards that you are used to. Quite often, there will be a sign explicitly asking you *not* to flush your used toilet paper. Also, women should never flush feminine products, whatever the modernity of an establishment (and this is true in the States as well). You may find this unpleasant but it's better than dealing with a room with a stopped-up toilet.

falafel. Most of the city's better eateries are located along and around the Plaza Borda in the center of town. However, notable exceptions include the restaurants located high above the city at the Hotel Monte Taxco. It's interesting that Taxco does not have the tradition of street vendors that you will find in many other Mexican colonial cities such as Guanajuato, Urúapan, and Oaxaca. However, whatever your budget, there are plenty of good restaurants to choose from in this lovely city.

DINING OUT (•) **Acerto** (762-622-0064; www.acertorestaurante.com) Plaza Borda #12, Taxco, GRO 40200. $$. MC; V. Open daily for lunch and dinner 11–11. This restaurant located right on Plaza Borda is hard to define because it is sort of an all-purpose hangout. From the street, it looks like it could be an upscale restaurant. The lovely arched entrance, impeccable view of Plaza Borda, and the menu, which has some nice entrées, supports this ambience. However, the dining room feels more like a cafeteria and it also doubles as an Internet café and sports bar. Nonetheless, this is a great place to relax and enjoy the view. It's also a good place to meet fellow travelers. This restaurant is well known for its pizza, though they do have an extensive menu, including espresso drinks and desserts.

Aladinos (762-627-6170), Calle Benito Juarez #19, Taxco, GRO 40200. $$. Open daily for breakfast, lunch, and dinner 9 AM–midnight. This restaurant offers a variety of Italian dishes

There are other differences that you are likely to run into when you are out and about and discover that you need to use the public restroom. First of all, janitorial work is largely considered "women's work" in much of Mexico. Therefore, it is always possible that men may be surprised by an elderly female janitor entering the restroom while they are taking care of their business. If this happens, do your best to maintain a blasé attitude, remembering that you're not doing anything she hasn't dealt with before. Also, you will likely find well-stocked facilities in high-end establishments that cater to tourists; however, you cannot always count on this. More often, public restrooms will cost a few pesos and an attendant will hand you a few squares of toilet paper when you enter. There are still other places where you will find no toilet paper at all and perhaps even the toilet seats will be missing. It's best to be well prepared, especially if you are traveling with children, who seem to have the habit of having to go at the worst possible moments. Be sure to pack a roll of toilet paper or—even better—a travel pack of baby wipes before you leave your hotel for the day. It is also a very good idea to also bring along a small bottle of disinfectant lotion, which you can pick up at any drugstore or pharmacy. This will go a long way toward making sure you don't pick up any of those nasty digestion problems that Mexico is so famous for.

ALADINO'S PATIO PROVIDES NICE VIEWS OF TAXCO AND THE SURROUNDING AREA.

as well as some interesting soups and energizing juices. While the menu does feature several classic Mexican dishes, some of the most popular menu items here are the *spaghetti boloñesa* and hand-made pizzas of all types. They also have a full bar here with a good selection of beers and wines, as well as homemade cheesecake and espresso drinks. For the best seating, continue through the first dining area all the way to the rooftop patio where you will dine under the shadow of the Santa Prisca Parish Church.

El Atrio (762-627-3655) Calle Estacadas #32, Taxco, GRO 40200. $$. Open daily for breakfast, lunch, and dinner 9 AM–10 PM. This pretty little restaurant is located near the Ex Convento de San Bernardino de Siena. The dining room is located in a long room framed with a series of arches with a couple dozen wooden tables topped with linen tablecloths. The menu here is rather eclectic with such items as Greek salad, Parmesan chicken, and French onion soup. To be

sure, the menu has many traditional Mexican items as well. For dessert, you will delight in the caramel crepes and espresso drinks.

Café del Convento (762-622-3272), Calle Estacadas #32, Taxco, GRO 40200. $$. MC; V. Open daily for breakfast and lunch 7:30–5:30 and dinner 6–10:30; brunch Sun. 8–noon. This restaurant offers an interesting blend of classic Mexican dishes and unexpected international fare. For example, you may be in the mood for some traditional *bistec a la tampiqueña* or perhaps for something from north of the border, such as filet mignon . . . or maybe a more Mediterranean flavor such as shish kebab. This restaurant can accommodate any of these urges. They also offer a selection of salads and seafood dishes. The rooftop patio offers a wonderful spot to linger over a dish of ice cream or an espresso drink in the evening. Guests of the Hotel Posada San Javier may order poolside service off the menu as well.

Café Sasha (762-627-6464), Calle Juan Ruiz de Alarcón #1, Taxco, GRO 40200. $$. Open daily for breakfast, lunch, and dinner 8 AM–midnight. Looking for some variety? Well, this restaurant offers dishes from around the world, including Thai chicken, French crepes, vegetarian curry, chow mein, and falafel. As you can see, many of the dishes here are vegetarian classics, making this a good selection for the meat-averse traveler. They also have a selection of desserts, coffee, and espresso drinks. On Saturday nights, this restaurant also features live music with local talents.

Del Angel Inn Restaurant (762-622-5525), Calle de Celso Muñoz #4, Taxco, GRO 40200. $$. AE; MC; V. Open daily for breakfast, lunch, and dinner 8 AM–10 PM. This lovely restaurant is located right off Plaza Borda and has a rooftop terrace that provides beautiful views of the city. Likewise, the inner dining area is also attractively decorated with stone columns and angels painted on the walls. The menu features a nice combination of Mexican specialties such as Oaxacan enchiladas and tortilla soup, paired with international favorites such as shrimp scampi and T-bone steak. The ambience will make you want to linger, so follow up with a coffee and dessert. There is also an extensive wine list featuring both Mexican and international selections.

Sotavento Restaurante-Bar (762-627-1217), Benito Juárez #12, Taxco, GRO 40200. $$. MC; V. Open for breakfast, lunch, and dinner Tue.–Sun. 8 AM–11:30 PM. This stylish restaurant features an attractive inner dining room as well as a lush garden patio with beautiful colonial architecture. It makes a good choice for anybody looking for a nice restaurant to have a romantic meal. The extensive menu features a selection of Mexican and Italian specialties such as tortilla soup and spaghetti with cream sauce. They also offer crepes and salads as well as vegetarian selections. Additionally, they offer a good selection of wines and beers.

(((•))) **La Terraza** (762-622-0663), Plazuela Borda #4, Taxco, GRO 40200. $$. AE; MC; V. Open for lunch and dinner noon–11. One of two restaurants within the Hotel Agua Excondida, the rooftop La Terraza offers a beautiful view of the Plaza Borda and the surrounding city. The menu offers a wide range of cuisine with everything from grilled pork chops to chicken fajitas to breaded veal. And while this restaurant offers a romantic ambience for dinner, it is a very popular place to enjoy an espresso drink or an after-dinner cocktail. There are patio umbrellas for shade during the day and at night it is a nice place to sit back and do some star gazing. Bring your laptop because there is also free wireless Internet here.

Toni's Restaurante (762-622-1300), Lomas de Taxco, Taxco, GRO 40210. $$$. AE; MC; V. Open for dinner Tue.–Sat. 7–1. Located high above the city at the Monte Taxco Hotel, this steak and seafood restaurant provides diners with a beautiful panoramic view the surrounding countryside. The restaurant's dining area is located inside a huge palapa with about a dozen tables topped with linen tablecloths. The menu is mostly variations on steak and shrimp, including such standbys as prime rib and rib eye, though you will not be disappointed. Reservations are recommended.

La Ventana de Taxco (762-622-0323), Lomas de Taxco, Taxco, GRO 40210. $$. AE; MC; V. Open daily for breakfast, lunch, and dinner 9 AM–11 PM. This is another one of the restaurants at the Monte de Taxco Hotel. It provides diners with a spectacular view of the city as well as a nice change of pace from the standard Mexican fare that is available everywhere else. The ambience here is fairly casual, though it does make a nice fine dining option, with Italian and Mexican cuisine. The best way to get here is by cab.

EATING OUT (((•))) **Café Punta del Cielo** (762-627-2722), Plaza Borda #4, Taxco, GRO 40200. $. MC; V. Open daily for breakfast, lunch, and dinner 9:30 AM–10 PM (Thu.–Sat. until 11 PM). This coffee shop serves high-quality coffee and provides wireless Internet access to the road weary traveler in need of a good cup of joe. So settle in with your laptop and enjoy a latte and a pastry, or a cappuccino and a sandwich, whatever your preference may be. It is conveniently located on Plaza Borda right in the middle of the action, making this a great spot to plan your day. And if you happen to be staying in the city center, the café will deliver your order right to your door.

Cielito Lindo (762-622-0603), Plaza Borda #14, Taxco, GRO 40200. $$. Open daily for breakfast, lunch, and dinner 9 AM–11 PM. Probably the most popular place in town to stop for lunch, this restaurant features an extensive menu that features everything from soups and salads to roasted chicken and steak to tacos and enchi-

ladas. However, the best dishes here are traditionally Mexican. If you like chicken mole, this is a good place to treat yourself. If you show up in the afternoon, expect to wait because the tables are always full.

La Parroquia (762-622-3096), Plaza Borda, Taxco, GRO 40200. $$. MC; V. Open daily for breakfast, lunch, and dinner 8 AM–10 PM. Located across the Plaza Borda from the Santa Prisca Parish Church, this intimate restaurant offers an enjoyable dining experience in a relaxed family-friendly atmosphere. Be sure to get a seat at one of the restaurant's mini-balconies that look onto the plaza. From this spot, you can do some serious people watching. The menu features all of the traditional Mexican favorites such as *chilequiles,* enchiladas, and chicken mole. They also offer some more

THE MINI-BALCONIES AT LA PARROQUIA PROVIDE LOVELY VIEWS OF PLAZA BORDA.

familiar comfort foods, such as club sandwiches and hamburgers. Their menu has a good selection of beers and spirits and they also have some delicious dessert choices along with espresso drinks.

Pozoleria Tia Calla (762-622-5602), Plaza Borda #1, Taxco, GRO 40200. $. Open daily for lunch and dinner 11 AM–9 PM. This restaurant specializes in the traditional pozole soup. Despite being located on Plaza Borda, there are no magnificent views of the Santa Prisca to be had here, only good food. Also, it is not a big restaurant and it does tend to get crowded. However, for a quick, traditional meal that is also delicious, you can't go wrong here. The traditional pork pozole is the most popular, though the chicken pozole verde is a very nice choice.

Restaurante Ethel (762-622-0788), Plazuela de San Juan #14, Taxco, GRO 40200. $. MC; V. Open daily for breakfast 9–noon, lunch 1–5, and dinner 6–9. Located a block off Plaza Borda, this is a great place to come for a simple, inexpensive meal that tastes as though it is home-cooked. In fact, the entire restaurant has a home-cooked feel to it, with colorful tablecloths and rustic furniture. For a good, hearty meal, order the *comida casera,* which features soup or pasta with a small meat dish, followed up by dessert and coffee. Vegetarian offerings are also available. Although their specialties are traditionally Mexican, they also offer a selection of more familiar dishes, such as breakfast omelets, hamburger with fries, as well as a pork chop dinner.

NIGHTLIFE Taxco has many places to enjoy a drink and live music. Plaza Borda has several Bohemian cantinas with laid back atmospheres while there are several small discos south of the *zócalo* along Avenida de los Plateros . These clubs are generally only open on weekends and during major festivals. However, when they do open their doors, they get surprisingly lively. Some charge an all-inclusive cover that pays for your drinks while others charge a smaller fee to get in and charge for drinks on top of that. These dance clubs get going late, around 11 PM and keep going until the wee hours of the morning.

Amnesia (762-627-1664), Plazuela de Bernal #15, Taxco, GRO, 40200. Open Thursday through Saturday from 9 PM to 4 AM. This club is one of the trendier night clubs in Taxco. This means that the crowd tends to be very young. Despite this, there are people of all ages. The music here is a mix of techno and pop tunes. If you decide to give your ears a break, the open-air terrace provides a beautiful view of the city. There is a full bar here serving a good selection of beers, spirits, and wine, as well as mixed drinks.

▼ **Aztec Disco** (762-627-3833), Avenida de los Plateros #184, Taxco, GRO. Open Thu.–Sun. 10 PM –3 AM. This gay-friendly disco features drag shows and a lively dance scene.

Bar Bertha's (762-622-0172), Plaza Borda #9, Taxco, GRO, 40200. Open daily 11 AM–8 PM. Opened in 1930 by a woman named Bertha, this is Taxco's oldest bar. The walls are decorated with items such as swords and spurs, making it seem just about as old as it actually is. Since those early days, this bar has been famous for a concoction called the Bertha. It is a mixture of club soda, tequila, lime, and honey. After a few of these, Taxco may seem significantly more uphill than normal. This bar is located right on the zócalo near the Santa Prisca Parish Church, so be sure to get a balcony seat so you have a view overlooking the plaza. It is a popular gathering place for locals and tourists alike.

La Bodega (762-622-0063), Cerro de la Misión #32, Taxco, GRO, 40200. Open daily 5 PM–11 PM. This piano bar located at the Posada de la Misión Hotel offers a relaxed atmosphere combined with tranquil rhythms. Located right off the hotel pool area, it is a good place to enjoy a cocktail and talk about the day's explorations. The bar's intimate setting also provides a nice setting for a romantic night out.

La Concha Nostra (762-622-7944), Plazuela de San Juan #7, Taxco, GRO, 40200. Open daily 8 PM–1 AM; Fri. and Sat. there is live rock music by local talent. This cantina is located on the second floor of the Casa Grande Hotel in the Plazuela de San Juan. It has an attractive colonial atmosphere, with thick, wooden tables and handmade chairs. Get a seat on the balcony for a good view of the street action below. Their menu features a nice selection of Italian and Mexican specialties and they are well-known for their pizza.

Ibiza (762-627-1664; www.ibizataxco .com), Avenida de los Plateros # 137, Taxco, GRO, 40200. Open Thu.–Sun. 9 PM– 4 AM. This popular night club attracts locals and tourists alike. It features a modest sized central dance floor flanked by a row of tables and there is a large television screen on one of the walls. Closely surrounding this on all sides are several levels of terraces with disco lights flashing down from the scaffolding above. This gives the place a fairly claustrophobic feel when it is really crowded. On nights like this, the clientele tends to skew very young with a lot of kids in their late teens and very early 20s. However, the club occasionally features live Latin music that attracts an older crowd. On nights such as this, Ibiza presents a very enjoyable, intimate atmosphere.

Windows (762-622-1300), Lomas de Taxco, Taxco, GRO, 40210. Open Fri. and Sun. 9 PM–3 AM. This nightclub, located way out at the Hotel Monte Taxco, is a popular hangout for tourists and locals alike, though it is big enough that it seldom gets really crowded. Friday night is meringue night as people do their best moves to the Latin rhythms. On Saturday nights, the music goes retro, with hits from the '70s, '80s, and '90s. The hotel also offers a buffet on Saturday nights, as well as a fireworks display. $5 cover.

✳ Selected Shopping

Because Taxco is the main silver producer in Mexico, you will have absolutely no trouble finding quality silverwork in shops and stands throughout the city. Some visitors are lucky enough to get to watch the artisans at work making their impressive pieces. And because there is so much competition in this town that seems to be overflowing with silver, you will find that the prices are extremely reasonable.

However, besides its silverwork and jewelry, Taxco has much more to offer. For example, located directly behind the Santa Prisca Parish Church, you will find the Mercado de Artesanías, or Crafts Market. This collection of street stalls offers every-

A VENDOR AT THE CRAFTS MARKET BEHIND THE SANTA PRISCA PARISH CHURCH.

thing from inexpensive silver jewelry to handicrafts made of wood, clay, and bright fabrics. For example, you will find a good selection of lacquered wooden boxes with painted designs, which are typical in the state of Guerrero. Also, you will find carved wooden masks and colorful *talavera* ceramic ware. This market is a good place to practice your bargaining skills with the vendors. Keep in mind that you can also barter in many of the silver shops around town, even when they display price tags. Also, if you happen to be in town on a Saturday, be sure to visit the Tianguis de la Plata (Silver Street Market). Here, the city's handicraft workshops bring their wares out of the shop and display them in a collection of stalls. Take advantage of the excellent prices and purchase everything from silver jewelry with crystal inlays to complete silver tea sets.

CERAMICS AND FOLK ART

D'Elsa (762-622-1683), Plazuela de San Juan #13, Taxco, GRO 40200.

Open daily 9 AM–7 PM. This shop features a nice selection of quality handicrafts as well as a collection of women's clothing inspired by the indigenous style. Prices are reasonable.

TAXCO HAS MANY CRAFT STORES SELLING ALL MANNER OF MEXICAN FOLK ART.

Naivir Galería y Plata (762-627-6777), Calle Benito Juárez #7-B, Taxco, GRO 40210. Open Mon.–Fri. 9 AM–2:30 PM and 3:30 PM–7 PM. This rustic shop features a wide variety of quality Mexican handicrafts, including silver jewelry, handmade lamps, and intricately painted clay jars.

La Tienda del Taller (762-622-4320), Calle Palma #2, Taxco, GRO 40200. Open daily 9 AM–7 PM. This shop features a nice collection of the traditional miniature *artesenías* depicting old-fashion kitchens, mariachi bands, and other traditional scenes. There is also a unique selection of necklaces and bracelets that integrate pieces of Mexican tile. In addition to jewelry and crafts, the shop carries bottles of local mescal and perfectly spiced *sal de jumil*, seasoning salt made from a local insect.

TAXCO'S SHOPS OFFER ALL MANNER OF SILVER JEWELRY.

JEWELRY Adaami Orfebres (762-622-2330), Cuauhtémoc #3, Taxco, GRO 40210. Open Mon.–Fri. 9 AM–3:30 PM and 5 PM–8 PM. This shop specializes in silver necklaces, earrings, and bracelets. Come here to find designs that are unique but solid and fairly simple. The jewelry is not over-ornamented but the quality shows through in the work.

Angel Ortiz (762-622-3858), Plazuela de los Gallos #5, Taxco, GRO 40210. Open Mon.–Sat. 9 AM–3:30 PM and 5 PM–8 PM. This elegant jewelry store offers a relatively small selection of high-quality silver necklaces and bracelets. Many of the pieces are composed of many individual pieces intricately linked together.

Daniela Plateria y Exportaciones (762-622-1495), Calle Miguel Hidalgo #36, GRO 40210. Open Mon.–Sat. 9 AM–7 PM. This shop buys and sells silver jewelry. They have a large selection of silver necklaces, many inlayed with semiprecious stones. They will also make you a piece if you have a specific design in mind.

Eva (762-622-8188), Calle Benito Juárez #9, Taxco, GRO 40210. Open Mon.–Sat. 9 AM–7 PM. This small shop is strictly a silver jewelry store. They sell pieces designed and produced by local artisans.

Galerías Taxco Centro Joyero (762-627-3954), Avenida de los Plateros #278-C, Taxco, GRO 40210. Open daily 9 AM–7 PM. This large store has a bit of a warehouse feel to it. The spacious showroom contains rows of glass cases from which to select pieces. The selection is not limited to jewelry. You will find handicrafts here as well. There is even an on-site restaurant upstairs just in case you work up an appetite from all of the shopping.

Magic Joyería Fina (762-622-5660), Calle Benito Juárez #13, Taxco, GRO 40210. Open Mon.–Sat. 9 AM–7 PM. This shop specializes in necklaces, earrings, and other jewelry made of 0.925 quality silver. Many of the pieces are inlayed with semiprecious stones.

Paloma (762-622-0191), Calle Benito Juárez #12, Taxco, GRO 40210. Open Mon.–Sat. 9 AM–7 PM. This shop specializes in jewelry made from 0.925 quality silver. The pieces here are solid, high-quality, and made with precision. They have many matching earring, bracelet, and necklace sets and their prices are reasonable.

Rya de Taxco (762-622-7946), Calle Benito Juárez #23, Taxco, GRO 40210. Open Mon.–Fri. 9 AM–3:30 PM and 5 PM–8 PM. This jewelry store offers a wide selection of necklaces, earrings, and bracelets. Many of the pieces combine silver with semi-precious stones. There is also a large collection of necklaces of shell and other materials.

Spratling Ranch (762-622-6108), Km. 177.5 Highway 95, Taxco el Viejo, GRO 40321. Open Mon.–Fri. 8 AM–1 PM and 2 PM–5 PM, Sat. 8 AM–1 PM. This ranch was once the home of William Spratling. Today it is a workshop where you can watch craftsmen creating silverware and jewelry. These high-quality pieces are a bit more pricy than most, ranging from $100 to $3,000. This shop is located about 15 minutes south of Taxco de Alarcón and can be reached easily by taxi.

THE BELLS OF THE SANTA PRISCA PARISH CHURCH.

✳ Special Events

January: Jan. 17–18—**Fiesta de Santa Prisca**: On the 17th, parishioners bring their pets to the parish for blessing, and on the 18th, the *zócalo* (town square) fills with pilgrims there to honor Santa Prisca; the day is celebrated with folk dancing inside the church.

November: On the first Monday, the **Fiesta de los Jumiles** is celebrated in Taxco, in which people feast on raw or roasted *jumiles* (crickets). **Nov. 28—Feria Nacional del la Plata** (Silver Fair) is A celebration of Taxco's silversmiths.

CHILPANCINGO

The state capital of Guerrero, Chilpancingo is a small town burdened with a city on top of it. Located 62 miles from Acapulco, it has a population of around 200,000. However, Chilpancingo has relatively few hotels. For this reason, it is a good idea to make your reservations at least a week in advance, if possible. Despite this demand, accommodations here are cheap, with no hotel charging more than around $50 a night. Most of these are business hotels with few frills. The Jacarandas and Parador del Marqués hotels are exceptions, though they are also located well away from the city center.

✳ Lodging

Hotel Alameda (747-471-7649), Abasolo #38, Chilpancingo, GRO 39000. $. Located near downtown Chilpancingo, this three-story, white colonial building with arched windows and wrought-iron balconies offers 27 rooms and suites. The rooms here are simply appointed but clean and comfortable, furnished with either a king-size or two double beds, with ceiling fans to circulate the air. All rooms are also equipped with cable television, though most channels are in Spanish. Suites come with an additional sofa bed as well as a refrigerator, a microwave oven, and a small dining area. An unusual amenity of this hotel is an on-site car-washing service. If you are not in the mood for microwaved food, there is a restaurant-bar that serves traditional Mexican specialties daily 7 AM–9 PM.

Hotel del Parque (747-472-2547), Calle Colón #5, Chilpancingo, GRO 39000. $$. This modern hotel, in a four-floor building just one block south of the *zócalo*, has 30 rooms and suites with shower baths and double-glazed windows to cut down on the street noise. The rooms are clean, comfortable, and nicely decorated in modern Mexican style. On the ground floor you will find the **Taco Rock Restaurant,** open daily 8 AM–10 PM, which serves Mexican and international dishes and is popular with the locals. There is no parking on site, though there is a nearby lot where you can park your car for an extra $5 a day.

(((•))) .**Hotel Presidente** (747-472-9731), Calle 30 de Agosto #1, Chilpancingo, GRO 39000. $. This hotel is located a block from the bus station in a white rectangular building with large tinted windows and terraces that look onto the street. The rooms are fairly small and feature a gaudy décor but they are clean. Most are furnished with double beds, including some rooms that have three beds, though there are suites with king-size beds. Downstairs, you will find the Café Green, open daily 7:30 AM–10 PM, which serves good Mexican cuisine. Also, if you need to use the Internet, there are a couple of computers just off the lobby that are open to guests of the hotel. Other amenities include room service and laundry service.

↝ **Hotel Jacarandas** (747-472-4444), Avenida Ruffo Figueroa, Chilpancingo, GRO 39000. $. AE; MC; V. About 1.5 miles south of the city center, you will find this resort-style hotel. It is located on a lush property filled with jacaranda trees and offers 66 rooms and suites. These rooms have plenty of space; they are whitewashed with tile floors and have large windows to allow in lots of light. Standard rooms come furnished with two double beds; master suites, with two queen-size

beds; and the Presidential Suite, with two king-size beds and a private terrace. There is also a good-size swimming pool on the property, as well as an event room for special occasions. The hotel restaurant serves traditional Mexican and international fare daily 7 AM–11 PM.

↝ (ɰ) **Hotel Parador del Marqués** (747-472-6773; www.paradordel marques.com), Boulevard Vicente Guerrero km. 276.5, Chilpancingo, GRO 39000. $. AE; MC; V. Located about 2 miles south of town, this resort hotel has 38 rooms and suites that are very spacious and feature tasteful modern furnishings. Most standard rooms come with two double beds. The hotel also offers standard rooms with three double or with a king-size bed. Suites are also furnished with one king-size bed. The hotel grounds are attractively festooned with tropical plants. The swimming pool is not overly large but it's sufficient for the size of the hotel. **La Cava Restaurant,** open daily 7 AM–11 PM, serves traditional Mexican cuisine as well as a choice of international dishes.

IGUALA

Usually overlooked by tourists, Iguala de la Independencia is a historic patriotic center. It was settled in 1750 and named in honor of Agustín de Iturbide's Iguala Plan, which spelled out his plan for independence. With a population of just over 110,000, it is the third-largest community in Guerrero after Acapulco and Chilpancingo. It lies along the Cocula River and is an important regional communications and commerce center. Products from throughout Guerrero, such as corn, beans, sugarcane, lemons, and rice, are gathered in Iguala and distributed to the cities of Mexico's inland plateau. Despite the lack of tourists, Iguala has a pedestrian-friendly downtown area and several good restaurants. All of the hotels in this city worth recommending are less than $50 per night. If you plan on staying in the city during the hot months of April, May, and June, you will probably want to splurge the few extra bucks it will cost to get a room with air-conditioning when renting your hotel room.

✳ Lodging

⚑ Hotel Maria Isabel (733-333-3233), Calle Constitución #5, Iguala, GRO 40000. $. This is probably Iguala's best hotel, conveniently located near the downtown area. It is an older hotel and its 60 rooms are clean, if slightly worn. They feature dark paneling and each is furnished with two double beds. Some rooms have air-conditioning. If possible, request one of the upper rooms located at the back. These are the quietest rooms and have balconies overlooking the hotel's modest swimming pool. Downstairs, the hotel's restaurant serves traditional Mexican cuisine daily 8 AM–10 PM.

Hotel Señoral (733-332-5250), Avenida Vicente Guerrero #37, Iguala, GRO 40000. $. Conveniently located in downtown Iguala, this simple business hotel has 30 rooms that are small but sufficiently comfortable. They are simply appointed in a rustic style. Some have air-conditioning. Standard rooms are furnished with a sitting table and mirror and either a king-size or double bed. There are also rooms with either two double or a king-size bed plus a single bed. Triple rooms have two double beds and a single bed.

Hotel Valesco (733-332-0566), Bandera Nacional #3, Iguala, GRO 40000. $. Situated two blocks east of the *zócalo* this is a budget hotel in just about every sense of the word but it is clean and will suffice if you find yourself in Iguala looking for a room. Its 36 rooms are small and simple but feature shower-baths, hot water, and ceiling fans. Some have air-conditioning. Standard rooms have one double bed and larger rooms have two double beds. These rooms are configured in a two-story building around an open-air courtyard. Noise from the street can be a problem here so be prepared to deal with that until around 11 PM. Also, none of the staff speaks much English.

INDEX

214